Will Rogers

Between filming scenes on the Fox studio lot, Will Rogers pecks out another newspaper column. (Will Rogers Memorial Museum)

Gary Clayton Anderson
The University of Oklahoma

Will Rogers
and "His" America

THE LIBRARY OF AMERICAN BIOGRAPHY

Edited by Mark C. Carnes

Prentice Hall

Boston Columbus Indianapolis New York San Francisco Upper Saddle River Amsterdam
Cape Town Dubai London Madrid Milan Munich Paris Montreal Toronto Delhi
Mexico City São Paulo Sydney Hong Kong Seoul Singapore Taipei Tokyo

Executive Editor: Ed Parsons
Editorial Assistant: Amanda A. Dykstra
Senior Marketing Manager: Maureen
  E. Prado Roberts
Marketing Assistant: Marissa O'Brien
Operations Specialist: Renata Butera
Cover Designer: Karen Salzbach
Creative Art Director: Jayne Conte
Manager, Visual Research: Beth Brenzel
Manager, Rights & Permissions: Zina
  Arabia
Manager, Cover Visual Research &
  Permissions: Karen Sanatar

Cover Illustration: Will Rogers
  Memorial Museum
Full-Service Project Management:
  Joseph Barnabas Malcolm,
  PreMediaGlobal
Composition: PreMediaGlobal
Printer/Binder: Edwards Brothers/
  Lillington
Cover Printer: Lehigh-Phoenix Color/
  Hagerstown
Text Font: Sabon

Library of Congress Cataloging-in-Publication Data

Anderson, Gary Clayton
Will Rogers and "his" America / Gary Clayton Anderson.
  p. cm. — (The library of American biography)
  Includes bibliographical references and index.
  ISBN-13: 978-0-205-69506-5
  ISBN-10: 0-205-69506-X
  1. Rogers, Will, 1879–1935.   2. Entertainers—United States—Biography.
3. Humorists, American—Biography.   I. Title.
  PN2287.R74A82 2010
  792.702'8092–dc22   2010010646

Photo credits and acknowledgments borrowed from other sources and reproduced, with permission, in this textbook appear on appropriate page within the text.

Material taken from James M. Smallwood & Steven K. Gragert, eds., *Will Rogers Weekly Articles* and James M. Smallwood & Steven K. Gragert, eds., *Will Rogers' Telegrams* in chapters 3–7. reprinted with the permission of Will Rogers Memorial Museum, Claremore, Oklahoma.

Prentice Hall
is an imprint of

ISBN-10:   0-205-69506-X
ISBN-13: 978-0-205-69506-5
www.pearsonhighered.com

To my children
Kari, Evan, and Jon

Contents

Editor's Preface

Think of humorist Andy Rooney, political satirist Stephen Colbert, and TV journalist Anderson Cooper. Imagine them morphed into a single person. Then you will be close to envisioning the Will Rogers of this biography: a pioneer in journalism who inaugurated the transition from print to electronic media, an iconoclastic and funny pundit who shaped public opinion in the fateful decades of the 1920s and 1930s.

Readers may be surprised by this Will Rogers, because the popular version is somewhat different. That Will Rogers is a lariat-twirling cowboy turned B movie actor, master of homespun one-liners such as "The income tax has made more liars out of Americans than golf." But few know about Rogers the journalist, the man whose column was regularly read by nearly every adult American during the social, political, and economic transformations of the Roaring Twenties and the Great Depression.

In funny and memorable ways, Rogers described the American nation and its people during a time of great hardships. He also influenced events. Rogers preached calm during the worst of the economic storms and exuded confidence in FDR's proposals to expand the role of the federal government in people's lives. As the Great Depression worsened, Rogers came to believe that government should feed desperate people and provide them with jobs. His common sense, laced with humor, did much to change the political attitudes of an American people who had always believed that the common man should pick himself up by his own bootstraps. Indeed, Rogers was arguably the most effective proponent of liberalism of his age—perhaps surpassing even Franklin Delano Roosevelt. For his part, Roosevelt borrowed some of Rogers' techniques, including homespun humor and radio-broadcast chats with the American people.

Veteran biographer Gary Clayton Anderson first became interested in Rogers because of his humor. Anderson, who is George Lynn Cross Research Professor at the University of Oklahoma, was also drawn to Rogers because Rogers, a Cherokee Indian, was from the Indian Territory in remote eastern Oklahoma. Anderson was astounded that Rogers could rise from such obscure origins to journalistic prominence, surpassing in readership two of the titans of print journalism of the twentieth century: Walter Lippmann and H. L. Mencken.

Anderson has the good sense to allow Rogers, a master of the one-liner, to speak for himself; few biographies, consequently, are as consistently fast-paced and amusing as this one. Yet Anderson also advances a thesis of enduring relevance. Nowadays pundits bludgeon their way to public notice; but Rogers realized a deeper truth: the best way to change people's minds is to get them to laugh.

Rogers delivered an emblematic "gag" when he tried to interview Leon Trotsky in the Soviet Union in 1926. Being disappointed by the strongmen in power, Rogers simply wrote that he would like to have met Trotsky, "for I have never met a man that I didn't like." It was that attitude, the belief that everyone had a story to tell, that there were always positive and negative sides to every story, that make Rogers a house-hold name.

MARK C. CARNES
ANN WHITNEY OLIN PROFESSOR OF HISTORY
BARNARD COLLEGE/COLUMBIA UNIVERSITY

Acknowledgments

Those who have helped formulate my rendition of *Will Rogers* include a host of professionals both in publishing and in the academy. Michael Boezi, formerly the U.S. History editor at Pearson Longman, and editorial assistant Amanda Dykstra, both saw the biography as ideal for the Library of American Biography Series and supported it from the start. Those of my colleagues who have read sections and offered criticism include my good friend Richard Lowitt and University of Oklahoma colleagues Robert Griswold, David Levy, Richard Lowitt, Brad Raley, Ben Keppel, and William Savage. Perhaps no one knows as much Oklahoma history–and thus Will Rogers history–as Bill Savage. Several of my graduate students have found time in their busy schedules to read and critique. They include Emily Wardrop and Catharine Franklin.

My close friend Charles E. Rankin, Editor in Chief at the University of Oklahoma Press, has been a wonderful foil for discussing Rogers and national politics. Chuck has also graciously allowed me to use quotations from the press's recent publication of the *Will Rogers Papers*, in five volumes, a magnificent achievement that took ten years to put together. I also wish to thank Steven K. Gragert, Director of the Will Rogers Memorial and Museum; in addition to supplying photographs, he kindly allowed me to quote from two wonderful but poorly known publications of Rogers' articles and telegrams, the *Weekly Articles* (in six volumes) and the *Daily Telegrams* (in four volumes). While all of this material was originally published in newspapers, bringing it together into two publications makes it so much easier for scholars to pursue research on the views and impact of this very interesting American. The Will Rogers Museum is located in Claremore, Oklahoma, and maintains an active publishing agenda.

As usual, my lovely wife, Laura, has been there through it all, watching and helping with the pacing—or, rather, the thought process—that comes with writing.

GARY CLAYTON ANDERSON
GEORGE LYNN CROSS RESEARCH PROFESSOR
THE UNIVERSITY OF OKLAHOMA

Introduction: Will Rogers and "His" America

On a tense evening, May 7, 1933, the phone rang at NBC studios in New York. An aide to President Franklin Delano Roosevelt at the White House wanted to speak to someone in charge. Will Rogers was on the air giving his weekly radio address, and Roosevelt wanted the script for Rogers' show sent to him immediately. Roosevelt went on later in what journalists called "a fireside chat," a radio address to the American people. The President had no intention of contradicting Rogers, who had become an oracular icon in America. While these two men, Roosevelt and Rogers, had markedly different backgrounds, one coming from the wilds of Indian Territory in Oklahoma, and the other growing up on an estate in upstate New York, there were striking parallels. In 1933, both spoke to the average person in America, those suffering from the Depression that had struck three years before. Both spoke with a down-to-earth, almost melodic style, and both had huge audiences that could change public opinion overnight. No wonder Roosevelt wanted to know what Rogers had to say.

But who was this man Will Rogers? How did he come to have so much influence in the United States that presidents would hang on his words? There is no question relative to his substantial influence in the print industry. Indeed, the leading columnists of the day, Arthur Brisbane, H. L. Mencken, and Walter Lippmann, all agreed that Rogers dominated the newsprint industry through his daily and weekly columns. What gave him yet more appeal was his role in the movies; by the 1930s, Rogers' contract with Fox Studios called for at least three movies a year. In 1932, he was the highest paid actor in the country, and the most recognizable. Yet, by this time, he took more pride in being a journalist than a comedic actor. Rogers, more so than any other writer, actor or politician in America, had his finger on the pulse of America at a time of immense turmoil and growing economic chaos. His worldview molded the opinions of millions of Americans.

That worldview included a critique of America's role in the world, just as it offered an ordered and simplistic understanding of the political forces that dominated the United States. The average American generally agreed with Will Rogers. He offered a down-to-earth assessment of many issues, in particular the Great Depression and the governmental officials who implemented the New Deal which was supposed to solve these economic problems. Rogers exposed the great divide between rich and poor. But he also kept people informed about the doings of Hollywood actors and New York financiers, and he even, to a small degree, illuminated the country's struggle with race relations. This is not to say that Rogers was always correct in all of his assessments. But like no other source, through Rogers' eyes we can see the events of the first one-third of the twentieth century unfold much as an average American viewed them, much as that American would have discussed them in a common, comfortable setting. Indeed, in an age when newspapers dominated the "information network," some forty million readers—during a period when the total adult population of the country consisted of little over a hundred million—generally turned first to Rogers' column before surveying the rest of the news.

Rogers' rise to prominence did not start in a Hollywood studio or even through becoming a cub reporter. He started in vaudeville as a comedic entertainer, doing rope tricks and telling one-liners, or what he called "gags." It was a tough business, often dominated by acrobatic teams, operatic singers, and fall-down comics often doing "Black Face." Fortunately, such a motley crew did not duplicate the uniqueness of Rogers' performance, and he survived in the business, moving on to motion pictures and writing a column in 1921. As Rogers matured as a performer, he increasingly offered up political humor, reading newspaper after newspaper to collect his material. By the 1920s, a man with little education and a penchant for misspelling words had secured for himself a remarkable career, as a budding successful journalist/entertainer. It was this Rogers—thoughtful and funny, charismatic and charming—who worked his way to the top of American journalism.

Along the way, Rogers jettisoned his provincial view of the world, which came with an Oklahoma upbringing. Once in Hollywood, he went through an intellectual renaissance that led to a commitment to a different America than that often characterized by writers during the "Roaring Twenties," a period of self-indulgence and rampant materialism. But while he developed new views of the nation, he remained passionate in his support for the capitalistic system. This enabled him to be friends with the very people who became symbols of the reigning, materialistic creed, which sanctified the rich, and their fortunes, and virtually ignored the downtrodden. In deference to them, Rogers called for moderation and compassion, for government to assist those who were down and out. He even challenged the tax system that existed in America, one that had led to the rich getting richer, the middle class remaining as a minority, and continued suffering for a majority of Americans whose income failed to support a typical family. This contradictory ideology, developed by Rogers in the late 1920s, embracing capitalism while calling for government intervention to assist the needy, ultimately epitomized the modern liberalism of Franklin Delano Roosevelt's New Deal.

Nevertheless, some in America thought Rogers to be far too uneducated to become a spokesman for any group or ideology. Some columnists claimed that he lacked the knowledge to comment on either domestic or world events. Newspaper editors, including those at the *New York Times,* occasionally edited his columns. This rather mild censorship reflected more so upon the intellectual snobbishness of the eastern, establishment press than upon Rogers' views. Rogers countered such criticism by seeing firsthand what was happening in the world—he traveled constantly to compare his views of America with that of other countries, circling the globe on three separate occasions. At one point, he devoted three months to visit the capitals of Europe, and spent several days with the Italian dictator Benito Mussolini.

He traveled through the communistic Soviet Union twice, when most Americans could not even get a visa, commenting on the nature of the evolving communistic system. Rogers made two separate trips to Manchuria to observe the tension that existed there among the three contending powers, Japan, China, and the Soviet Union.

While politics ran in his veins, Rogers also found time to comment on various personalities, on unique people such as actors, writers, European royalty, and the titans of American industry. He had close relationships with Henry Ford and John D. Rockefeller. He poked fun at Democratic and Republican politicians, both groups of which had turned decidedly conservative in the 1920s. He particularly berated Congress, being one of the first critics to suggest that the nation was better off when it was not in session. At the same time, he commented on the lady-troubles of friends such as Fatty Arbuckle and Charlie Chaplin. In essence, Rogers knew everyone in America who made his or her way into the newspapers.

Through his connections in industry, Will Rogers also experienced the many new innovations of the age. He enjoyed large cars and, especially, fast airplanes. While not a pilot, he pioneered in the airline industry, catching rides with air-mail pilots when such trips were dangerous, and he later pushed for the development of national air carriers, constantly assuring his readers that air travel was safer than riding in a car. Rogers hailed progress in America, indeed gloried in it, at the same time that he stressed the need to maintain traditional values.

In truth, Will Rogers will never be imitated again in America, primarily because he successfully spoke for so many different and varied people. His political humor, which lacked meanness of spirit, often had politicians begging for his attention. His astute assessment of the country's needs had presidents courting his help. While he is no longer a household name, for a brief time in the nation's early twentieth-century history, Will Rogers helped remake America into a country that offered more compassion and more justice to all, at the same time that he emphasized the traditional principles of hard work and dedication to fairness that he believed good countries must exhibit. And he always stressed the notion that individuals made a difference in his many "gags." "No man is great if he thinks he is."

"It's great to be great but it's greater to be human." And, "Everyone is ignorant, only on different subjects."

Now it is time to sit back and enjoy the many sides of Will Rogers, the comedian, the actor, the political scientist, and, as the newspaper often portrayed him, "the Cowboy Philosopher." Given his connections and like-ability, he had the best view in the house, one envied by every journalist, actor, and comedian in America. And he used a special language to forecast his thoughts on matters of importance, a language that is preserved in this biography, with all its euphemisms, exotic spellings, and incorrect capitalization. Will Rogers would have wanted it that way.

Promotional poster for Will Rogers' vaudeville act,
circa 1910. (Will Rogers Memorial Museum)

Will Rogers, the Opening Act

One April morning in 1905, the New York *Morning Telegraph*'s entertainment section applauded a new vaudeville act that had appeared the previous evening at Madison Square Garden. The performer was Will Rogers, "a full blood Cherokee Indian and Carlisle graduate," who proved equal to his title of "lariat expert." Just two days before, Rogers had performed at the White House in front of President Theodore Roosevelt's children, and theater-goers anticipated his arrival in New York. The "Wild West" remained an enigmatic part of the world to most eastern, urban Americans, and Rogers was from what he called "Injun Territory." Will's act met expectations. He whirled his lassoes two at a time, jumping in and out of them, and ended with his famous finale, extending his two looped lassoes to encompass a rider and horse that appeared on stage.

While the *Morning Telegraph* may have stretched the truth—Rogers was neither full-blooded nor a graduate of the famous American Indian school, Carlisle—the paper did sense the importance of this emerging star. The reviewer especially appreciated Rogers' homespun "plainsmen talk," which consisted of colorful comments and jokes that he intermixed with each rope trick. Rogers' dialogue revealed a quaint friendliness and bashful smile that soon won over crowds as did his skill with a rope. His earthy, western voice, slowed by a cowboy drawl, was disarming and infectious, displaying the personality easterners expected from a western cowboy.

Unlike most vaudeville performers who learned the trade, Will Rogers experienced early success, even in New York. He performed alongside the greats of the vaudeville era—Houdini, Al Jolson, the "Three Keatons," Josephine Cohan, Fred Niblo, and Earnest Hogan. Each show consisted of many acts, some with vocalists, others of a minstrel variety, and still other groups doing skits or acrobatic tricks. The most rowdy of the vaudeville theaters were saloons, where drinking and scantily-clad women danced as comics told off-beat jokes, waitresses hawked drinks, and prostitutes cornered customers. Rogers, on the other hand, often worked for Benjamin F. Keith, who created more refined shows that appealed to the middle class. He went on the circuit, appearing in the best theaters of Philadelphia, Boston, and Detroit. By 1906, his roping act made him $75 a week, a considerable salary in an age when it took factory workers a month to make the same income.

Will Rogers had begun an astonishing rise as an entertainer. By 1907, Will appeared in his first play, *The Girl Rangers*, with Reine Davies. In 1916 he joined the Ziegfeld *Follies*, where he performed for a decade, on and off, with the likes of W. C. Fields and Eddie Cantor. By the early 1920s, while continuing to work with the *Follies*, Rogers went to Hollywood, California to make motion pictures. More important, he started writing a weekly syndicated column. Rogers literally invented the modern monologue, so popular on late night television today, with its common assessment of American politics and life. He took this public discussion to the airwaves, doing a weekly radio show by 1930. Will Rogers became the most read comic, the most important political satirist, one of the most successful actors, and the most significant friendly commentator in America by the early 1930s. He left a legacy of "gags," as he called them, or one-liners, that still get quoted today.[1]

Along this long road to fame, Rogers went through a slow metamorphosis. He left Indian Territory, or Oklahoma, as a young

---

[1]See Reba Collins, ed., *Will Rogers Says . . . : Favorite Quotations Selected by the Will Rogers Memorial Staff* (Oklahoma City, Oklahoma: Neighbors and Quaid, 1993).

man with all the biases and racist views that most of his fellow Oklahomans held. He had considerable difficulty conquering his inbred prejudices. As a young man, he performed so-called "coon" songs—derogatory ballads that denigrated Black Americans—both at home and later while on stage. He was roughly one-quarter Cherokee Indian, but at times he rejected his Indian identity and sought acceptance in a purely white world. While over time he developed sympathy for most people of color—he especially came to appreciate the people of Mexico and the Caribbean Islands—he often wrote disparagingly of the Chinese in America. Like most liberal white Americans in the 1920s and 1930s, he struggled with the conundrum of race, condemning especially lynching but not yet recognizing the equality of colored people.

Rogers' need for acceptance led him to court important people, something that ultimately provided considerable fodder for his weekly columns. He ultimately considered himself a Progressive of a southern, Democratic persuasion. He supported Woodrow Wilson, Al Smith, and adored Franklin Delano Roosevelt. Yet he frequently parodied Congress, often distrusted government, and occasionally spoke highly of Republicans such as Calvin Coolidge and dictators such as Benito Mussolini, whom he interviewed in Italy. Perhaps worse, as a young man Rogers seldom, if ever, recognized the discrimination against Native people in America, or the terrible conditions in which they lived. He poked fun of their "Injun" behavior. He regretted this insensitivity later in life.

But who was Will Rogers? He was born in Indian Territory, Oklahoma on November 4, 1879, to Clem V. and Mary Schrimsher Rogers. Everyone knew the Rogers clan in Cherokee land as important political supporters of the so-called "Ridge Party": the group that had finally agreed to the Cherokee removal treaty of 1835, which forced Cherokees from their homeland in Georgia and North Carolina, west, into Indian Territory. Some evidence suggests that early Rogers family members migrated to Indian Territory before the treaty was signed. Progressives (in the sense that they worked within a fledgling market economy) and slave holders, the Rogers clan united with the Schrimsher family in 1858, when Clem married Mary at Fort Gibson, Oklahoma Territory.

The Schrimsher family had similar political views and roughly the same Cherokee blood quantum as the Rogers, but Mary maintained some degree of Indian tradition in the household. She frequently spoke Cherokee and her son, Will, undoubtedly learned some of the language, although he apparently never used it as an adult. Clem was far more engaging, although gruff and blunt. His political contacts led to a strong relationship with William Penn Adair, the brilliant Cherokee soldier and statesmen. Clem and Mary, like many mixed-bloods of their age in Oklahoma, had mostly abandoned the communal lifestyle and associated with merchants, or in Clem's case, ranchers. There is no evidence that either of them encouraged their parents to come live in their new household, creating an extended kin group.

The young couple, Clem and Mary, settled into a log ranch house on open, tribally owned, Cherokee land in the Verdigris River Valley of northeast Oklahoma near the community of Oologah. Clem received 200 head of cattle from his mother for the ranch and two slaves, Charles Rabb and Houston Rogers—a clear indication of considerable wealth. These two Black men and their families helped build the Clem Rogers ranch into a successful operation in a few years. Elizabeth Rogers was born on the ranch in 1861. She came into the world, however, at a difficult time. The political conflict between the North and South had entered Indian Territory. The American Civil War swept the Rogers family into the turmoil that spring.

The Civil War destroyed Indian Territory. The various tribes split into factions, and in a tragic fashion, Cherokees fought Cherokees, Creeks fought Creeks, and so on. Some Cherokee factions fled south and west where a large Creek town had declared itself to be neutral. Most members of the Treaty Party—those who had negotiated removal from Georgia, including Clem, sided with the South. He joined the rebellion because he strongly supported slavery, as did his closest allies. Within months of the outbreak of war, Clem and his young family fled their ranch. Clem joined Cherokee Confederate General Stand Watie's Mounted Rifles, rising quickly to the rank of captain. While in the Confederate Army, he watched as soldiers from both sides, as well as bushwhackers, ravaged Indian Territory. The latter were outright cattle thieves and robbers who took what they wanted and left behind starving people. Clem's ranch along the Verdigris River was completely destroyed. Clem protected his family, settling them into a refugee camp near Bonham, Texas. At Bonham, in December 1863, Mary and Clem had their second child, Sarah Clementine, born amidst the hardship of war.

After the war ended, Clem resettled on a rented ranch near Fort Gibson. Another son, Robert, was born, but barely reached adulthood, dying of scarlet fever in the mid-1880s. Yearning to rebuild, Clem and Mary returned to the Verdigris River and started over again. The cattle business suddenly turned prosperous as railroads entered Kansas and then Indian Territory, bringing markets. But the times also were difficult; bushwhackers, thieves, and murderers ran roughshod over Indian Territory. Many had scores to settle from the Civil War, and no one went to bed at night without covering their windows.

By the time young Will Rogers came into the world in 1879, the violence had somewhat subsided. Clem and Mary lived in a well-built, two-story frame house. Clem had also entered politics, becoming a judge for the Cooweescoowee District and later a senator in the Cherokee government. Interestingly, the majority of support for Clem came from the Gooseneck Bend district of northern Indian Territory, a region with a substantial African-American population. Clem had reassessed his views regarding slavery and he provided plenty of whiskey and barbeque in the days before the vote, courting the votes of former slaves who were enrolled Cherokees. Clem's status and business acumen also led to the control of considerable land, the ranch at one point reputedly covering 60,000 acres of Cherokee tribal range. This land had to be protected from interlopers and Clem used his political capital to maintain some semblance of authority over the spread. This, at times, involved gunplay.

The Rogers' ranch felt like paradise to young Will. His playmates were the children of their former slaves, Rabb and Rogers. He learned to ride almost as quickly as he learned to walk. He was addicted to roping, often corralling anything in range. These were heady days for the young future comedian and showman. He came to feel a sense of security on the ranch, an impression he never really could recreate anywhere else. Handling horses and cattle came naturally. But Will's parents expected more of him, perhaps because he was the only surviving son. He needed to be prepared to take over the ranch. Will's parents soon uprooted him to live with his older sister and her husband in a nearby town and attend a local school. Most of his fellow classmates were full-blood Cherokees, and Will felt out-of-place. As he later said: "I had just enough white in me to make my honesty questionable."

Both Clem and Mary Rogers had some formal education. They met and courted at school in Tahlequah, Oklahoma. Mary attended the Methodist mission school and was by all accounts a devoted Methodist. Clem studied for several years at the Cherokee National Male Academy. Both parents wanted their son to have a similar experience, and when Will was nine, they enrolled him at a much better school: the Harrell Institute at Muskogee, Oklahoma. Once again, most of his fellow students were American Indians, but he got on well with them. Unfortunately, Will avoided the opportunity to learn, especially after his mother, Mary, died in 1890. Will left school, returned home, and grieved.

Just what kind of impact his mother's death had upon him, Will Rogers never revealed. He never wrote or said much about his mother again, though he adored her. Clem had simply been too busy expanding and protecting the ranch to spend much quality time with his son. And Clem's political career kept him away from home for months at a time. After Clem remarried his new wife, Mary Bible, was much younger than Will's mother Mary. Will was openly resentful. He refused to mention his step-mother's name, as if she did not exist. Will never spoke of her again.

From what is known, Mary had been the communicator in the family, the peacemaker as well as the disciplinarian. She insisted upon grace at the dinner table and kept a spotless house. She very likely maintained some aspect of Cherokee avoidance, a practice that evolved with the matrilineal social organization of Cherokee society. In such a household, it was polite to speak only at the proper time, especially to a relative, and on certain occasions it was improper to speak at all. While the latter rule had mostly been abandoned by Will's time, one simply did not "babble on" in a Cherokee household, but thought carefully before offering something to say. This carefulness with language was one of Will

Rogers' most enduring assets. While Clem was blunt, gruff, and at times argumentative, son Will was the opposite. He was his mother's son, a trait that served him well later in life.

Perhaps Will's adoration of his mother stemmed from her own self-assuredness and dedication to family. "A tall, slender girl with dark hair and flashing black eyes," as a friend once described her, Mary was "witty" and disciplined. When first meeting Clem, she made it clear that he might court her, but he must prove himself before offering a marriage proposal. Mary was every bit the equal to the young, dashing, Confederate captain, Clem. As a mother, Mary read constantly to young Will and insisted that he attend school. Will dutifully obeyed, at least while she was alive.

It is plausible that Will's cautious, non-vociferous, sense of humor derived from his mother, a Cherokee woman who, while mostly white, maintained some vestiges of Cherokee social mores. It was simply impolite for Cherokees to speak evil of people, and when offering criticism, careful humor became the indirect tool used most frequently. Indeed, criticism was best displayed through stories and comparisons, placing oneself in a critical light in order to offer judgmental comparison of another person. This use of comparisons, sometimes displayed in the form of opposites, constituted standard Indian dialogue and humor. At its core was humility, an example being Rogers' 1924 critical "gag" of politicians:

> With every public man [politicians] we have elected doing comedy, I tell you I don't see much of a chance for a comedian to make a living. I am just on the verge of going to work. They can do more funny things naturally, than I can think of to do purposely.

Later in life, Rogers attributed this comedic sense of humility to his mother. Perhaps following Mary's last wishes, Clem convinced Will to return to school in 1891. He did opt to stay closer to home, however, agreeing to attend the Methodist Academy at Vinita, called Willie Halsell College, located some forty miles northeast of the Oologah. He convinced the administrators to let him keep his horse, a decision they came to regret. While on horseback, nearly everything became a target for Will's rope, including schoolgirls. On one occasion, he roped a colt, which was initially easy prey. But the colt darted this way and that and finally dashed off onto a tennis court causing general havoc.

At Vinita, Will showed the first signs of the oratorical skill that would make him famous. He was cast in a number of plays and he enjoyed performing in front of an audience. Will's experiences at Vinita blossomed to a greater extent when his childhood friend Charley McClellan joined him at school in 1893. Charley had Cherokee blood, about the same quantum as Will's, but Charley's father was white. The young man seemed rebellious, even militant. Charley wore his bright black hair long, braided into a ponytail and dressed in breechclouts, leggings, and moccasins. Charley helped re-introduce the Stomp Dance, imitating a Shawnee version that came from the small reservation of those Indians found in northeast Indian Territory, a mere fifty miles away. Will was initially averse to joining in these antics, but Charley convinced him and a large number of boys and girls to don headdresses, paint their faces, and then dance like plains Indians, howling war whoops.

Had Will wanted to rebuke such behavior—and he likely did—such a thing ran counter to his personality. The play-acting, while the machinations of a mere fifteen-year-old, had definite meaning in race-conscious Indian Territory. Cherokees, who identified themselves as being members of a "civilized" tribe, looked down on Plains Indians from the West, or "Blanket Indians," who painted themselves and danced. Charley's costumes mocked them, though the dance he used was eastern. Perhaps the antics did more to reveal Charley's rebelliousness than Rogers' views toward Indians. But later, Will Rogers would also distance himself from those Plains Tribes who he viewed as "uncivilized."

Rogers' schooldays at Vinita included one more learning experience. Charley, who spoke fluent Cherokee, started giving lectures in Cherokee at school, and Rogers interpreted them. While this suggests that Will had considerable understanding of the language, his translations of Charley's somber Indian rhetoric, while undocumented, likely were far from the substance of the lecture.

Will's father sent him on to more demanding schools, leaving Charley behind to continue his stomp dancing. Will first entered the Scarritt Collegiate Institution in Neosho, Missouri and then, a year later, Kemper School, in Boonville, Missouri. Clem's young wife likely appreciated keeping Will out of the house. At these schools, Will experienced racism from the other side, being generally dubbed the "wild Indian" by his fellow white students. Other nicknames were more demeaning—especially "swarthy," as some students called him. His style of dress likely encouraged the name-calling. He arrived at Boonville in 1897 wearing, according to one account, a "ten-gallon hat, with braided horse-hair cord, flannel shirt with a red bandanna handkerchief, highly colored vest, and high heeled red top boots, with spurs." The boots were the trademark that he most relished. Expanding on his experience with Charley's dialogue, Will made friends among the white students by telling jokes, offering a monologue or two of his own, and acting as the class clown, when he attended, which was not always the case.

At Kemper School, where he lasted for less than a year, Will also experienced his first failure in wooing a girl. She was Margaret Nay, a local member of his class. Rogers asked her for a date, and rejection was swift and complete. Margaret wanted little to do with the "wild Indian" from Indian Territory. In desperation, Will used his skill to write a letter that at its core revealed the disarming personality of his eighteen-year-old self, carefully choosing words in a satirical attempt to display his human feelings. Among these feelings was experimentation with alcohol, a fact that young Margaret found disdainful; indeed, Will and a few classmates had apparently gotten hold of some liquor and had an all-night bash.

In his letter to Margaret, Rogers got right to the point—he admitted that he was a "drunkard" and a "fool," and, coming from Indian Territory, a "wild and bad boy." But the point of the self-criticism was to show the opposite—that he was really not that bad of a boy at all. Disarming or not, Margaret rejected Will a second time. There would be no date with Margaret, who in later life suggested that she had hardly known the young Will Rogers. There is no doubt though that the rejection by a white girl had an impact on Rogers. Thereafter, he became determined to marry a woman who moved in the very circles that had rejected him, and he did.

Overall, Rogers' school years were mostly wasted. Just why is difficult to determine. Certainly his constant movement from one school to another demonstrates restlessness, or an uncertainty. This would occur in later life as well. Considerable white immigration into northeastern Indian Territory also must have been troubling. The Missouri Pacific Railroad had cut a line directly through the Rogers' ranch in 1889; the future of ranching in general seemed in doubt. Other Indian reservations across America were divided into farms, and Will Rogers came to loathe the notion of simple farm life. The changes in the land, his mother's death, and his father's frequent absence made it difficult for him to concentrate at school. His constant work with the lariat proved doubly distracting, but also allowed him an escape into a almost make-believe cowboy life.

Rogers left the Kemper School unexpectedly in March 1898, before graduation. He likely felt unwelcome there. Will also might have feared the consequences his 150 demerits would carry at a military school. Later in life, Will noted that he and the commandant at Kemper, Colonel Johnson, could never agree on how the school should be run, and he had therefore decided to leave. Rather than return to Oologah and his step-mother—or have a confrontation with his father—he headed west into Texas, failing to inform his father of his departure or whereabouts. When Clem Rogers learned of his son's flight, it certainly bothered him, but he said little about it. Will was nineteen years old, and young men often went out on their own at that age, or even sooner. Also, confrontation of this sort was simply not the Cherokee way. Once reaching the Southwest, Will participated in one of the last trail drives of Texas cattle into the Kansas railhead at Medicine Lodge, an experience he richly cherished later in life.

While on the high Plains, Rogers was in his glory. He ate out of a chuck wagon and slept on the ground. He sat around the fireside at night and told stories and listened to old cowboys tell their own. The men who worked with him that summer later disagreed on the amount of labor performed by the young comedian. But the ranch owner, E. P. Ewing, later paid him a full cowboy's wages—if nothing else, he kept the entire workforce in stitches with his many jokes. Yet Will remained restless, looking for some excitement in his life. Hearing of the out-break of the Spanish-American War, and of Theodore Roosevelt's recruitment of cowboys, Rogers quickly offered his services to the regiment in Oklahoma City. But being small of stature and young, the recruiters turned him down. Ultimately reconciled with the need to go home, Will returned to the Oologah ranch, somewhat repentant, late that fall.

Once back on the ranch, a number of decisions were made, regarding both Will and his father's future. Will would run the ranch and his father would move to town. Clem was advancing in politics and in age, and he had always been involved in business. The nearby town of Claremore had been growing, and Clem became a partner at a bank there. This was ideal, at least on the surface, given Will's interest in ranching.

Clem also had been elected to a new commission that was designed to negotiate with the federal government over the issue of Cherokee communal lands. Congress passed the Curtis Act that summer, in 1898, which abolished tribal law and mandated allotment. A large number of whites had moved into the territory after the Civil War. By 1900, their populations exceeded by a considerable margin those of the Indian tribes located there by a considerable margin. The whites wanted land and the Cherokee Nation owned vast amounts, including the 60,000-acre Rogers ranch. Clem had watched as other tribes across America had been forced to "allot" their lands. In other words, the government made contracts with tribes in which each Indian head of household received a 160-acre farm and the reservation was thereafter broken up. While the Cherokee Council fought this new assault on their sovereignty, they ultimately signed the agreement, ending their communal ownership of much of northeast Indian Territory.

The Rogers family, like other Cherokees, took allotments, preserving their homesteads. Given the fact that the family also had money, Clem eventually added to the ranch by purchasing land, something that Will would continue later. The Rogers family also turned to raising more desirable short-horn cattle, which were more marketable. The ranch they maintained, though substantially smaller, was now fenced in barbed wire, and it continued to be successful despite the loss of considerable open range. But Will Rogers remained unsatisfied, almost disdainful toward his ranch duties. Clem had recruited a family from Illinois to take over the ranch house during one of Will's frequent absences, and Will found them disagreeable. He moved out of the house and built a twelve-foot-square cabin on a hillside, overlooking his rangeland. His cousin Spi Trent moved in with him and served as a cook. This arrangement worked, at least for a short time.

Despite being the boss, Will Rogers was footloose and constantly on the move. He never really committed to the sort of careful management that came with turn-of-the-century ranching. Prior to 1885, ranchers let their herds roam at will, rounded them up in the spring, and kept only a sleepy eye over them through the summer. This had changed. Ranchers now maintained fences, and they constantly monitored markets. Cattle had to be vaccinated for disease and hay stored for the winter months when grass disappeared. Cowboying had once been somewhat idyllic, or so Will thought; it was now hard work and required attention.

Just when such concentration was necessary, Will often left the ranch, riding the range rather than taking care of business. He also took advantage of the recent access to new train service. Will and a friend frequently hopped a train for Kansas City or St. Louis to take in a play or a performance. Along with these distractions, Rogers entered roping contests in nearby towns, emulating a showman who had become an idol: Vincente Oropeza, perhaps the greatest roper of all times. Will had seen him perform in Buffalo Bill's Wild West show in 1893 at the Chicago World's Columbian Exposition. Rogers was enthralled, and it motivated him to work harder at his roping skills.

Despite his lack of interest in business, Rogers' ranching years offered plenty of opportunity to enjoy life. He re-introduced himself to dancing, joining Charley, his old school friend, at Cherokee stomp dances, or, just as likely, Rogers joined other friends at a square dance. These affairs sometimes went on all night. Considerable courting—and sometimes considerable drinking—occurred at these dances, for young people. The dances often turned into sing-fests, where the newest music was the rage. Will led the others in song, frequently becoming the center of attraction. These events created a fiendish desire to collect the newest songs, especially so-called "coon" songs, or Black minstrel songs.

The "coon song" mania that hit America in the late nineteenth and early twentieth centuries led to a plethora of new music known later as ragtime. It started in vaudeville with various acts putting on "black face," and doing syncopated numbers in the dialect of what whites assumed was African-American slave language. A second, refined rendition of the coon song consisted of the so-called "cake walk," or a dance with an animated high step that again supposedly imitated the actions of Black slaves. The cake walk hit Claremore just as Will Rogers had accustomed himself to performing in front of a crowd. A newspaper reported that at one such affair, he had won the grand prize for his cake-walking—a ginger cake. Likely he won others as he honed his cake-walking and singing ability.

Despite their general popularity, coon songs denigrated African Americans. They used the slang language of former slaves to demonstrate the perceived ignorance and incompetence of Black people, something that Rogers at this young age likely did not dispute. Such songs depicted Blacks as lazy or dishonest individuals. The worst of them projected Blacks as sexual predators. Rogers knew better—a Black woman had played a major role in raising him after his mother took sick, and Black men had built the Rogers' ranch. But he persisted in singing these songs and while traveling, continued to collect them and send them home to his sisters. To him, they were amusing and entertaining, and he lacked a sense of concern regarding their message. It should be noted that some Black vaudeville performers also performed the songs—either lacking concern regarding their message or sublimating those concerns because of the need for money. Bert Williams, for example, a Black entertainer whom Rogers later met and worked alongside, commonly sang coon songs.

Rogers met his future wife, Betty Blake, while singing coon songs at a dance. Betty played the piano while Will sang. She came from a modest upbringing in Arkansas, but she was Anglo, and it took time for Will and Betty to accommodate this racial divide. Will's correspondence with Betty reveals a confident but careful young man, yet someone who likely still smarted from his rejection by a young white girl in high school. His letters played upon Betty's visits to the "wild tribes" of the west, as if Claremore was more wild than Arkansas, Betty's home state. He mildly complained of being viewed as an "Injun cowboy," and warned Betty that the pictures she sent might end up in "an Indian wigwam." And in a particularly revealing note, penned in March 1900, Will wrote to Betty: "I know it would be a slam on your society career to have it known that you even knew an ignorant Indian cowboy," as if Will Rogers was ignorant or a simple cowboy.

Though he was just twenty-one, Rogers sensed the higher status that came with being born into an Anglo ethnic world, especially given his upbringing in Indian Territory, a place with a multi-cultural population. But he was intent upon using his own charm and perseverance to move beyond such ethnic limitations. Will never let Betty's Anglo ancestry serve as an obstacle to the relationship. His identity, at this young age, then, was tied to a pragmatic sense of an ethnic hierarchy, but one that projected himself near the top of this hierarchy. He would ultimately overcome this concern with racial status, but much later in life. He attended Indian dances because he enjoyed them, dancing and singing with Indian women, but he would court an Anglo woman, who seemed at least open to a writing relationship.

Will's singing and dancing hardly pleased his father, Clem, who was above all a hard-driving businessman. Clem's sense of his only son's early lack of direction is revealed in only one or two instances. Clem simply did not criticize. However, he once commented to a friend, "Willie ain't never going to amount to nothing." Will's decision to enter more and more roping contests—some of which in far-off Kansas City or Memphis—likely sent Clem to worry more. Worse, on July 4, 1899, Will won first prize in a steer-roping contest in Claremore. Will later proclaimed that it was the "first thing I ever did in the way of appearing before an audience."

Rogers' success at roping at times consumed him. But Will found the business fun and entertaining, certainly not the sort of occupation that led to a career, at least in early 1900. Part of the problem was his size. Ropers who made a living at the sport by appearing at rodeos nationwide were simply taller, stronger, and more willing to take chances. Realizing this limitation, and perhaps after some careful prodding from his father, Rogers decided to travel and find the perfect ranch land to develop. He realized the impossibility of recreating the old Rogers' ranch, with its endless vistas of open grassland, in northeastern Indian Territory. At first, Clem approved of this idea. At least it beat roping and rodeo-ing.

Will and Clem both spent part of 1900 in New Mexico, where some open range land still existed. At the time, however, title to this endless land remained in dispute as rings of lawyers busily wrested it, one parcel at a time, from the hands of Indians, Hispanic New Mexicans, or anyone else. This did not matter to Will and Clem, for they found nothing that approximated the rich grassland of eastern Indian Territory. In a rather romantic surge of near-desperation, Will turned to Latin America, a land that he anticipated would have plenty of opportunity. This spontaneous decision perhaps was a result of the expansion of American business into the Caribbean world at the end of the Spanish American War.

Rogers, who enjoyed the thrill of roping cattle but failed to show promise as a rancher, left the comfortable confines of the family ranch in spring 1902, bound for Argentina, the land of the *gaucho*. His letters home reveal a young man on the make, an expectant capitalist who thought that the open range, much like the Cherokee communal lands, could be recreated in South America. He financed the trip by selling most of his cattle, garnering $3,000. Clem talked him out of selling the ranch along with all the cows, sensing that the young romantic might need something to fall back on. After some careful thought, Rogers talked yet another friend, Dick Parris, into coming along. Will agreed to pay his passage just to get some companionship.

The folly of the trip became quickly evident; once in New Orleans, Rogers discovered that no boat sailed directly to Buenos Aires. The only way to reach Argentina at the time was through New York and thence on to London, where ocean-going vessels regularly set sail for the lands south of the equator. Stuck in the Louisiana city for a few days, Rogers quickly found the best shows in town and took them all in. One in particular impressed him—*When Knighthood Was in Flower*, starring Julia Marlowe. The play involved political satire, a Victorian critique of political authority. Rogers loved the drama of the play combined with the political lessons that it revealed, but attending plays was expensive, consuming more of the cattle cash than he had anticipated.

The two world travelers caught steamships to New York and then London. Once over the seasickness that plagued him throughout the trip, Will sat down to write a few letters to his sisters and father back home. In England, he found the money and the language more than he had bargained for. After striking up a conversation with a street fellow, Will hardly got a word in edgewise, and mused to his sisters: "I was perfectly willing to pay him for his over time if he would kindly relate it over again." And he never did figure out the money. After eating, he simply handed the waiter a pound and "trust to the lord that they will take pity on me and do me half right." He ended up with a bag full of coins, or "money in bulk," as he put it, about enough "to make the first payment on a soda cracker." Little did he know that the letters were a hit back home in Claremore, as both his sisters and his father had them published in the local papers. They constituted Rogers' first published attempts at humor.

During the sea trip to Argentina, the pair of Oklahomans quickly consumed much of what was left of the cattle money. The two travelers took a few days to look over the prospects of ranching in eastern Argentina and gave up the idea. Argentina had experienced a ranching boom much like Oklahoma's, with modern railroads moving into the interior that had adopted refrigerated cars. Land prices had doubled, and it required $10,000 to $15,000 simply to get a start. Worse, once arriving, and being away from home nearly two months, Will discovered that his friend Parris had tired of travel and wanted to return home. Counting the remaining dollars carefully, Will discovered that he had enough to send Parris home, but not himself. He bought a ticket for his friend and looked for work.

Rogers finally found a job doing what he knew best: punching cows on a ranch some 800 miles inland. But he discovered that the *gauchos* could lasso a cow nearly as quickly as he could, and the pay consisted of a mere five to eight dollars a month. Worse, the cattle outfits did not have chuck wagons. He yearned for the old cabin on the ranch, and his cousin Spi's cooking. In a rather desperate mood, Will wrote: "The country is overrated." The people were simply "a lot of *dagoes* [derogatory slang for Italians!] from all over the world, and all having a different lingo."

At most, Rogers' experiences in Argentina taught him something about poverty, which he carried into later life. He often struggled to acquire enough money for food and a place to sleep. Finally, he concluded that his prospects might improve back in Buenos Aires. He talked with the few English friends he had made, read the English-language newspaper, and discovered a slow boat sailing for South Africa with a load of cattle. Will signed on, hopeful that South Africa might have workable ranch land. Before departing he wrote his sisters back in Indian Territory a revealing letter. He admitted to spending money foolishly in New York and London and feared that family and friends might think less of him for it. He hoped that his sisters did not think of him as a burden, and he admitted that they "have done everything in the world for me and tried to make something more than I am out of me."

Rogers was fortunate to survive the trip across the Atlantic. The cattle ship leaked and nearly went down in a storm. Will became terribly sick, and when he did recover, he found out that most of the crew's food was gone. But the old steamer made a landing at Durban after thirty-two days of hell, and Rogers agreed to help his new boss drive the cattle herd to his ranch in the interior. Along the way, he witnessed the ravages of the Boer War, and laughed heartily at the incompetence of the British Cavalry that still had a duty of preserving the peace. Purchasing agents had bought horses off the ranges of western America—they were so wild that Rogers declared it "suicide" to simply get on one. After hollering "Company Mount," in a few seconds you could see "nothing but loose horses and Tommies coming up digging the dirt out of their eyes." The British recruits had as much chance staying on the horses as "a man would have sneezing against a cyclone."

Rogers' sense of the war in South Africa never reached the point where he openly took sides, but the struggle left a deep impression on him. The Boers, Dutch settlers who had defied the British, had been badly treated by their British conquerors to the extent that concentration camps had been used to control populations. Perhaps a hundred thousand Boers and African allies died in the camps, many of them women and children. Much of Boer land was ranching country, not unlike the open spaces of Indian Territory, and the similarities between how Great Britain had treated the Boers and how the American government had treated the Cherokees were obvious. Yet Rogers saw himself as a visitor who said little, testimony to his mother's impact on his upbringing. Later, he would admit that the trip had brought him to think hard about his own nation. Ironically, rather than make him more cynical, he came to appreciate Indian Territory to a much greater extent after traveling through these foreign lands and witnessing what the British had done to the natives. American treatment of Indians could have been much worse!

By December 1902, Will's wanderings led him to Johannesburg, still looking for opportunity and perhaps a grub stake to get him home. He learned quickly of a traveling Wild West Show scheduled to go on that evening. Texas Jack, a colorful figure whom Will Rogers set out to meet, ran the show. Near the show grounds, he saw a lean, willowy figure in cowboy boots, spurs, and jeans. It turned out to be Jack, who indeed was a Texan (and acted like one), who met young Rogers with a square jaw and an open smile.

Jack had an interesting life, being the adopted son of a more famous "Texas Jack" who had initially performed alongside Buffalo Bill Cody in his first Wild West performance in Chicago in 1872. His father had led his adopted son into the business. While Rogers knew little of the lineage, he quickly stepped forward and asked Texas Jack for a job. After explaining that he had done some roping, Jack handed him a lariat. Seeing Rogers smoothly make a big loop, and jump back and forth through it, Jack's face broke out in a big grin. "You go on tonight," he said.

With just 35 people and 23 horses, the show was short-handed. But everyone got into the act, Rogers playing a screaming Indian during one of the scenes. "I screamed so loud that I like scared everyone out of the tent," he later quipped. The show lacked the "real" Indians of Buffalo Bill's rendition—a number of Englishmen with strong accents had to play the parts. But after the bucking broncos, an Indian fight, a stagecoach robbery, and the like had all finished, Rogers came into the arena and did his short act. He was an immediate success and his salary increased to $20 a week, quite a bit more than what he had made as a *gaucho* back in Argentina. Jack came up with a name, the "Cherokee Kid," and Rogers received billing as one of the premier acts in the show. Jack took advantage of

Will's singing ability, having him add a coon song and do an occasional cake walk.

These performances were the first of any sort in which Rogers did an act in front of a crowd in which he made serious money. And he studied that crowd quite carefully. He found it to consist of Afrikaners, or white descendants of the first western Europeans to settle Cape Town, Englishmen, and a combination of Black Africans often called "Kaffirs" in the day and age. A derogatory term, which was outlawed in the 1970s, Rogers had little difficulty in using it, despite its comparison to "nigger" back in Indian Territory. When he dressed up in black-face and sang coon songs for the audience, they roared in approval. "My appearance amused the natives and Kaffirs greatly," he announced in a letter to home. Afrikaners, Englishmen, and Africans alike must have been amused to see a white man, who was really part Indian, dressed and painted as a Black man, singing and dancing on stage.

Jack and Will got on famously, sharing a common background and good humor. Jack saw Will as more of a partner than an employee. Jack even offered Will the show, an inducement to keeping him in South Africa. But when Rogers had earned sufficient money, he boarded a ship to Australia and eventually, home. Jack took the rebuttal in stride as he convinced Will to look up the Wirth Brothers Show, which had just reached Australia. Will, Jack thought, could work the circus while seeing Australia. Jack gave Will a letter of introduction that stressed Rogers' work ethic, his sobriety—which might have been a stretch—and the fact that he was a champion lasso thrower. He caught up with the show in Sydney, was quickly given a job, and traveled with it to New Zealand.

Nearly everywhere he traveled with the show, he found notoriety. In Auckland, there seemed to be an insatiable desire for "anything American," Rogers noted. The January 20, 1904 *Auckland Star* suggested that Rogers' act was, "like most of our new things, American." It described Rogers as "the Cherokee Kid," a gentleman "with a large American accent and a splendid skill with lassos." Rogers had been honing his rope skill while on this two-year trip, working frequently with two ropes which mystified audiences. The attention was not lost on Rogers who sent home the clippings to his sisters. Yet Rogers yearned for

Indian Territory, and despite his new-found success, he booked passage on a ship for San Francisco thereafter.

While he had left Indian Territory traveling first class, his ticket back to the United States was below deck in Third Class. And when he arrived, he hopped a freight train across the Rockies, finally landing in Claremore. Rogers was a changed person. He came back with barely a nickel in his pocket. His father Clem seemed somewhat amused and hopeful that the trip had cured Will of his wandering spirit. He also hoped that Will would get an honest job. Will was "so broke," his father told a friend, "that he was wearing overalls for drawers." Yet the hopeful Clem faced yet another disappointment. Rogers had changed but he had also discovered that he could make a living as a showman. It certainly beat hard labor, as he later was fond to say.

Despite the similarities between the British treatment of the Boers and the American treatment of Indians, Rogers came away from his travels with a deep appreciation for the United States. Many of the men he met in Africa and Australia reassured him of these views. "I was always proud in America to own that I was a Cherokee," he wrote Clem from Australia on September 28, 1903, "and I find on leaving that I am equally as proud to own that I am an American." He confessed to his father that he had arguments with "every nationality of man under the sun," and most of the time, he found himself defending America. Will Rogers had taken a strange progression of thought, especially for a part-Indian person who had just lost a huge ranch to an imposed government policy. Perhaps it had something to do with the downtrodden condition that most people of color lived in around the world. The *gauchos*, poorly paid and poorly dressed, had impressed Rogers with their ropes, but not their humanity, nor had he found much sympathy in the suffering of the Boers or the "Kaffirs," people who had been oppressed by the English. But his ethnic and economic stature as the son of a successful Cherokee politician in Indian Territory, suddenly had more meaning when he compared his plight with so many other unfortunates.

This defense of a homeland came naturally as Will slowly discovered his own identity. But it came as well from Will's separation from the Civil War politics of his father, a veteran officer in the Confederate Government. Being Cherokee and American at the same time offered few contradictions for Will Rogers as he departed New Zealand, a dual identity that many American Indians, especially those of mixed heritage, had trouble digesting. Rogers sensed that others in the world were not as fortunate to live in a country like the United States, though it was a country that had humbled the Confederacy and the Cherokee Nation.

Though Will Rogers had seen the world—or at least Argentina, South Africa, Australia, and New Zealand—he still had much to learn about America. He would soon embark on new adventures into the heartland of his own country. His upbringing had left him with a mild nature, a strong, likeable, personality and a thoughtful presence. But there was still an important identity debate that would occur within his soul. And he struggled with the issue of race—not unlike most thoughtful, thinking Americans of that age.

Indeed, Rogers lived in a racist age; Indian blood ran in his veins at a time when being Indian was not particularly attractive or acceptable. This early identity challenge and all that came with it, his racism, his Americanism, would enter a new phase in 1904 when he entered the entertainment business. As the ropes twirled, Rogers told one-liners to the considerable amusement of his audience. And these quips drew upon his upbringing, as he poked fun of himself in order to get a laugh. This humor led to a new Rogers' identity, one bound up in the age of vaudeville, where comics were outsiders—many of Jewish or Irish extraction—and successful comedians seldom were viewed as sober, "true Americans." How Will Rogers successfully coped with this new challenge says much about him as a person—both an Indian and an American—as well as much about early twentieth-century America.

Will Rogers, circa 1915. (Brown Brothers)

CHAPTER

The Pursuit of Fame

The Cherokee Kid returned to America with a name and a reputation for showmanship. Texas Jack's show and the Wirth Brothers Circus were both well-known and successful venues, and Will Rogers name gained the notice of one of the key figures in the industry—Zack Mulhall. An irresistible opportunity also beckoned young Will. St. Louis planned to host the upcoming World's Fair of 1904, with pavilions from around the world and a considerable number of large shows. Frederick Cummins, Jim Gabriel, and Mulhall all had Wild West performances scheduled, and they required the expertise of a roper like Rogers. By April, twenty-five year-old Will Rogers had hopped on a train to St. Louis.

The fair offered excitement and entertainment only dreamed of in Claremore, Oklahoma. Among the pavilions that caught Rogers' eye were the so-called "Indian Building," and the large compound nearby that housed a contingent of natives from the Philippines. American Indians appeared in many places, performing in shows and working booths at the pavilion. Another thousand Filipinos manned various venues, displaying art, pottery, furniture, and other wares from their country. To many of the visitors, the Indians and the Filipinos came across as simple "primitives," from the far-off reservations of the American West and from the strange world of the Pacific Islands.

At the Indian Building anthropologist W. J. McGee held sway, offering a simulation of a paradigm borrowed from the works of Herbert Spencer's "Social Darwinism." The building reflected the stereotypical images of evolutionary progress that dominated the age. American Indians represented "savagery," some of whom had arrived at a more progressive position of "barbarism," but none of whom had reached the point of civilization. The gradual extinction of such people, Filipinos and Indians alike, denoted progress. At the fair, they could be seen perhaps for the last time. The lesson was not lost on Will Rogers, who within weeks of arrival stopped referring to himself as the "Cherokee Kid." The term would re-emerge later in Rogers' career, but for the time being he wanted nothing to do with being Indian.

Rogers worked mostly for Mulhall, who had several different venues that summer, and for Frederick T. Cummins, who called his show the "Wild West Indian Congress and Rough Riders of the World." While the Rough Riders supposedly included the famous band of soldiers who served with Roosevelt, most attention fell on the Indians. The latter consisted of a large contingent recruited from the reservations of the West, many of them Lakotas and Comanches. Nevertheless, Chiricahua Apache leader Geronimo remained the most famous among them, and the most feared, despite his advanced age of eighty-seven. Next in importance was Chief Joseph, the Nez Perce chief from the Pacific Northwest. Both had defied the American army and captured the imagination of the American public, but both had been forced to surrender and were still incarcerated. While Joseph had little fight in him, Geronimo had arrived from Fort Sill, Oklahoma with two army soldiers as guards. They stayed with him at all times, watching as he made arrows and sold them while sitting quietly in the Indian pavilion.

Rogers kept his distance from these more famous Indian men. The Cummins show that Will had joined had its Indian battles and stagecoach robbery, the typical entertainment for Wild West shows. Rogers' act remained isolated from these events. He did rope tricks and rode with the rough riders. At one point, however, he donned the dress of George Armstrong Custer and simulated the death of the last man at "Custer's Last Stand." As imaginary bullets pierced his body, he fell across his horse and slid to the ground. Wild Indians surrounded him and did their war dance over him. On another occasion, an Indian participant entered the area with a loaded pistol and fired it off near Roger's head. While this random shot went harmlessly into the air, it likely only confirmed Will's general bewilderment of his Indian partners in the show.

Rogers worked best alongside Mulhall, a determined plainsman from Oklahoma whom Will openly admired. This affection only strengthened when Mulhall, supposedly confronted on a street one afternoon, pulled a gun and shot three people—one of whom had tried to kill him. While Will thought afterwards that it might have been better had "the Colonel," as Mulhall was affectionately called, only knocked the man down, Roger remained convinced that Mulhall had acted appropriately. Weeks later, Rogers joined the Colonel, who had been released from jail on bond, in a roping contest at the Delmar Race Track and reputedly "broke the world record" of thirty seconds for downing a steer. The event also featured roping by Geronimo, who snagged a steer on his first try and wrestled it to the ground. Rogers failed to reference Geronimo's efforts, which made the newspapers, in his letters home to his sisters.

To what degree Rogers crossed the road to visit the Indians who participated in the various shows is not revealed by his letters. He does refer to the group as "Blanket Indians," a term commonly in use at the time. The term was employed by the "civilized" Cherokee and other such Indians to describe plains groups such as the Kiowas and Comanches, whom they generally disliked. This racial, or more correctly, ethnic conflict had historical roots in Oklahoma. Cherokees had migrated into the region from North Carolina and Georgia after 1805; others were forced to join these early arrivers after Indian removal became law in 1830. Cherokees fought with the indigenous tribes of that region for control of land, a conflict that produced deep animosity. Rogers no doubt heard old stories of this conflict during his childhood. He inherited a built-in racism against "Blanket" Indians, which took years to overcome. It showed no sign of abating in 1904.

Public accounts show that "Blanket" Indians often did double duty, performing for the Cummins show as well as working within the Indian Building, doing dances that attracted audiences, revealing spiritual ceremonies, and like Geronimo, selling their wares. A number of Indian women had joined this group, some of whom prepared food while others did beadwork and leatherwork, which sold quickly in the festive atmosphere. Rogers no doubt saw such trivial economic pursuits as degrading, certainly unbecoming the so-called "civilized" Indians such as himself.

After appearing with several different shows for nearly three months, Rogers moved on to a burlesque theater in downtown St. Louis, called *The Standard*. Here, Rogers honed his "cowboy persona," improving his double roping skills; according to one account, he was the only cowboy who could successfully whirl two ropes at once. Yet he realized that the act needed something else. While standing in the wings one afternoon, a dog darted across the stage, escaping its responsibilities in an act, and Will quickly roped the small animal. That night, he realized that his tricks could include the roping of a horse, if he could actually accomplish the feat on a small stage. Borrowing a horse from Mulhall, Rogers practiced with it, and the new act materialized, with a horse as the needed prompt.

As he worked on his roping routine, Rogers moved on to Chicago and then the East Coast, once again joining Mulhall, who had convinced a jury of his innocence. On the way east, in April 1905, Will Rogers, the Cowboy from Indian Territory, got the chance of a lifetime—he performed for President Theodore Roosevelt's children at the White House. Tom Mix, another famous cowboy entertainer, who Rogers had met in St. Louis, had also been invited to the event. Attired in "cowboy boots and hats," the two men did tricks to the great delight of Roosevelt's children. A reporter from the *Washington Times* noted on April 23 that Rogers was "one of the few cowboys who can use two lassoes at once." While the President did not attend, Rogers would later meet and become a great fan of Teddy Roosevelt.

Just two days later, the Mulhall entourage opened at Madison Square Garden in New York City. Lucille Mulhall, a trick rider, received star billing, but Rogers remained a close second. Yet his fame did little for his private life. He had reunited with Betty Blake from Arkansas at the St. Louis Exposition, but Will failed to move the relationship forward. Betty returned to Arkansas. Thinking that his notoriety might help his courting, he confided to roommate Mix that he might introduce himself to one of the young "cowgirls" who performed in the act. After the next night's show, Mix was surprised to see a downtrodden Rogers come into their room, his hat back on his head, his eyes glistening over, and his mind distraught. Rogers had overheard one of the girls talking about him. She had admitted interest in the cowboy at first, but finally said that "she could stand being entertained by the darkest inhabitants of Africa, but an Indian went against her nature." Will went back to work, conscious of the liability his ethnicity carried in some circles. He continued on with Mulhall, sharing a hotel room with his friend Mix.

As the Madison Square Garden shows prepared to close, a strange event put Will Rogers back on the front pages of the New York newspapers. At the last performance, as the crowd settled into their seats, a steer broke from the herd, hurled itself over the wooden barricade, and forced women and children alike to run for their lives. Vendors dropped their confections as the steer bounded up the stairs into a hallway. While what happened next is open to conjecture, a story in Joseph Pulitzer's *New York World* reported the next day that a young performer named Will Rogers had lassoed the animal and brought it back into the arena. Other papers suggested that the steer returned of its own accord, but the event thrust Rogers back into the limelight. He took advantage of it, remaining in New York after Mulhall's departure and trying his hand at working in vaudeville. While he did not enjoy immediate success, the king of vaudeville in New York, Benjamin F. Keith, finally signed him to a contract. Yet Rogers sensed that his own act had limited appeal. It needed some innovative changes.

Keith owned nearly two dozen theaters, located mostly in eastern cities. He had been responsible for developing a more modest, middle-class show. Rather than the bawdy, dance hall atmosphere of most typical vaudeville theaters, where women sold drinks and served as prostitutes, Keith offered good clean fun. His show appealed to both working-class and middle-class families, and children also attended. It featured acrobats, who juggled and tumbled to drum rolls and rim-shots, followed by singers and dancers, comedians, and an occasional short play.[1] Will Rogers often performed the last act, and he discovered that the roping aspect of it, while crucial, became more entertaining as he joked and talked with the audience. While newspapers in 1905 identified him as the "Lariat King" of vaudeville, reviewers of his performance within the next year or two increasingly mentioned his "plainsman talk."

Will's dialogue played on the same prejudices common to all performers of the time. He often joked about Jewish and Black Americans, who were a common target of comedians. At one point, he added to his routine the imitation of a "Yiddisher Cowboy," which apparently brought the house down. Keith's theaters attracted the very best that vaudeville had to offer, and the King of Vaudeville refused to allow bad language, which led to more singing and clean humor. Rogers fit well into this vaudeville genre. After missing a rope trick one night, he quipped: "I'm handicapped y h'yar [you hear], as the manager won't let me swa'ar when I miss." Rogers used this mild joke over and over again, bringing down the house nearly every time.

Keith had a host of successful acts under contract. These included Harry Houdini, the Three Keatons, Josephine and George Cohan (a sister and brother dance team), Fred Niblo, and Earnest Hogan. One in particular, Louise Henry, was a comedic singer whom Rogers became somewhat enamored with. They took walks together, had dinner, and had a brief affair. Notes kept by Rogers during his months in Australia and New Zealand reveal similar trysts with female performers, one of whom wished to run away with him. Henry, however, was married. While it is uncertain to what degree the relationship matured, in later letters to his future wife, Betty Blake, Will confessed to a fling or two although he never mentioned Henry's name.

The demands of his rising career separated him from Henry as Rogers headed off to Philadelphia to perform. His act was such a hit that theater owners competed for his services. By summer of 1905, Will appeared in several of the best theaters in New York, accruing the astonishing sum of $75 a week. Shortly thereafter this

---

[1]A good description of Keith's role in changing vaudeville is found in M. Alison Kibler, *Rank Ladies: Gender and Cultural Hierarchy in American Vaudeville* (Chapel Hill: University of North Carolina Press, 1999), 24–27.

figure rose to $150 a week. His rise to stardom likely surprised him, as he had intended to go home after appearing at Madison Square Garden but found the money too enticing. By fall of 1905, the legendary William Morris Agency signed him, and his salary again nearly doubled, to $250 a week. Others in the business made more—a few star attractions paid upwards of a thousand dollars a week—but some successful vaudeville performers often received only 15 to 20 dollars a week. Rogers was doing well.

Such a handsome fee required that the Rogers act settle into a routine, one that theatergoers would pay to see. It generally started with Will walking onto the stage while doing a few simple twirls with his rope. He always dressed the part, wearing buckskin trousers, a red flannel shirt, cowboy hat, and large handkerchief. With a signal, his new partner Buck McKee rode onto the stage on Teddy, the horse will had first practiced with and later purchased from Mulhall. Will then roped them both with two different ropes simultaneously. Following this, Will did some simple tricks, jumping in and out of a loop that he twirled. The act's finale involved Will mounting Teddy and making a huge loop with his lasso that twirled above his head for some time and then encompassed both the performer and the horse.

Rogers' ability to poke fun of his mishaps gave the act more appeal—he occasionally botched a trick in order to comment on it. He developed a list of one-liners to use when his rope missed its target. Some were simple, such as being "handicapped" and not able to swear. Others were ad-libbed. After following an archery act, in which the Teutonic performer opened by suggesting that he "nefer" made a "meestake," Rogers followed him by admitting that he sometimes made "meestakes." Audiences universally came to love his human persona and boyish demeanor. Rogers commonly got three curtain calls by fall 1905, which was unheard of in the business.

In these early years, Rogers faced the reality of vaudeville politics. Theater owners dominated the business—the two most prominent being Keith and his partner, Edward Albee—and sometimes took advantage of performers. Just getting paid could be problematic. And when actors complained, they could be "blacklisted," or denied work. A few efforts had been made at organizing performers into a union but Keith and other theater owners broke up the first effort in 1901. Another group called the White Rats replaced the broken union in 1907. It was eventually affiliated with the American Federation of Labor. The owners eventually broke it too, after a bitter strike in 1917.

In typical fashion, Rogers generally avoided politics as it smacked of confrontation. There is no indication that he ever joined the White Rats, or had his name attached to any of the many blacklists that theater owners collected during the period. Rogers was able to remain independent primarily because of his act's success. He even forgave theater owners who canceled his act despite having a contract that obligated them to pay him. He had a unique act that could not easily be copied, and it sold well. It allowed him to play the consummate outsider and remain above the struggle that often separated performers from theater owners. Whether his attitude represents general apathy on his part for union activity, or downright disdain for it, is impossible to determine. On the other hand, since vaudeville was dominated by performers from working-class and immigrant backgrounds, and the White Rats considered their organization to be somewhat of a fraternal order, perhaps Rogers never felt welcome in it.

Rogers did enjoy the camaraderie that came with being a performer. Performers faced constant insecurity, and they clung together. They shared advice on improving parts of their acts, and generally saw their performances as that of "them," being the entire show, versus the audience, which could at times be noisy, critical, and mean. Two who studied Rogers and his unusual delivery of jokes were George Jessel and Eddie Cantor. Rogers formalized many different friendships with performers such as these, a number of whom were Jewish. Rogers came from a state and region that elected a number of politicians who belonged to the Ku Klux Klan—which persecuted both Blacks and Jews—and these relationships broadened his sensitivity to various ethnic groups that he had little contact with in the past.

Rogers developed an affinity toward fellow actors and actresses reminiscent of his days around a campfire with cowboys, not knowing what challenges would appear the next day. Vaudeville was a rowdy life of adventure and travel that appealed to Rogers. He also believed that it was temporary and that he should take from it as much as he could, as quickly as he could.

Within a few years, he had sent home thousands of dollars, having his father buy up acreage in and about Claremore.

Will's success also allowed him to continue his exploration of the world. In 1906, Rogers recruited a troupe to tour Europe. The group, with Rogers as the main attraction, performed for several weeks in Berlin to hugely appreciative crowds. He met, or at least nodded to, Kaiser Wilhelm, who rode his horse daily in a park named Tiergarten near the theater. The trip allowed him a stopover in Paris, where he, like all travelers of the age, marveled at the Boulevards and the crowds that they attracted. The Parisians walked slowly along the tree-lined streets, gazing at the artists who hawked their paintings. To a cowboy from Indian Territory, the scene was so civilized. Understandably, Will also enjoyed the nightlife, which never stopped. He was so impressed during this first trip that he returned again in 1907, this time performing in London. Since he had recruited the troupe that went with him, however, Will discovered that simply doing the act was considerably easier than planning and financing such a trip. He made little money for his efforts and returned to the security of Keith's theaters.

Earning money of the sort that Rogers made for a fifteen-minute routine—albeit often doing it two or three times a day—required more than simply performing. Theater owners wanted publicity, and Rogers took on a new role of promoting the show a day or two before it opened. While on the road in Toledo, Ohio, in October 1905, he gave his first major interviews with both the *Toledo Times* and the *Toledo Bee*. Now far away from the Wild West Shows that had launched his career, Rogers re-embraced his Cherokee background. The *Times* reported that Will was "a full-blood Cherokee" from Indian Territory, who came from an elite family. His father Clem was President of the Claremore Bank and a member of the Cherokee Senate.

The *Bee* went further, quoting Rogers on the issues of the day, especially the treatment of Indians. While Rogers seldom identified with Indians in general, at least this once he wryly commented on whether they were "getting a square deal." He did not belabor the fact that he believed otherwise, moving on to play his audience and drum up excitement for the show. Will grudgingly noted, in typical western fashion, that "eastern folks" were "all right." Yet he claimed to be different: "when a man's system gets inoculated with the life o' the plains," and finds himself in an eastern city, "he's like a sailor ashore." Regardless, Rogers well knew that the open range that he promoted had long since vanished. To keep up with the changes, Will kept sending checks back to his father with which to buy land.

Ironically, as the West he knew disappeared, Rogers played on its popularity in the East. He often entered a new city by riding down main street, dressed in fringed leather breeches or chaps, a fiery red flannel shirt, complete with a sombrero hat, whirling his lariat as he went. Rogers had supplanted his Cherokee identity with a Western identity. The *Lowell Daily Courier* noted that to meet Will Rogers was "as good as reading a half dozen chapters of Owen Wister's 'The Virginian.'" This wildly popular novel was written by the Harvard-educated friend and classmate of Theodore Roosevelt, Owen Wister, in 1902. Wister, to easterners, was the West personified, and he played the theme to the hilt.

While his western identity mostly dominated his behavior, at times Rogers returned to a dual identity, suggesting that he had once lived in a tepee. In interviews, he occasionally admitted to being "a quarter-breed," and to being proud of it. "I'm a Cherokee and they're the finest Indians in the World. No 'Blanket Indians' about them," he raved. Cherokees were civilized and educated. Indeed, Rogers claimed that the government would not allow the Cherokees to go to such Indian government boarding schools as Carlisle. "They're for the ignorant kind [of Indians]." Cherokee schools in the territory, however, were "just as fine as any in the country." If the "boys" from Cherokee country wanted a better education, their parents sent them east and paid their tuition. At a time when many of his friends were Jewish entertainers, Rogers built a wall between himself and the majority of Indians in America. But in all fairness, most Cherokees in Indian Territory viewed western, or "Blanket," Indians as virtually another race.

In these many interviews, Rogers also continued to explore what he clearly perceived as an evolving, unique persona, comprised of genuine, marketable components. While an elite Cherokee Indian—not a "common" Blanket Indian—he also revealed himself as a "real" cowboy, not an invented one. This especially became clear when he commented on the novel *The Virginian*. In a rather remarkable contrast, Rogers did his best to distance himself from "the Virginian," and what he perceived as Wister's invented cowboy. And along the way, he created a new, powerful image of how a westerner should act. The Virginian was a cardboard cowboy to Rogers, created by an eastern writer for an eastern audience that did not know better.

"There ain't no such West as them fellows that wrote say there are," Rogers once proudly proclaimed to the *Baltimore World*. The Virginian, quite bluntly, was a fraud. "There ain't a man in the West who would do a pal as dirt as the Virginian did," Will proclaimed. The Virginian had "no spirit," no affection for his "bunkie," and he had no sense of western morality and justice. In the real West, men were left alone out of respect, including "outlaws," as long as they did not bother a person. Will claimed that many an outlaw had come to the Rogers' ranch and received the same treatment as a common traveler.

The last statement rang true. Will's father had once been charged with murder, or at least collaborating with outlaws who arranged a murder, a charge that never stuck. Such occurrences were common in Indian Territory. Outlaws gunned down several of Rogers' relatives in the violence that dominated the territory in the late nineteenth century. Accordingly, as Will saw it, the Virginian demonstrated a lack of understanding of right and wrong when he gave into the pressure that resulted in the hanging of his friend, though the friend was a rustler. True cowboys simply did not participate in such a disloyal act. Rogers claimed that while he sat with cowboys beside a camp-fire one night, when one of the men in the group reached the hanging scene in the book, he threw the novel into the fire in disgust. No westerner could stomach such a thing.

Newspaper editors across the land relished such interviews. They gave flavor and substance to Will Rogers' persona as a western Cherokee Cowboy; an outsider who honorably clung to the morality of a past world. These interviews also revealed a man who was gaining confidence on stage and in dealing with reporters. By 1911, Rogers abandoned using a horse on stage, doing the act solo, and using more homespun humor than rope tricks. The rope tricks became a way of spacing out the humor. He easily transformed his show from a novelty act to a comedic monologue.

A reviewer from the Chicago *Inter-Ocean* aptly described the genius of Rogers' act. "In place of trying to nourish the sympathies of his audience," he began, Rogers "contrives to make them sorry for his stage fright . . . and his lariat tricks and apparently unstudied conversation score the more heavily for that feeling of pity for his embarrassment." But the "feature" of his act was not the "cleverness with the lariat; it is the surprising manner in which he plays upon the sympathies of an audience willing enough to be sorry for a stage fright that doesn't exist."

This led to more political dialogue; risky, perhaps, given the age, and also somewhat new to vaudeville. But Rogers, with his "stage fright" appeal, discovered that audiences were ripe for political banter in an age when politicians were often larger than life.

Rogers virtually brought his audience to apoplexy when he contrasted Theodore Roosevelt and William Howard Taft, the two Republican frontrunners for the Presidency in 1912. He frequently provoked the audience by musing over what had ever happened to Theodore Roosevelt (who in fact had been hunting in Africa for two years after leaving the Presidency). "You must remember Roosevelt, don't you?" he started. "I wonder what has happened to him?" Then a short rope trick followed. "Sometimes they come back," he quipped. This brought a strong "huzzsa" from the TR supporters who had come to hate Taft. And then he quickly followed with "sometimes they don't," which brought a crush of applause from the Taft supporters. Being a folksy cowboy allowed for such banter. Rogers went on to admit that he might have to vote for Democrat William Jennings Bryan, who had run for President a decade before. To fail to do so would have resulted in a thrashing with a "neckyoke" from his father, he once told an amused audience. Rogers, viewed as the "sage from the Plains," could approach such subjects without retribution. Other comics, who lacked Rogers' boyish appeal and his western, other-worldly persona, could not do it as easily.

This ability to comically compare himself with other people allowed him to address religious issues. He once castigated Taft for being "wishy-washy" on religion, because he was supposedly a Unitarian. Rogers declared that his father had been a Unitarian and that this was hardly a religion at all. Will had "chucked" all religion. "Like myself," Will mused, "he [Taft] doesn't know what he is." Rogers' mother had been a devoted Christian and Will had attended Christian schools, yet his meandering into religious subjects had some personal meaning; Rogers had gradually abandoned organized religion; he apparently never joined a church. Perhaps it had something to do with the friends he kept—many of whom were non-Christians—and his work on the road or perhaps his early religious schoolings had been too strict on a less-than-dedicated student.

These attempts to discuss religious and political issues contrasted so markedly with the routines of other comics. W. C. Fields and Nat Wills, so-called "tramp comics," did juggling and rude commentary that appealed to the lower classes. Good friends such as the Jewish joke-tellers Jessel and Cantor also offered far different routines. They, along with many urban comics, often appeared in "blackface," the most common comedic routine of the age.

Blackface comedy became an important entertainment form in America, appearing as early as the 1830s. It involved painting one's face black, setting out one's eyes and lips in white paint for grotesque contrast. The common routine imitated Black slaves on plantations and their supposed, comic, childish behavior. The comedy took a new form in the so-called "dandified *coon*" of eastern, urban America, who appeared in blackface, wearing a woolly wig, gloves, and black tailcoat. He danced and sang minstrel songs. This completely American "art-form" perpetuated racist views world-wide, becoming immensely popular in England after the turn of the century. Blackface ethnic comics had created characters that had eastern, urban, ethnic identities. They lacked wholesomeness, and thus, had to remain mostly non-political, for their comedy often was what many Americans perceived as being "un-American."

While Rogers occasionally added a "coon" song to his roping act, he usually came off as a folksy, rather patriotic songster rather than a typical "coon" singer. On a few occasions he dressed in blackface for a performance, trying new ideas, but he usually thought it best to leave such "professional" singing to the experts such as May Irwin, Marie Dressler, or Sophie Tucker. At one point, he even added George M. Cohan's "You're a Grand

Old Flag" to his repertoire and cake-walked around the stage. In reality, these heady years on the vaudeville circuit slowly had made Rogers into a "cowboy philosopher," or as one reviewer named him, "The Droll Oklahoma Cowboy." Regardless of the name, Rogers became expert at judging his audience.

As Rogers became more a monologist than a physical performer, his ability to play the audience had much to do with timing, as with all comedy. While his act was disorderly at times, and he appeared unprepared or frightened, this was a ruse. Rogers left many written examples of how hard he worked at the proper timing and placement of his gags. He even conspired with the orchestra to perfect his timing. He would introduce a rope stunt by stating "I tried it last week and spilled it all over the place." Then the orchestra would abruptly play, and Will, acting annoyed, would break them up. "Wait a minute. I haven't got to it yet. You horned in with that music too soon." Rogers timed his jokes for the greatest impact, and most were used over and over again in town after town. He poked fun of this repetition, once announcing on stage that "you can tell that's a new one . . . every time the orchestra laughs."

His act, with its occasional patriotic flair, avoided the often crude, scandalous, ethnic banter of the Jewish and blackfaced comics. This remained mostly true also in his personal life, which took a turn to the better in 1908. He had occasional affairs with female performers, but had always been careful—in later years when fellow actors or performers wrote their memoirs, his friends seldom had any details to record regarding Rogers' female companions. By 1906, once Will had become successful, he made a serious effort at courting Betty Blake. He saw her after returning from Europe and again, the next year, returning to Arkansas for brief respites. But the courting went slowly; Betty appeared unwilling to join the nomadic theater scene, or perhaps she still had some reservations about marrying an Indian from the territory.

This finally changed in 1908 when Betty consented to marry Will. Betty was twenty-nine, an age that at the time signaled the approach of spinsterhood. Other offers might not come. The agreement hinged on Will's willingness to give up vaudeville and settle on what had become a rather substantial ranch that he had acquired near Claremore. He had money in his father's bank. Betty agreed to join Will in one more tour of the East after the wedding, allowing Will to fulfill his contracts. With the deal in place, Will, two of his sisters, and his father Clem journeyed to Rogers, Arkansas. The blessed event occurred on November 25 at the Blake home with a Congregational minister officiating. The new family departed that afternoon for New York.

While the marriage might easily have failed under the hardships of road life, Betty rather quickly abandoned her conventionality. Betty Blake was a product of the Victorian Age, of the "Cult of True Womanhood," as it was often called, of nurturing family and keeping house. To Will's happy surprise, Betty realized that her life in Arkansas had been dull. In New York, she discovered the opera (which she dearly loved and Will generally loathed), and visited Wall Street, the Bowery, and the Statue of Liberty. These two soul-mates, both twenty-nine years old, had to make up for lost time. The transition was complete when a female friend visiting Betty from Arkansas voiced serious complaints about the fact that Betty and Will had dined at the Metropole Café, a place where sports betters, prizefighters, and actors converged. Betty had even shaken hands with a prizefighter, something respectable women from Arkansas did not do. Betty was unrepentant.

The wedding and Betty's rapid adjustment placated Rogers' once pervasive fear that as an Indian, he could not enter the white world. The break with his ethnic identity rushed to the forefront while he and Betty were touring the West; there, Will first visited the Pueblo Indians of New Mexico and Arizona. His description of their ways led to his complete abandonment of his modest amount of "Indianness." All Indianness, after assimilation into the white world, through marriage, became ugly to him, at least for a time thereafter.

This ugliness was most apparent when Will and Betty visited the New Mexican Pueblo San Ildefonso. Will poked fun of the gorgeous black pottery that these people made, calling it "a cheap grade." Will sent a postcard to relatives from another pueblo, that of Isleta, on which he had written above the image of a pueblo woman who was weaving, "Me Heep Big Injun." In all fairness, the New York art crowd had yet to discover the beauty of New

Mexico, its unique and exquisite Indian art and tapestry. In an interesting contrast, which clearly reinforced his need to be seen as a white person, Rogers became a staunch friend of the cowboy artist Charlie Russell, who he had met in New York in 1904. Russell's art depicted the last of a fleeting frontier and the disappearance of the Indian. Rogers collected many of Russell's doodles, especially those on postcards and visited Russell in Montana on occasion. Later, Russell frequently stayed at the Rogers' home in California and Will and Betty helped market his art.

After several years of traveling, Will and Betty settled into permanent housing, taking a place on Long Island, and they started a family. William Vann Rogers arrived in 1911, followed by Mary Amelia Rogers, who was born in May 1913. The family added another boy, young James Blake Rogers in 1915, and finally Fred Rogers, in 1918. Will's joy at parenthood was tempered in late October 1911, however, when news arrived that his father Clem had passed away in his sleep. Fortunately, Clem had lived to see Will's success and had sent along presents for young "Willie" after his birth. Yet another devastating blow came a few years later when Fred, only an infant, caught diphtheria and died. In the typical Cherokee fashion of avoidance, Will never spoke of his father or Fred again.

Spending time in both New York and Arkansas, the family thrived, yet Rogers' act appeared to near its end. By 1915, Will found it difficult to get engagements as vaudeville was in its last throes. Theaters were running new motion pictures, which were being mass produced across America. While some larger theaters in New York continued to offer plays and some vaudeville, many, at least of the sort that had thrived in local, community venues, were turning to "silent" motion pictures with piano players who put music to the action on screen.

Will worked harder to find engagements, and lowered his fee. When this failed, he turned to friends such as Fred Stone, an actor, who lived next door on Long Island. Stone had become one of Rogers' best friends; they often rode horses together and enjoyed each other's company. More important, Stone knew people on Broadway, and this helped lead to Will's first part with a new musical, *Hands Up*. The show lasted less than a month, but it led to a part in what was then the most important show in New York, the *Ziegfeld Follies*. Rogers did not start at the matinee, but rather was hired to work the *Midnight Frolic*, which occurred on the roof of the Amsterdam Theater where the *Follies* performed. Patrons sat at tables, danced to an orchestra, and listened to light comedy. The *Frolic* had literally become the "in place" in New York for the mostly young and middle-aged rich.

Since regulars often frequented the *Frolic*, Rogers had to find new material. While he had worked prodigiously in the past to develop new routines for vaudeville shows, his efforts had usually lasted for at least a complete season. The principal writer for the *Follies*, Gene Buck, suggested that Rogers turn to the newspapers for new jokes. Will already read many newspapers, and he realized that they offered plenty of gossip and news. Out of this combination of comedy and newspaper stories, the modern monologue was born, with its political and social commentary. It was an immediate hit.

The *Follies* and the *Frolic* had become institutions in New York by the time Rogers joined them. The show had originated in 1907, under the direction of Florenz Ziegfeld, Jr., the son of a German immigrant who might easily be judged the greatest showman of all time. After honing the show in Atlantic City, Ziegfeld moved it for the summer to New York, and thence went on the road come fall, hitting the biggest, eastern cities. The one consistency of the show was Ziegfeld's inclusion of dozens of girls in a variety of costumes, some quite modest and others, rather scandalous.

At first, most of the girls had plenty of ostrich feathers to provide strategic coverage; as the *Follies* progressed, year after year, the girls were less attired. When designer Ali Haggin joined the show in 1918, he seized upon mixing sex and art. Kay Laurell had her début as "September Morn" that fall. Posed completely nude on top of a huge globe, she sat motionless as soft lights and music swirled around her. The next day, a writer in the New York press dubbed her the new "American Venus," and the nude revue was born. During one season, Ziegfeld had several nude girls posed in silence, like a Michelangelo statue, iconic works of art that never moved a finger, as other female dancers from the revue strutted in feathers about them in what became the "Grand Revue."

Rather than middle class, the act was high-brow and it attracted the very crème de la crème of Eastern Seaboard society.

Ziegfeld promoted the revue by advertising it as showcasing the most beautiful women in the world—and it likely did, at least those to be found in America. To become a Ziegfeld girl quickly became the dream of many young women. Ziegfeld actually auditioned 15,000 girls every year for several dozen slots in his show. He often gave interviews on how he picked the girls—they had to have perfect figures, bust 36, waist 26, hips 38. He then dressed those selected in ermines, sables, and mink coats, and demanded that the girls be immaculately dressed wherever they went. The girls themselves became instant stars, icons of wealth and fashion, and an instant advertisement for the show. Many, including Irene Dunne, Fanny Brice, Paulette Goddard, and Helen Morgan, went on to Hollywood careers. While tickets to the *Follies* cost considerably more than a simple vaudeville performance, they sold out while the smaller theaters were closing their doors.

While the girls likely brought in much of the crowd, Ziegfeld quickly realized that the show needed entertainment. He added new faces every year, corralling a bullpen of talent. Famous singers and comics included Jessel and Cantor, as well as Bert Williams, Ann Pennington, Ed Wynn, and W. C. Fields. Contemporary short plays and skits often poked fun at politicians and wealthy patrons. The show had everything—comedy, beauty, grace, and glitter!

While the *Follies* remained a solid part of the entertainment scene in New York into the late 1920s—and Will Rogers its star comedic attraction for years—the *Frolic* on the rooftop became the place where rich New Yorkers took their out-of-town friends. There, comedians such as Rogers could rub shoulders with the elite of America. An astonishing list of celebrities showed up at the mid-night shows. It included America's leading business elites, and their sons and daughters, such as the Harrimans, the Vanderbilts, the Goulds, and the Morgans. The mayors of New York, John Purroy Mitchel and John F. Hylan, occasionally the brunt of jokes, nonetheless came. More important, while such men came to the *Frolic* to be entertained, Ziegfeld also realized that his acts must remain at least on the border of respectability. Jewish comics in blackface, with their often off-colored humor, were inappropriate. Rogers was not.

While Rogers started with the *Frolic*, within a year he also toured with the *Follies*, often for six months at a time. Besides the dozens of girls, the cast just during the years 1916 to 1918 included Bert Williams, who may have been the best pure comic of his age, Ed Wynn, who did a "buffoon" act that often brought down the house, and W. C. Fields, who played a scruffy tramp who juggled everything from cigar boxes to pool balls. Cantor, a Jewish comic from New York, occasionally did black-face comedy and became one of the leading songsters of the day. Later, he became famous on Broadway performing the hit song, so typical of the 1920s, *Makin' Whoopee*.

Offstage, Fields begrudged Rogers' popularity and his close friendship with Cantor. Fields often played rude jokes on Rogers, at least at first, and lied about him behind his back. Fields, who professed to have an English noble background, was in fact ignoble; he drank too much, and he could be terribly impolite. Rogers got on with him despite these character flaws and ultimately won over his friendship. Later in life Fields visited the Rogers' ranch, staying for days at a time, and Rogers helped him break into films in the 1930s. While Will Rogers coined the saying, "I never met a man I didn't like," Fields often tested the theory.

The gaudy nature of the *Follies* also likely tested Will. Most of the theaters played on the road had nominal dressing room space. The main comics, such as Fields, Cantor, and Rogers, got their own rooms, but the girls in the revue were often forced to dress in a hallway or in a large room, where common access was possible. Fields frequently waited until one or several of the girls were *au naturale* to grab Will and turn him the right direction. According to Cantor, Rogers promptly turned red, tore himself from Fields' grip, and ran away. Fields roared with laughter, and so did Cantor, who noted that Rogers fell for the gag over and over again.

When not sparring with Fields, Rogers worked on his material hour after hour. Special targets were Theodore Roosevelt and William Jennings Bryan. Roosevelt had pushed for American involvement in World War I, which had broken out in Europe in 1914, while Bryan remained reticent. As Rogers read their words from the newspapers on stage, he followed with: "Bryan says that he will go to war if they want him, but Roosevelt says he will go whether they want him or not." More ammunition came from President Woodrow Wilson, who stood for re-election during the summer of 1916. Besides the campaign, Wilson was then dealing with the Pancho Villa raid into New Mexico, an American invasion of Mexico to try and capture the so-called "bandit," as well as with German submarines, which occasionally attacked neutral shipping, including some flying the American flag. Likely reeling from the many problems at hand, to the surprise of all, Wilson grabbed a train to Baltimore one evening expressly to see Rogers' act. It was an electrifying night for all.

Knowing that the audience included the President sobered Rogers. It was the first time a President in attendance had faced political comedy. Once on stage, Will slowly turned on the charm: "I am kinder nervous here tonight." Everyone laughed, including Wilson. Then he moved on, mentioning Bryan, who had been Wilson's Secretary of State; he recently had left the cabinet in a huff. Rogers turned to his now familiar "I wonder what has become of him," which broke the ice and brought a round of laughter. Taking on General "Black Jack" Pershing, who headed up the American forces in Mexico, Rogers made several quips about how the newspapers in the morning clamored with news regarding the capture of Pancho Villa, while those in the afternoon explained how he got away. The final line that brought the President to a belly-laugh came when Rogers brought up the continued "note" exchanges, or diplomatic efforts, then underway with Germany that went on in a dizzying fashion after each submarine attack. "Do you realize, people," Will slowly explained, "at one time in our negotiations with Germany, he [Wilson] was 5 notes behind." It brought the house down and later earned Rogers a brief interview with the President.

The *Follies* allowed Rogers considerable freedom, and he relished it. He occasionally used racial jokes with political overtones. Rogers consistently poked fun at the Mexican army and the country that tried to support it. "The Mexican soldiers get 10 cents a day for serving in the army. And the only day they earn it is the day they try to collect it." On another occasion he pointed out that the Mexican soldiers, unlike those in Europe, did not fight from trenches. "That's right," Rogers matter-of-factly noted,

"They'd rather be shot than dig a trench." The *Follies'* jokes, then, were something a father would have little difficulty in letting his children hear, while at the same time, they had a maturity that made them unusual for the day and age.

One more aspect of Rogers' act says much about entertainment in America during this age. While doing his *Frolic* or *Follies* routine, he made a point of asking celebrities in the audience to stand and then he roped them, adding a mild joke that they found amusing. It soon became a tradition, for getting roped by Rogers made the newspapers, and important people liked being in the news. Rogers rewarded ushers at the theaters who informed him of celebrities who came in unannounced. Actors Douglas Fairbanks and Mary Pickford were victims. Democratic governor of New York, Al Smith, also went along with the gag. Rudolph Valentino, perhaps the hottest sex symbol in Hollywood, took the rope. And minions of industrial leaders bowed to Rogers' rope. One of Rogers' biographers, Ben Yagoda, has noted that the thrill that Rogers received from being in the company of such people vindicated his decision to go into show business. It also demonstrates that Rogers had a considerable amount of insecurity, as happens to be the case with most comedic entertainers.

Perhaps this insecurity is best displayed in the issues that Rogers avoided. New York at the time of Rogers' rise to prominence was the intellectual center of America. Writers and artists flocked to the city where patrons often gave them refuge. The most remarkable patron of the day was Mabel Dodge of the famous automobile family. She had opened a salon at number 23 Fifth Avenue, in Greenwich Village. Here the elite of America's writers and thinkers came together, including D. H. Lawrence, Walter Lippmann, Max Eastman, Lincoln Steffens, Sinclair Lewis, Eugene O'Neill and John Reed, the indomitable Marxist, who ultimately joined the Russian Revolution, died of fever, and was buried in the Kremlin. These intellectuals, through their novels and letters, became the social critics of the day, exposing an America that was too materialistic, and too industrial to be culturally vibrant.

Such critics thought that the United States was a nation developing without a soul. World War I only confirmed for them the cultural decay as millions of troops were cut down from machine guns, tanks, and mustard gas. The critics sought many remedies for the overall problem, including investigating one of the leading issues of the day: race. Salon regular Carl Van Vechten first took on the issue in 1912 when he convinced Dodge to allow several Black performers from Harlem to sing in her salon. This was a novel idea. They were part of what became the "Harlem Renaissance," a parallel movement to the Greenwich Village group. While Dodge initially was not impressed—she later expressed considerable anxiety over the "Negress" who had sung too passionately for her in high boots and visible stockings—the exchange continued. The Harlem group had launched the Apollo Theater by 1912, on 125th Street, a venue that offered an entirely new entertainment concept, ultimately helping spawn the "Jazz Age," as F. Scott Fitzgerald called it ten years later. Like the pottery at Pueblo San Ildefonso in New Mexico, the Harlem group was on the cutting edge of entertainment by the time Rogers reached the *Follies*.

What made this collision of culture so unique was its focus on race. Dodge eventually had to choose between being a patron of the new Black culture or that of the American Indians. She eventually chose the latter and moved to Taos, New Mexico where she married a Pueblo Indian named Tony Luhan. Dodge's Taos salon had coalesced by 1920 into what was likely the most famous collection of intellectuals in America—Lawrence came west, along with Willa Cather, Margaret Sanger, Greta Garbo, Ansel Adams, Thorton Wilder, Mary Austin, Georgia O'Keeffe, and the young John Collier, who would transform American Indian policy in the 1930s. Their views varied, but perhaps salon member D. H. Lawrence put it best: "white men have probably never felt so bitter anywhere, as here in America [in particular, the American city], where the landscape, in its very beauty, seems a bit devilish and grinning." There is, he continued, a "desire to extirpate the Indian, and the contradictory desire to glorify him." While the landscape of New Mexico appeared "culturally" pure—unlike that of the barren, smoky, New York City—the Indian was part and parcel of this brave new world and salon members embraced him.

Individuals connected with this new, western salon would eventually cross paths with a curious Will Rogers, who ultimately reassessed his own values. Yet as he lumbered on, night after night, at the *Follies*, and the war in Europe slowly came to a close, Rogers remained oblivious to the new literary and intellectual world that was emerging around him. He certainly had abandoned all that was Indian, virtually ignoring the issue in his letters and his nightly routine. He said nothing of the coming together of the final curtain for Buffalo Bill's Wild West Show in Denver in 1915. The politics of Washington, D.C. and the struggle in Europe became wonderful distractions that led him astray from his roots and any serious questioning of his identity. He was, as he said, an American, plain and simply so.

This satisfaction with his own position in society led Rogers to ignore another group that appeared on the scene just before the war. It came together at Washington, D.C. in 1911, and ultimately called itself the Society for American Indians (SAI). Organized by such leading American Indians as Charles Eastman, author of many famous books, including *Indian Boyhood* (1902) and *From the Deep Woods of Civilization* (1916), the group sought publicity at every turn, publishing magazines and writing newspaper articles. Eastman, a Dakota or Sioux Indian, was typical of the group, being both a medical doctor and a writer. He was the best-known Indian in America; someone who Rogers surely knew of but never spoke of.

A host of other important men and women joined Eastman in the SAI. Carlos Montezuma, from Arizona, castigated the Bureau of Indian Affairs on a regular basis. He authored a famous piece printed in the *New York Tribune* in 1905—and many others in years to come—which Rogers surely read. Arthur Parker, the nephew of an earlier Seneca Indian who had been Commissioner of Indian Affairs, also had considerable visibility. These men saw citizenship as a crucial need in America for Indians, but they could agree on little else. They all criticized the American Indian policy of the age, and many wrote extensively about it. A good example of such a critique came from SAI member William J. Kershaw, who published "The Red Man's Appeal, Being an Address to the President of the United States," in 1914. Rogers, who read every newspaper he could get his hands on, could hardly avoid seeing the critique of these so-called "Red Progressives," yet he ignored them in his evening monologues.

Rogers remained aloof when it came to all "progressive" issues. But in fairness, he had come of age professionally and politically in 1915, after much of the progressive agenda had run its course. Roosevelt had created the United States Forest Service and had set aside large amounts of western land as National Forests and parks a decade earlier. The Pure Food and Drug Act dated as well a decade before Rogers' *Follies* routine. And most of President Wilson's progressive agenda dealt with banking and taxes, issues that Rogers generally avoided.

Not all progressive issues had been settled. Rogers, for example, ignored the so-called New York Settlement House movement and the controversy it created over immigration, a debate which continued unabated into the 1920s. The controversy addressed the merits of allowing more foreigners into the United States, especially people from eastern and southern Europe. Such issues were simply too confrontational for Will Rogers. The best that can be said of Will was that with an income of between $50,000 and a $100,000 a year, Rogers did devote a portion, about 10 percent, to charity. His contributions went mostly to the Red Cross, a mainstream organization that he publically supported.

Perhaps the only glimpse into Rogers' cautious mind came during a series of comments made in Minneapolis, Minnesota, and later recorded in an interview with the *Kansas City Star* on March 11, 1919. While in Minneapolis, he spoke at a dinner reception in which the mayor preceded him. The mayor's comments riled Rogers, for he noted that "some good people from the South were with us, too [in World War I], for the South now is part of the United States." Rogers, always the folksy gentlemen, this time could not help himself; "I am glad to be back in Minneapolis again," he started. "The last time I was here was the year they started teaching English in the Minneapolis public schools." The crowd did not like the comment, which referenced the deep Scandinavian brogue spoken by the mayor and many residents of the city. Rogers still was sensitive about his southern background.

Perhaps his southern background explains why a man like Rogers would avoid Harlem, despite the reputation of the Apollo Theater as a place of entertainment innovation. His prejudice against Blanket Indians also likely explains his lack of interest in the SAI, which often met in New York. But a likelier reason for Rogers' reticence lies in his non-confrontational nature and dislike of controversy, though he certainly had not forgotten what the federal government had done to the Cherokee Nation, forcing it to give up vast amounts of land, including the beloved Rogers' ranch. Will's success, his hobnobbing with celebrities, and his acceptance into the Anglo world, at least in the late 1910's, made it easier for him to ignore the reality of life for the downtrodden in America.

Certainly Will's new celebrity friends sincerely supported him. As the war came to an end and the hardship of doing two shows a day took its toll, Rogers made a snap decision to move to Hollywood, California. Fairbanks and Pickford were instrumental in this decision and the Rogers family bought land that allowed for the stabling of horses, just down the road from the Fairbanks estate. Fairbanks and Pickford, the most successful stars in Hollywood silent films at the time, helped get Will a role in his first movie in November 1918. He stayed on in the business for a few more years, but he then discovered the liabilities of filmmaking. It did not pay as well as he had hoped. Rogers returned, at least briefly, to the *Follies* in 1922. But California quickly became the Rogers' home and it remained so for the rest of Will's life. He and his wife never did return to the Oklahoma ranch that Betty had anticipated when they married.

While this transition occurred, Rogers took his initial stabs at writing a daily column. This would lead to a more stable income and help defray the expenses of living in California. The "Philosopher of the Prairies," as he was on occasion called, wrote short pieces about almost everything, starting in 1918. Most were commentaries on the war, the peace, Prohibition, which offered considerable material, and baseball, one of his favorite sports. His writing had the usual flair for comedy. Remarking on the Peace Commission that went to Europe under Wilson's hand, Rogers noted that the Democratic President had brought along one Republican, to "wait on the Peace table." When American troops stayed on in Siberia in 1919, Rogers suggested that they were simply waiting "for their mail" to catch up with them.

With the possible exception of his jab at the mayor of Minneapolis, Rogers' humor never hurt people and often gave them recognition. Celebrities liked being called out of the crowd. In his last years in office, President Wilson appreciated Rogers' light-hearted assessment of the war, and Rogers' humor, if just so slightly, gave the *Follies* the respectability that it needed for success. And politicians had been fair game in newspaper cartoons and commentary for many years. While Rogers might have made their views on certain issues seem like nonsense, his persona as a cowboy comic, one who lacked sophistication and used an unusual vocabulary, made such humor acceptable in America.

At the point the Rogers family moved to Hollywood, Will's life had been an attempt to enter and become successful in the mainstream white world he admired, perhaps especially the capitalistic side of that world. Once in Los Angeles, however, Rogers met and became friends with the mostly Jewish filmmakers and writers who dominated the scene. These relationships accelerated a steady change regarding Rogers' inner thoughts about people, race, and the country that he so fervently embraced. The Roaring Twenties was not a particularly placid period in America, either in terms of politics, or especially in terms of race. One historian has dubbed it the "Nervous Generation." The surging Ku Klux Klan took over states such as Texas and Oklahoma. Race riots broke out just after the war in several major cities, including a terrible incident in Tulsa, Oklahoma, when whites burned out the Black community of Greenwood in 1921. This was close to home.

Perhaps more of a concern was the moral decay that infested the politics of the country. The beloved Teddy Roosevelt died in 1919. His successors in office, Republican William Howard Taft, whom Rogers had immeasurable fun with, and Democrat Woodrow Wilson, were honest and decent men. But after the war, the new Republican administration of President Warren G. Harding, during 1921 to 1923, proved to be one of the most corrupt in American history. Big business and big banking followed suit, showing little concern for ethics.

How would Rogers, the bashful, folksy entertainer turned writer who found criticism difficult, respond to this new age in America? Could he be a successful commentator without responding to such excesses? Fortunately, the California air was rife with new ideas being pushed by new, exciting people. Newspapers were often unattached to the politicians of the age, conscious of their role in a rapidly changing and new society. Will Rogers was about to get the education that he had so successfully avoided during his youth. It would lead to his renaissance.

The Renaissance

California had become an American Mecca when the Rogers family departed for the West in 1919. Los Angeles, a bustling city of over 300,000 people, possessed mountains, Pacific Coast beaches, and a wonderful climate. The move to Los Angeles went smoothly. The family rented a house downtown. Will and Betty actually arrived a few months before Mary Pickford and Douglas Fairbanks, who had encouraged them to look for land outside the city in Beverly Hills. There, in 1920, Will and Betty bought a well-developed house on eleven acres, with stables and a pool. It was located just behind the famous Beverly Hills Hotel.

The land had at one time been an oil patch, but its value increased with each passing month. The purchase convinced Rogers of the potential for real estate investment in California. The construction of "Pickfair," the Pickford/Fairbanks estate, was underway not far from Will and Betty's new house. Despite its location in a bustling new Hollywood community, the land surrounding Rogers' new home looked similar to northeast Oklahoma, with range land to exercise the horses, plenty of sun, and a moderate temperature. Only the mountains and the ocean made it different, a refreshing change from the smothering heat of the summer on the central prairies.

Rogers immediately fell in love with California, which had become a capitalistic speculators' paradise. He bought land in an almost fanatical fashion. He quickly financed three lots in Beverly Hills and then purchased a whole block on the corner of

Wilshire Boulevard and Beverly Drive. Rodeo Drive, which would be one of the most famous avenues in America, intersected with this new purchase. A few years later, Rogers bought another large tract of land that later became Santa Monica. Will had learned from his father the value of land, and he turned to it for his future security rather than to the stock market, which at the time had become accessible to individual investors. Indeed, the market would become a target for much of Will's future comedy, but then, so would Hollywood realtors, whom the humorist considered a questionable breed.

Others promoted California along with Pickford and Fairbanks. Fred Stone joined the Rogers family in the West. Stone's sister-in-law had convinced a newly successful movie producer to see one of Rogers' shows at the New Amsterdam Theater. The man in question was Shmuel Gelbfisz, originally from Poland, who changed his name to Sam Goldfish, once in America, and later to Sam Goldwyn. Partnering with director D. W. Griffith, they made a film called *The Birth of the Nation* in 1915, which eventually made the astonishing sum of fifty million dollars. This capital funded Goldwyn Studios. Goldwyn signed Rogers to do *Laughing Bill Hyde* in the fall of 1918 just before the move to California. The story of a friendly escaped convict in Alaska, who proves his worthiness while on the lam, the film made money. This led Goldwyn to sign Rogers for two more years at a salary of roughly $9,000 a month, nearly three times what he was making with the *Follies*. The films were made in California.

The money proved irresistible and it allowed for considerable land speculation, but it did not match what leading actors in Hollywood were paid. Both Charlie Chaplin and Roscoe "Fatty" Arbuckle took home an astonishing million dollars every year, and Fairbanks and Pickford likely doubled that figure. Ironically, Goldwyn signed Rogers to do melodramas rather than comedy. At one point, Will donned a blond wig and played a Swedish fisherman. Rogers showed surprising abilities in front of the camera. He quickly perfected the broad grin, the scratch of the head, and a quizzical look that were standard silent film gestures. He received good reviews, some critics comparing his realistic portrayals with those of Hollywood mega-stars. But he lacked the sexy box office appeal of Rudolph Valentino, whose two films,

The Sheik and *The Four Horsemen of the Apocalypse* both appeared to rave reviews in 1921 (Valentino became the ideal "romantic" idol to many young women, who flocked to his movies), or the absolute comic relief of Chaplin. After making a dozen films in two years, Goldwyn failed to renew Rogers' contract. One criticism tells all: the film committee of the Methodist Episcopal Church recommended all his films, for families.

Rogers did return to films and made dozens in the years to come for a variety of producers. But his film career and the money that came with it temporarily ended in 1921. He headed back to the stage, returning to New York and the *Follies*. Nevertheless, he kept most of the California land he had bought and his family stayed there as much as possible. This led to a life of constant travel, back and forth, between the two coasts.

The movies had boosted the fame of the still young comedic actor. Rogers discovered that Ziegfeld was willing to pay him $3,000 a week, more than the movie studio contract. Working in the *Follies of 1921*, he suddenly was the highest-paid comedian in the show and, of course, its star attraction. While Rogers continued to use his tested rendition of calling famous people up to the stage, he also added new material with guests in occasional comedy skits. While the melodramas and comedy skits lacked originality, they led the way for the later success of comics such as Red Skelton and Carol Burnett. Ziegfeld, on the other hand, helped further the risqué morality that became synonymous with the "Roaring Twenties." His girls appeared on stage completely nude, a situation that ultimately brought Rogers to protest. The girls of vaudeville had always been vulnerable, some being sexually exploited by managers. While this was not the case with Ziegfeld, Rogers, who looked out for the girls, finally put his foot down, refusing to perform under such circumstances. Ziegfeld relented and provided some modest cover-ups.[1]

Rogers' apparent embarrassment fit well with the traditional elements of his comedy routine. He often noted that he was "the

---

[1]On several occasions, union activists seized on the exploitation of young women in vaudeville to organize theater performers. Rogers had nothing to with such unions, despite his individual efforts to protect female performers. See Kibler, *Rank Ladies*, 171–184.

only man who came out of the movies with the same wife he started with." He also built into those values a certain nationalism, and he became uncharacteristically angry at those Americans who were pushing the phrase "100 percent Americanism," a term that appeared in the aftermath of World War I. They were usually the same people who also called for the deportation of people who were not "American," or people of an ethnic origin other than Anglo. Political debate and politicians beckoned Rogers ever more as the decade moved on and he started to show an interest in ethnic issues, including ones that reflected upon the citizenship of Poles, Slavs, Greeks, Russians, or Italians.

The Rogers kept company with people of a political persuasion that is described generally as "progressive," whether Democrats or Republicans. While in Washington, D.C., Rogers often dined with Theodore Roosevelt, Jr. and their close friend Congressman Nicholas Longworth. Theodore Jr.'s father had frequently spoken of Rogers before his death in 1919. Former President Roosevelt had suggested that Rogers, more so than anyone else, understood the "American mind." Rogers' comedy in the *Follies* reflected the fairness and decency Roosevelt appreciated. Of this comedy, Rogers later noted: "I have cracked quite a few jokes on public men here, both Republicans and Democrats, I hope I have not given any offense. In fact, I don't believe any *big man* will take offense."

Upon rejoining the *Follies* in 1921, Rogers recouped the money that had suddenly disappeared from his movie contract. Over the next few years, Will continued with the *Follies*, did an occasional film, and turned to writing weekly newspaper columns of a light-hearted nature. While the films and the weeks on the road probably made more money, especially early-on, the weekly column came to epitomize Will Rogers, and his views on America, especially regarding politics, foreign affairs, American society, and race.

The United States was entering a rather unenlightened period in its history—one initially dominated by the Red Scare of 1919 to 1920. Some leading Americans had adopted a definition of "Americanism" based on the belief in the superiority of the white race, and on the fallacy that a nation built mostly by immigrants should expel newly arriving Europeans or Asians who were somehow un-American. Some of these groups—as well as Black and Indian Americans—were even blamed with fomenting social declension, or a decline in the moral standards of the Victorian Age. Finally, the twenties were a materialistic decade with rampant greed, as exhibited by the stock market craze and political corruption.

Perhaps the most perplexing of all these issues remained a "progressive" one that went back several decades—Prohibition. Will Rogers mostly disagreed with so-called "teetotalers," or people who abstained from drinking. He consumed hard liquor as a youth and had worked many a vaudeville halls where bartenders sold drinks in excess. He had difficulty adhering to the new morality of the age, that of abstinence. But it descended upon the nation like a thunderclap in 1920 when a constitutional amendment was adopted that prohibited the manufacture, sale, or transportation of liquor, followed the next year by the Volstead Act, which put enforcement under the authority of the Department of the Treasury. American feminists, among others, had pushed the legislation for years, under the belief that it would cure unemployment, a serious affliction that undermined the family. The war also played a role in passing the legislation, as most brewers were German Americans, with names like Ruppert, Pabst, Lieber, and Schmidt.

While supporters of the law approached the new decade with great optimism, Americans openly violated Prohibition. Brewers turned to producing "near-beer," which could be "enhanced." And ships congregated off shore along New England's coast, beyond the three-mile limit, off-loading liquor onto high-powered speed boats, which smuggled it ashore. Some 2,000 cases of Jamaican Rum and Canadian Whiskey entered New York state every day. "Speakeasies," or illegal saloons, appeared off dark alleys in nearly every American city. Rogers noted in his column that senators and congressmen consumed liquor while on the floor of Congress.

Rogers found himself in the middle of this age—explaining the reactionary politicians, the greed, the muddled foreign policy, the perceived declining morality, and the hypocrisy of Prohibition— trying to make sense of it all. The first opportunity to comment on these issues in print came when a film company he had worked with hired him to provide fifteen witty sayings, or "gags," a week, at a salary of $750. Initially, he thought only of using material from his *Follies* routine, almost all of it political in nature. The upcoming Republican convention in Chicago that summer, in 1920, offered the cowboy comic what he needed. The front runners were the Progressive Senator Hiram Johnson from California and General Leonard Wood, who had subdued the Philippine Islands in 1902 after a rebellion by natives. While Rogers could not attend the actual convention, he wrote extensively about it, concluding, after Johnson and Wood had done considerable damage to each other, that Warren G. Harding would be the victor. "The Delegates vote the way their people tell them the first ballot," Rogers informed his new readers. "But after that they sell to the highest bidder!"

While hardly a novel notion, Rogers told the truth. Within a year, his columns were longer and more interesting, and they had been syndicated, or carried in a variety of newspapers. The columns slowly matured primarily because of the friends that Rogers made in California, both in and out of the movie industry. They did much to alter his world-view. For a young man from Oklahoma with little education, whose father had owned slaves, this transformation was nothing short of a renaissance. Newly made friends brought Rogers to re-evaluate much of what he thought—or he had never considered important—about the rich, the middle class, and the working men and women of America, some of whom lived day by day. Between 1919 and 1925, Rogers metamorphosed from a one-dimensional comic and writer who covered politics at a superficial level to a confident commentator on the rich, the industrial entrepreneurs of the age, European royalty, politicians, Hollywood mega-stars, and especially the common man. He kept his columns at a stylistic level that the average reader could appreciate.

Just how this change came about is still difficult to determine, as Rogers never mentions his influences in his letters or writings. One Francis Fletcher Lummis played a major role. Rogers had met Lummis in California while on tour in 1907, and they resumed their friendship in 1919. Lummis was brilliant, eccentric, committed to preserving the West, especially its Indian and Hispanic heritage, and a famous journalist. He wrote extensively for the *Los Angeles Times* in the 1880s to 90s, penned a monthly called *Out West* by the turn of the century, and in between, published numerous volumes on history and anthropology. Most important, Lummis had a cadre of friends and followers who simply could not resist his electrifying personality.

Lummis could make words do things that Rogers only dreamed of, and both Betty and Will were enamored with him. They frequently attended his parties, held at the Lummis house, called "El Alisal," located just west of downtown Los Angeles. Indeed, Lummis dubbed Betty "Bonnie Betty," and the two often spent hours in the kitchen getting ready for the evening. At El Alisal, a hacienda style ranch house, visitors found hundreds of artifacts from Lummis' many trips into the Southwest. He especially collected Pueblo pots—and the most spectacular pieces of the age from new archaeological digs. The collection became the foundation for perhaps the most complete rendition of Southwestern Indian pottery in the United States, housed today at the Southwest Museum in Los Angeles, an institution that Lummis nurtured. Rogers must have been shocked to see that such a cultured man collected such "Indian" artifacts, items that he had considered "second-rate" just a few years before.

Lummis grew up in Massachusetts, went to Harvard, and there met the revered anthropologist Frank Cushing. Cushing enthralled Lummis with his stories of life with Indians, and when Harrison Gray Otis of the *Los Angeles Times* offered Lummis a job—literally the chance to see Cushing's West— Lummis leaped at it. Walking across the West to his new post in 1885, Lummis entered Pueblo lands. He would return again and again to New Mexico and Arizona, becoming an expert on native culture. At times, he moved into Isleta Pueblo and stayed for months on end. Rogers learned many lessons from Lummis, some of which he likely questioned. Lummis detested the crowded, teeming, slums of eastern cities—and perhaps their inhabitants to some degree—and he became a defender of the downtrodden, especially the American Indian and the Mexican American.

Rogers also learned much from the many friends, writers, scholars, and politicians that Lummis cultivated. Early on, these included President Theodore Roosevelt and the California environmentalist John Muir, powerful figures in the American "Preservationist" movement. Lummis convinced TR at one point to stop the Bureau of Indian Affairs policy of exporting Pueblo children to boarding schools outside of New Mexico. Lummis groomed young John Collier—a frequent visitor to El Alisal—who would eventually become the most important Commissioner of Indian Affairs in American History. Finally, Lummis ran with the crowd known in New Mexico as the protégés of Mabel Dodge Luhan—artists, writers, and intellectuals from a variety of backgrounds.

Lummis brought honesty to his friendship with Rogers and a critical, socially astute mind that Rogers had never been exposed to while in vaudeville. The two became fast friends despite Lummis' shifting family loyalties. He had already been divorced once when Rogers met him, and Will and Betty would witness two more breakups thereafter. Rogers had said mean things about a number of ethnic groups—especially Blanket Indians— when he first entered the Vaudeville stage. This aspect of his world-view changed dramatically thereafter. He also abandoned yet another viewpoint that was culturally a product of Oklahoma. While a young man, Rogers had tried valiantly to volunteer for TR's Rough Riders and serve in Cuba. Rogers also had been a supporter of American troops in Europe during the world war. He made jokes about getting them home after the war, but he had never seriously questioned Wilson's rationale for sending them. Lummis convinced Rogers to take a new look at world affairs, one far more critical of America's involvement beyond the country's border.

Lummis also forced Will Rogers to re-evaluate his views regarding race, whether dealing with Blanket Indians, Mexican Americans, or Blacks. Years before, when writing about the intent of the United States to bring "civilization" to the Philippines, after the Spanish-American War, Lummis' views on race were openly revealed. We would treat the Filipinos, he prophesied, "as philanthropically as we treat the Chinese— proscribed, disenfranchised, and occasionally mobbed. As philanthropically as we have treated our Southern Negroes . . . herded apart as if they were pariahs, and lynched every week in the calendar." Lummis changed minds with his pen and with his commitment to fairness and he preached an openness regarding sexuality that Rogers had been forced to reckon with while in the *Follies*. Such views, cynical but compassionate, weeping at times with overt criticism, rubbed off on Rogers, almost immediately after he reached California.

Will and Betty Rogers attended dinner parties frequently at Lummis' ranch between 1919 and 1923. The guest list included Charley Russell, Rogers' already-famous artist friend from Montana, who spent the summers in Los Angeles. Tom Mix, the cowboy now turned actor, Rogers' friend from Vaudeville, as well as close friends Mary Pickford and Douglas Fairbanks, often showed up. In the fall of 1921, young Collier joined the dinners. In addition, Lummis constantly invited friends from New Mexico, including Margaret Sanger (who started Planned Parenthood), Ansel Adams (America's most famous western photographer), Mary Austin (the most famous and prolific female author in America), and Georgia O'Keeffe (the best known female western artist in America). Perhaps the most interesting of the lot—at least to Rogers—was the indomitable lawyer Clarence Darrow. Rogers met Darrow at a noise and liked him immediately. Darrow was perhaps the leading liberal of the age.

An indication of the impact of the "noises" on Rogers came one evening in 1921 when he spent the entire night talking with western novelist, Eugene Manlove Rhodes. At the time, Rhodes was likely the most famous novelist in America, publishing several novels before the war and several in the early 1920s. Many of his books were the basis for Hollywood westerns. Rhodes had a much better understanding of the West than Owen Wister, or so Rogers concluded. In *Bransford in Arcadia* (1914), Rhodes depicted a western cowboy, Jeff Bransford, who refused to compromise the woman he cherished though it meant facing the gallows. Bransford certainly had the grit that Rogers wanted to see in a cowboy.

Lummis, despite his amoral behavior, had connections, and Rogers found an enlightening "salon" at the Lummis house that had no equal in America. Those attending were an unusual lot, complete with a few who practiced free love, and others, who raged against the follies of American foreign policy. And finally, despite the ban on the production and sale of alcohol, which went into effect in 1920, the "noises" were awash in gin and whiskey.

This never seemed to bother Rogers or his wife, Betty, who patiently labored in the kitchen with Lummis, making dinner, while Will worked the crowd.

Will Rogers changed his views about a variety of issues during these heady years. The change likely came gradually from listening and cracking light jokes with new friends at Lummis' parties, rather than making brash statements. It was not the Rogers way to impose, intellectually, on other people, but rather to listen, absorb, and respond with deflecting humor. This intellectual trait—that of absorbing rather than arguing—worked extremely well in the diverse crowds that Lummis attracted.

The day and age may also have influenced Rogers. Called the "Jazz Age" by some, it was a time of cultural reassessment, one in which Victorian norms became outdated. Car ownership was exploding, and automobiles replaced more placid—and guarded—parlors when suitors came calling. Young women chose skirts with a hemline that rose above the knee, considered "scandalous dress" by many Americans. Anyone who read such noted cynics as H. L. Mencken, the Baltimore columnist who made fun of everything in America, including the Boy Scouts and Christians, or F. Scott Fitzgerald, whose novels *This Side of Paradise* (1920) and *The Great Gatsby* (1925) generally concluded that sex and greed had become the alter egos of the country, could hardly be optimistic. Yet Rogers never fell to such cynical levels, nor likely did the nation at large. His humor reflected the changes that were underway, rather than endorse them. Few people wanted to believe that the average American, as depicted in the sensational novel by Sinclair Lewis, *Main Street* (1920), was callous, narrow-minded, and dull, or dominated by some deviant sexual drive, as the immensely popular psychologist Sigmund Freud was then arguing.

Regardless of how change came about, Will Rogers, a man from a conservative, small-town background, embraced the issues of the new age. This transition became apparent when Rogers prepared a speech for a Los Angeles crowd and defended the almost indefensible actor Fatty Arbuckle, who had made millions of dollars doing movies. Rogers knew Arbuckle's reputation—Fatty was a sex addict, often satisfying himself by inviting young, budding actresses to his Beverly Hills mansion.

Unfortunately, several days after having what was likely rough sex with the rather corpulent Arbuckle at a hotel party, sometime actress Virginia Rappe had died of a ruptured bladder. It could have been coincidence—the district attorney, a budding politician, thought otherwise, and indicted Arbuckle for manslaughter. The press tried and convicted Arbuckle, depicting the good-natured comedian as a sex villain who had attacked Rappe with a soda bottle.

Hearing the horrid news, movie producer Jesse Lasky quickly hired Rogers to replace Arbuckle in two upcoming pictures. The charge ended Fatty's once-lucrative film career. This event, along with several other notorious indiscretions by Hollywood actors, led to the creation of the Motion Pictures Producers and Distributors of America, a commission which hired Will Hays, then a respected cabinet member of the Harding Administration, to act as moral policeman in Hollywood. Hays' commission set moral standards for films and it created a blacklist to rid Hollywood of any more Arbuckles.

Rogers quickly took over Fatty Arbuckle's roles and pocketed the money. Nevertheless, he also took up the Arbuckle case, making comedy of the affair and criticizing the political overtones of the prosecution. The story of Arbuckle's abuse of Rappe had no basis in fact. While Adam and Eve had "made the rib," Rogers quipped to a dinner crowd two months after the charges had been leveled, sooner or later the conversation about Arbuckle "drifts to the bladder, it has supplanted the appendix as a conversational." And he went on—"The district attorney has been promised if he can hang Arbuckle he will be Mayor." Women groups, Rogers noted, wanted a piece of the action and held meetings for the sole purpose of debating what charge to levy against Arbuckle. "Its just a nice day for charging something," Rogers lamented. In the end, Arbuckle's greatest crime, Rogers thought, was "being from Los Angeles," a town with a deviant reputation.

Rogers, who had a good sense of his own moral obligations to wife and family, found himself defending the creativity of what many perceived as a morally corrupt Hollywood. But the place also provided fodder for humor—the charge of bigamy leveled against Valentino in the early 1920s only reinforced the outrage regarding Arbuckle as well as the scandalous behavior of Chaplin, who had a penchant for teenage girlfriends. Rogers, on the other hand, enjoyed just as much bantering about Will Hays, the new Hollywood moral policeman. Rogers' comedy made Hays a household name in America, a status about which he never complained.

While the evidence is slight, it may have been Rogers' idea to hire Hays, whom the comic had known for several years. Hays had introduced Rogers to President Warren Harding in 1921, busting in on the President without any notice. The three men had an extremely pleasant discussion in the Oval Office, with Harding telling most of the jokes. When Rogers tried to chime in on the President by suggesting that he tell a few "political jokes," Harding quickly responded: "I know 'em. I appointed most of 'em!"

Hays, for his part, was not puritanical in nature. After he came to Hollywood, the Rogers and Hays families often dined together, and the wives of the two men became fast friends. Amazing as it may seem, Rogers could defend a rather deviant Fatty Arbuckle, or Valentino or Chaplin, at the same time that he helped Hays forge ahead with his job. Hays soon saved the movie producers millions of dollars, which only secured his job and the commission. Each state had censorship boards, charging the producers by the foot of film cut from each movie before releasing it for viewing. Hays created a negotiated standard that all the states accepted, which ended those fees. Reaching that balance regarding what constituted acceptable morality in America became yet another lesson for Will Rogers the columnist.

The friendship between Rogers and Hays also matured because they both belonged to the Friar's Club. At a Friar's "Roast" one evening, Rogers spoke for over an hour about the "three Czars" in America, one naturally being his friend Hays. The others included Judge Kenesaw Landis, who headed the baseball commission in the aftermath of the Black Sox scandal—a case where several players tried to fix the World Series—and Augustus Thomas, who pledged to clean-up the theater, taking aim at such productions as the *Follies*, an undertaking Rogers likely—but quietly—applauded. Rogers, unlike some artists, sensed the need for such controls over society and he never questioned them.

Indeed, when discussing personalities, he fashioned his column around the need to maintain a reasonable balance between praise and criticism.

Hays became literally the most powerful person in Hollywood, but he listened to Rogers. Rogers instilled in Hays a sense of compassion—the new "czar," after being lobbied by Rogers, later removed Fatty Arbuckle from his blacklist, partly because Arbuckle had been acquitted by a jury. Fatty was allowed to work as a producer, but not an actor. The Hays Commission did however place a number of actors on the list, and it set standards for studios. A "kiss," for example, could not go longer than seven feet of film; clergy could not be depicted as comedic characters or villains; and adultery was taboo along with nudity. Studios scrambled to push the limits of these prohibitions, but generally agreed to them.

While Hollywood remained, such as legend portrays it, a sort of Sodom and Gomorrah, Rogers worked above it and his influence with Hays certainly did not hurt his film career. Just how someone with Rogers' wit—and he used it on people, including his friends—could manage to keep so many diverse people as close friends is somewhat astonishing. Unlike Rogers, Will Hays never drank alcohol. There was little common ground between Charles Fletcher Lummis and Will H. Hays, two of Rogers close friends.[2]

Rogers defended the motion picture studios and their actors primarily because it reflected on his own chosen profession. But these first forays into social and moral criticism revealed something more significant. Was America becoming prudish, dull, or both, and politicians self-serving? To what degree had Prohibition become a disgraceful double-standard? Those with money and power had no difficulty getting liquor. The hypocrisy of the age became a central theme of Will's weekly columns. It served him well as a vehicle since he could always turn to self-effacing humor, emphasizing his humble and somewhat anti-intellectual upbringing in Oklahoma, a background from which a commanding intellectual awareness hardly seemed expected by the reading public.

---

[2]Hays' relationship with Rogers is documented in *The Memoirs of Will H. Hays* (New York: Doubleday & Company, Inc, 1955).

Gauging the morality of American politics became a central theme in Rogers' columns after Republican Warren G. Harding won the Presidency in November 1920. Harding had been part of a political machine in Ohio—his campaign was run by fellow Ohioan, Will Hays—and offered the country hardly anything in the way of innovative legislation or leadership. He ran simply on the platform of returning America to "normalcy." Once he won, many of the machine's top lieutenants promptly received jobs in the administration. Several, including two cabinet secretaries, would be forced to leave the administration amid cries of corruption. One, Albert B. Fall, served jail time.

Just as Rogers began writing his weekly columns the signs of this corruption appeared. It offered ample opportunity for jokes and these made Rogers a powerful enemy, his former friend President Harding. Taking a trick from his *Follies* routine, Rogers started his columns with the quip "all I know is what I read in the newspapers." Eventually he would dub the column the "Illiterate Digest," primarily because of his use of made-up words and euphemisms taken from "cowboy talk," which gave the column an earthy flavor. Politics became a staple in the weekly diatribe, and the Republicans were frequently his target. They were "mangey with dough," he once wrote of Harding and his friends, and the implication was that they bought elections. Approaching the issue fairly, however, Rogers then went on to suggest that maybe the Democrats should have a slush fund to help elect their politicians.

By contrast, Rogers believed that the Democrats had but one wealthy man, Will's friend Bernard Baruch—who he called "Barney" in his columns. Barney often came by the *Follies* to say hello, and pretended to be embarrassed when Rogers introduced him. A Wall Street speculator by trade, Baruch had ran Wilson's War Industries Board during World War I. Rogers believed that Baruch was already running for the Democratic nomination for President in 1923, and Rogers endorsed him in a humorous way one evening during a *Follies* presentation. While Baruch offered some balance for Rogers' attacks on the wealthy Republicans in America, that separation—rich Republicans and poor Democrats—formed the basis for many of Rogers' columns that appeared in the early to mid-1920s.

Wherever you found Republicans, Rogers believed, there would also be hordes of bankers. In the classic Jacksonian, southern tradition, Rogers loved to criticize bankers, as well as those who gambled in the stock market, who he considered much-akin to bankers. Indeed, Wall Street became to him a symbol of that Republican greed that pervaded America in the 1920s. One of his columns in early 1923 addressed the farm crisis, a problem that would grow in years to come, offering a sobering critique of the farm bill that congress had designed to allow farmers to, as Rogers put it, "borrow money on what's called 'easy terms.'" "Show me ten men that mortgage their land to get money," Rogers concluded, "and I will have to get a search warrant to find one that gets the land back again." Congress, he thought, would better serve the farmers by passing a bill that made it illegal for anyone to borrow money from bankers. Rogers wanted to do away with banks entirely. "If you think it ain't a sucker game, why is your Banker the richest man in your Town?"

Rogers had found a "populist" topic that the average American could fully understand though such a view seemed arcane from an economic perspective. In truth, very few Americans liked bankers—and they were often the richest men in town—and Rogers, despite his rhetoric, used bankers to purchase vast tracts of land in California. A year later, the theme of rich Republican bankers and their manipulation of people again filled his columns. In a description of a Senate investigation, one of the witnesses identified Andrew Mellon, the Secretary of the Treasury, and a banker, as a man who "backed the bootleggers," by loaning them money. Quite a charge for the day, Rogers then deflected the criticism, adding a gibe at Prohibition. "I know a lot of bankers out in the farming and the cattle country that have been loaning on farms and livestock that would like to have as good collateral as a few hundred barrels of Old Crow [whiskey]." If Mellon had loaned on such collateral—and Rogers made sure not to accuse him of such behavior—"I would call him a better banker than 90 percent of the rest of them."

Rogers had no leniency for Wall Street either. A few weeks after America had elected Calvin Coolidge President, in November 1924, Rogers roared in his "Illiterate Digest" against "the disgracefully rich, or Republican, element of the entire country." They celebrated the return of their party to power by buying stocks. In an exaggerated comment, Rogers roared that the stock exchange had stayed open twenty minutes longer just to accommodate the splurge in speculation. "It was one of the worst personal hardships that the Exchange members had gone through," Rogers bemoaned in his column, as most brokers missed their 3:00 P.M. golf games. People wired in, demanding, "buy me some stocks." The broker asked, what kind? "Any kind," the buyer responded, "The Republicans are in, ain't they [stocks] supposed to go up?"

Old friends from Hollywood joined in the craze. Rogers reported that Tom Mix, Gloria Swanson, Ben Turpin, and Rudolph Valentino, all bought stocks and were engrossed in the financial sections of newspapers. Many had invested in movie companies and had inside information on what would sell at theaters. Rogers, in a particularly funny column, speculated as to what might happen had Flo Ziegfeld offered his company to the stock exchange. Rogers then speculated on the impact that his jokes might have had on the investment. He concluded by asserting positively that there would be funnier material under a Republican Administration than a Democratic one, making an investment in the *Follies* a good one. The stock market, then, to Rogers came to represent some aspect of America's moral transformation from an earlier, more economically stable era, but he failed to recognize the dangers inherent in such speculation, as did virtually all other Americans at the time.

Rogers' comedic critique of the wealthy of America led also to some discussion of labor strife. On several occasions he wrote about the twelve-hour day, which industries such as steel mills commonly employed at the time. While he avoided commenting on the legitimacy of labor unions—a major controversial issue of the day—his targets in the debate became Judge Elbert Henry Gary, Chairman of the Board of United States Steel and Charles Michael Schwab, who founded Bethlehem Steel Corporation. His jokes embarrassed the men in question. Rogers especially lit into Judge Gary after he collapsed when reading an hour-long report at a banquet on the benefits of the twelve-hour day. Schwab had to finish reading the report.

Rogers began his assault by noting that Judge Gary had put considerable thought into his argument—he made his "report" so attractive that most workers "were apt to stay the extra four hours on their jobs, just through the health and enjoyment that they got out of it." Rogers concluded that he had never understood that steel work was so easy: "the advantages that they enumerated in this report would almost make a Bootlegger trade jobs with a steel worker." Of course, it seemed odd that Judge Gary, who wrote the report "couldn't work an hour himself," while he expected his workers to continue on to twelve. Rogers considered going to work for Gary and Schwab "himself," but he was "going to try to get them to let me work 18 at least, for I don't believe I would get enough pleasure out of just 12."

The same sarcasm emerged in late December 1923 when the issue of the "Bonus Question" appeared in the papers. Soldiers who fought in World War I had been promised a bonus, supposedly due at retirement in some twenty-five years. While the economy of the 1920s seemed quite robust, some unemployment existed, roughly hovering around 10 percent. Veterans and some politicians considered the option of giving out bonuses early (this would be reconsidered in 1931, when a "Bonus Army" marched on Washington, D.C.). Rogers promptly came out in favor of the bonus payment, once again charging that it was the "rich" in America who opposed it. "You promised them [soldiers] everything but the kitchen stove if they would go to war," he began, but critics instead argued that only "disabled" veterans should be eligible for assistance. Rogers found this suggestion, one offered by many Congressmen, disgusting. He countered: "when he [the soldier] went away you didn't tell him he had to come home on a stretcher before you would give him anything, did you?" Rogers seemed intent, on some occasions, to take over the acid pen that Lummis had wielded so effectively in years past.

Then Rogers turned to his comedic charm, absurdly comparing the soldier and a laborer who worked in a ship-building yard. He farcically argued that studies had shown that German soldiers fired 25 bullets at each American soldier each day. "Now the way to arrive at the worth of anything is by comparison. Take shipbuilding . . . by an odd coincidence, statistics also show that each workman drove at the rate of 25 nails a day."

The soldier was getting paid just $1.25 a day while the shipbuilder got $12.50. "I know that bullet stopping comes under the heading of unskilled labor, and that shipbuilding by us during the war was an art. But I don't think that there is that much difference." Readers loved such bantering, despite its foolish nature.

Far better material for humor appeared in late summer 1923, when news of the Teapot Dome scandal broke. The investigation continued into the fall and next year as trials got underway. Rogers promptly blamed rich Republicans in office. There were, he wrote, "lots of people that won't speak or associate with one [a Republican]. They think they would catch some grafting disease." That disease involved a scandal over oil. Harding's Secretary of Interior Albert B. Fall, after taking bribes, had secretly leased naval oil reserves at Teapot Dome, Wyoming, and Elk Hills, California, to oilmen Harry Sinclair and Edward Laurence Doheny. Federal prosecutors eventually convicted Fall and he received a one-year jail sentence and a $100,000 fine.

The comedy over the oil scandal went on for another year, great material for a column that lived mostly on political parody. Rogers quickly saw the comparison between the scandal-ridden Hollywood and the scandal-ridden White House, and he poked fun of both. He suggested that his friend Hays be appointed to sort out the mess. He had a better chance than the Senate, which, Rogers mused, has proven "that the surest way to get anything out of the public mind and never to hear of it again is to have a Senate Committee appointed to look into it." What is more, Rogers went on, while "Tea [had] started one war,"—the reference being to the Tea Party in Boston Harbor that helped start the American Revolution—"nobody ever thought that a Tea Pot would boil over enough to scald some of our most honorable financiers." Certainly, Rogers believed, Will Hays should be appointed as a "wet nurse [to] the oil industry, and see if he can keep their nose clean."

As ongoing news of the scandal reached the press, Rogers was amused by the number of politicians and oilmen involved. He told his readers that he was the "only person I know of that has not been mentioned as receiving something in the nature of a fee from some big corporation." Then, in tongue and cheek, he confessed that he too had been on the take, hoping that if he came out with it, that at least he would be viewed as an "honest man." But it was difficult to be honest in Washington. In yet another tongue-in-cheek gibe, Rogers mused that a man had come to the Senate hearings hoping to tell his story regarding the oil scandal and suddenly found "twenty-nine cabinet and ex-cabinet members in line ahead of him." Witnesses to the corruption of the Republican Administration had to get in line to tell their stories!

Rogers found some solace in the fact that Edward Doheny had been revealed as a bribe giver. Doheny was a Democrat, and as such, indicated that other Democrats had also been involved in the corruption. As Rogers saw it, Democrats "would have looked rather dumb to be standing around with these oily shekels falling all around them and not opening their pockets to catch a few." Americans, Rogers felt, could forgive almost anything "with the possible exception of stupidity."

As the Senate investigation went on into March 1924, Rogers turned to chastising the lawyers who represented all the accused men. "Just think," he wrote, "America has one hundred and ten million population, 90 percent of which are lawyers, yet we can't find two of them that have not worked at some time or another for an oil company." So many lawyers were engaged by oil companies that business literally could not be done without them. "Oil men engage their lawyers nowadays before they have leased the land." You would think after the lease had been arranged, Rogers went on, that at that point, honest men would get together and simply "do business." "Oh no, lawyers must do that." There had been, Rogers believed, "at least one lawyer for every barrel of oil that ever come out of the ground."

When Edward Doheny's corruption trial got underway in Los Angeles, Rogers milked it. He first described a fictional trip to the train station to see the lawyers disembark. In a piece entitled "Meeting 2½ Carloads of Lawyers," Rogers described the crowd that waited patiently for the cars to unload, noting that the first group that came off were the "little ones." "Chances are," he wrote, their fees ran no higher than "maybe 40 thousand a case." The second car had lawyers who "wouldn't argue even a speeding case for less than a hundred thousand." The third group contained the "heavy hitters." "Real Lawyers! Men who, on a case like this which involves perhaps about 400 million dollars, why they consider that slumming."

The oil scandals, however, only revealed what most Americans already knew—that the country was creating wealth and that the economy was booming. Rogers readily admitted that the stock market continued to go up and new fortunes were made every day. The best that Rogers could do, under such circumstances, was speak out for those who were not as fortunate. One of his best columns regarding this comparison came just after New Years in early 1924 when he playfully questioned the continued economic progress of the country.

The piece began by quoting many of the richest men in America and what their views were regarding the future economic growth of the nation. Secretary of the Treasury Andrew Mellon said he "was an optimist. I never feel pessimistic." Henry Ford too was "at heart an optimist," who had "great faith in the coming year." Ford had reasons to be optimistic. His company was selling over a million cars a year in the early 1920s, or one every sixty seconds. Finally, a favorite target, Charles Schwab, got his turn. "I am at heart an optimist. I think the coming year will be the banner year of 1924."

After rounding out an entire page of "optimistic" quotations from rich Republicans, Rogers then lit into them. "Why, in the name of common sense, don't they ask somebody else what they think of the coming year?" The rich had a right to be optimistic. "If we had their dough we would be optimistic too. I would not only be an optimist for that much Jack, I would even be a vegetarian." He then wondered why they had not bothered to ask Will Rogers what he thought. "I want to tell you that it don't look any too rosey [sic] from where I am sitting. With every public man we had elected doing comedy, I tell you I don't see much of a chance for a comedian to make a living."

Rogers' questioning of the economic vitality of the nation became more serious when he discussed his favorite martyr, the American farmer. He had faced nearly four years of declining prices for wheat and corn by 1924; the average farm income had fallen by 25 percent. The year before, Congress had passed the Farm Credit Act, which tried to aid farmers by making loans less costly. A short time later, Congress finally passed a bill that would use federal subsidies to bring farm prices back to "parity," or what the average price had been before the war. The legislation provided for a federal agency to buy up commodities until prices reached parity, and then the government would unload the products on the world market. Seeing this as government intervention in the market, President Coolidge vetoed the bill. "See what the farmer is paid every year for his optimism," Rogers ranted on, parodying the optimistic statements of politicians.

Rogers remained careful with such "populist" comments, words that might promote class conflict. He had often brushed shoulders with the rich during his vaudeville days, and his letters, the few that we have, suggest that the meetings fed his ego. Yet, Rogers' modest and mostly comedic castigation of the rich in America had foundation in fact. Of the 27 million families in America that filed an income tax return in 1924, some 12 million had income of roughly $1,500 a year, and six million had earned less than $1,000. Estimates suggest that a family of four needed $2,500 a year to sustain a descent standard of living. Rogers' columns remained mostly comedy where the exaggerations seemed obvious to everyone and serious banter, which included statistics such as those above, was studiously avoided. His criticism of the rich became more pointed as the decade passed.

Up to the point of the oil scandals, Rogers had avoided criticism of the White House and its occupant. Despite being introduced to Harding by his friend Hays, he ran afoul of the beleaguered president. The criticism of Harding's various cabinet officers likely did in the relationship, but Rogers also found Harding's campaign rhetoric to be insufferable—Harding had continued to parrot the "return to normalcy" theme into the second and third year of his administration, and he emphasized the moral stands that he took on various issues—especially Prohibition—at a time when his cabinet was under siege for corruption.

On his famous trip west in 1923, just as the Teapot Dome scandal hit the newspapers, Harding stopped to deliver a speech on "the enforcement of the law," in Denver, in particular the law against selling liquor. Such rhetoric sounded foolish to Rogers.

As he saw it, "the bootleggers all agreed with him [the president] that the stricter the law is enforced the better it will make prices. Why, in some places it was getting terrible; the prices had dropped to almost what they were before the law went into effect." Bootleggers, according to Rogers, wanted enforcement; it made their stock more valuable. The argument was tongue-in-cheek but held considerable truth. Later evidence would also demonstrate that Prohibition led to considerably more organized crime, which profited from illegal liquor sales.

At Salt Lake, the cynicism surrounding Harding's trip cut deeper. Harding spoke at the Mormon Tabernacle. Rogers, no fan of Mormonism, pushed the limits of his own civility in describing the theme of Harding's speech as, "Thou shalt have no other wives before thee." The Mormon population and the Mormon Church had generally been Democratic in politics well into the turn of the twentieth century, believing, as Church leaders did, that it was better to support a party that preached states' rights, as the Democratic Party did, and thus leave Mormons alone to practice their different marriage beliefs, rather than one that demanded an end to polygamy and used federal judges and officers to enforce bigamy laws. This changed, however, after the church denounced polygamy in the 1890s and Utah attained statehood. By the 1920s, Utah Senator Reed Smoot had moved the state into the ranks of the Republican Party. Harding's stopover—one certainly not predicated on lecturing Mormons on polygamy, as Rogers had mused—was a reward for Smoot's political support in Congress.

The President found less relief from Rogers while in Idaho, the state of long-time Progressive Senator William Borah. Borah was a Republican, but somewhat of an enigma. He had progressive tendencies yet remained conservative on many issues. "It was a wise move" on Harding's part, Rogers noted, to speak in Idaho, especially about the tariff, which the President and Borah both believed should be higher. "What the lately passed tariff bill had done for Utah and the sugar beet" was truly remarkable, Rogers thought. It had resulted in cheaply made Cuban sugar becoming more expensive—and partially damaged the Cuban economy, which led to instability—but as Democrats rightly charged, it also led to higher sugar prices in stores. Rogers made the point to his readers, asking quizzically regarding "what it had done to the Housewives." The tariff remained high during the entire decade of the 1920s, and was increased again in 1930—the bill being authored by Senator Smoot—doing serious damage to the economy during the first year of the Great Depression. While Rogers failed to understand the importance of banking and liquidity, he was determined to support open markets and free trade.

Harding never liked political satire despite his attempt to be funny with Rogers in the Oval Office some two years before. Rogers, who was likely the most popular comedian in the country, and was certainly the most read, also realized that the fun could go too far. After Harding died mysteriously of a heart attack on his return trip from Alaska, Rogers put the best face on their differences, noting in his column of August 19, 1923, that while "the diplomatic relations were strained between President Harding and some of my jokes," that the two actually had patched up their differences. Rogers said that he had met with the President on an earlier occasion and had explained that he also told jokes about the Democrats when they were in office, some of which were "even funnier." Showing respect for the office, Rogers then concluded by praising Harding, a President who would go down in history as having one of the most corrupt administrations ever. "HE WAS A REAL HONEST-TO-GOD MAN," the comedic columnist concluded. That, he may have been, but it's doubtful that Rogers believed it.

Rogers learned a valuable lesson from his criticism of Harding, as was demonstrated by his attempts to posthumously praise him. While they might seem rather tame in comparison to the political cartoons of present day, severe, straightforward attacks on a president's policies ran against Rogers' nature. Also, Rogers enjoyed having contact with powerful people. One did not get invited to the White House after attacking the occupant. As the new President, Calvin Coolidge, took office, Rogers developed more careful tactics in his political satire.

Despite his populist leanings, Rogers went out of his way to be kind to Coolidge. He developed an honest affection for the new President, and especially the President's wife, Grace Goodhue Coolidge, an extremely well-educated and cultured lady. Long after the Coolidges left the presidency, and the early death of Calvin Coolidge, Will and Betty remained close to the family.

Coolidge's appeal rested on a simple, ideological stand against radical change—as represented by socialism, labor strife, and the rejection of the liberal criticism of capitalism and an aggressive American foreign policy—and in an indomitable belief in small government. He represented stability, morality, restraint, and piety in the mid-1920s, when many Americans feared that the country had lost its way. The Harding scandals, the moral decay as represented by Hollywood, and the fashion revolt against Victorian dress suggested, as historian Michael Parrish has noted, that "a raucous hedonism permeated much of the culture." Will Rogers seemed less fearful of this decay than most, but he understood the changes that had occurred and mostly admired Coolidge for his clear opposition to them.[3]

Will's first foray into the Coolidge presidency came just two weeks after his praise for Harding. The column was entitled "Why Don't Coolidge Fix it?" Rogers had a litany of charges, most of a farcical nature. "First, take the farmer." There had been no rain in some states and too much rain in others. "Now you see, he [Coolidge] had been in there a month now and it's time he was declaring himself." He was either for more rain or against it! Worse, most of the rain had fallen in Republican states, and Coolidge needed to explain that. But it was not only the rain, how about the boll weevil, a small insect that infected cotton plants. "Other Presidents have settled the thing by coming out against them [boll weevils] and why don't he!" There were low wheat prices—"Why don't he [President Coolidge] issue a message and say wheat from now on is $1.50 a bushel." The railroads needed fixing, a coal strike was coming, the new Soviet Union wanted diplomatic recognition and virtually all of the European countries were at each others' throats over war reparations. Rogers even brought Rudolph Valentino into the discussion. The male "love goddess" of the age was losing his hair and "What had Mr. Coolidge done about that?"

[3] See Michael E. Parrish, *Anxious Decades: America in Prosperity and Depression, 1920–1941* (New York: W. W. Norton, 1992), 47–51.

After the comedy had ceased, Rogers portrayed Coolidge as a "quiet man," a "confident man." Yet the author of the *Illiterate Digest* could not help but criticize Coolidge after his first State of the Union Address, which was rather short. The delivery, Rogers thought, was also "rather amateurish." Nevertheless, "when you figure that the gentleman hadn't used his voice for months, why, any little defect in delivery can readily be overlooked." Coolidge was becoming "Silent Kal," to Rogers, a Vice President who became President by accident, but one who had considerable character. One of Coolidge's most redeeming traits, Rogers thought, was his ability to fix problems without "calling Congress." If Coolidge only made them stay home, "he would go down in history as another Lincoln!"

As talk inevitably led to the upcoming presidential election of 1924, Rogers found Coolidge to be more palatable than ever. While public sentiment suggested that Coolidge had made a good Vice-President, such talk had ended and many pundits suggested that Coolidge had become a stronger leader. Rogers lauded his handling of the coal strike. Coolidge had done something that "no other President had ever been smart enough to think of." He had appointed another man to settle the affair, staying above the bantering. As the election neared, Rogers attempted some analysis of the Coolidge platform. He wanted to help the farmer, but he did not want anyone "to pay more for food." He supported lower taxes, but Coolidge recognized the need for raising more federal revenue. He was, Rogers argued, "a very agreeable man," who if able to deliver on such promises "should be the next President."

Coolidge slowly gained support throughout the country and Rogers sensed the reason why: "Coolidge is the first President to discover that what the American people want is to be let alone." Republicans in general would "walk in" if they only "just keep from doing something." On the campaign trail, Coolidge appeared presidential. Only on one occasion did he attempt to argue for the accomplishments of the Republican Party, a disaster, as Rogers saw it. "If you say something, you are liable to say something foolish and the smarter you are, and the longer you talk the more fool things you will say." Coolidge reinforced this "silent" image, telling his Secretary of Commerce, Herbert Hoover, "If you don't say anything, you won't be called on to repeat it!" Rogers feasted on the "silent Kal" image that the President embraced and it only made Coolidge more popular during the presidential campaign.

What little Coolidge did say often became fodder for Rogers' jokes. When pressed during the 1924 campaign, Coolidge finally did say that his policy for the future would be based upon "common sense." Rogers could hardly help himself. "Well, don't you know the Democrats will claim that too? Do you think they will call their campaign "Darn foolishness?" Coolidge's Republican opponents on the left, some of whom still adhered to a progressive agenda, were quite clueless. Robert La Follette, who ran as a Progressive, wanted to abolish the Supreme Court and nationalize the railroads. Those were hardly issues, thought Rogers, but rather "grudges." And people saw La Follette's campaign as one that went too far in changing an America that did not want change.

As the Democrats gathered at Madison Square Garden for their convention in the summer of 1924, Coolidge looked stronger as a candidate given the massive problems within the ranks of the Democrats. The delegates split between the mostly Catholic "wets," who supported Al Smith of New York and the more conservative, southern Prohibitionists, who supported William Gibbs McAdoo. Neither side could gain a two-thirds majority of votes and the delegates finally turned to John W. Davis of West Virginia. Davis had the least appealing platform of all, according to Rogers. He was running on the policy of "honesty." That was just plain ridiculous, since Will was quick to point out that it would require "a miracle." Rogers then rhetorically asked if there were enough people who "believed in miracles" to elect Davis. He doubted it.

Rogers was fundamentally right about another issue—the wishes of the American people. President Wilson had promoted a crusade "to make the world safe for Democracy," and nothing of the sort had come out of World War I. As Rogers smugly noted, "there is no nation that ever tried democracy since!" By 1924, Americans wanted a President who said very little and who did virtually nothing. Coolidge fit the mold. He defeated both Davis and La Follette by wide margins in the Presidential election, winning more of the popular vote than the other two candidates combined. Rogers summed up the outcome in his usual style. "The people felt like trusting [Coolidge] . . . and he kept his mouth shut. That was such a novelty among Politicians that it just swept the country." As for the Democrats, Rogers thought they "needed a new act." They had continued to push Wilson's agenda, including joining the "League of Nations," which the Senate had rejected in 1920. They had also "pulled another bone head," Rogers thought, by concentrating on the oil scandals. People had forgotten the corruption of the Harding Administration by the fall of 1924.

Yet Rogers' political columns did avoid the hard issues; that became very apparent when he visited the Democratic Convention in New York City. At best he hinted at the reality of the situation, which became downright ugly. Rogers amused himself initially by noting the hours it took for politicians to simply nominate the two leading contenders, Smith and McAdoo. "It looked like they were going to run out of people" to do the nominating. This process went on for six days, and the convention remains as the longest in history. The names of some sixteen men were put in front of the delegates.

Just when it appeared like the convention would set records for boredom, Rogers witnessed what he came to call "the most exciting and dramatic night I ever saw." The debate, which started in the afternoon, went on into the wee hours of the night when the two sides involved collapsed from exhaustion. They argued over the "Klan," or more properly the Ku Klux Klan (Rogers usually identified it as the "Klu" Klux Klan). Rogers tried to make comedy out of it—without much success. "Alaska voted one Klu Klux Klan away up there," he retorted. "Can you imagine a man in all that snow and cold with nothing on but a thin white sheet and pillow slip?" A bit more humor emerged when William Jennings Bryan declared that if the Klan issue split the party—which it did—he was ready to lead a new one.

In reality, much like Prohibition, the Klan issue drove a wedge between northern and southern Democrats and when Forney Johnson from Alabama rose to nominate Senator Oscar Underwood, and mentioned the need to reject such secretive organizations as the Klan, the convention broke into chaos. Fist-fights broke out in cloak rooms and in the great hall. Southern states including Texas, Oklahoma, Georgia, and Kentucky had strong Klan contingents. They generally supported McAdoo, and they wished to have no mention of the Klan, or reference to its intolerance, in the platform.

Delegations from northern states, such as New York and Massachusetts, wanted the Klan condemned. While a young soon-to-be governor of New York, Franklin Delano Roosevelt, put Smith's name into nomination, given the Klan debate, it received boos from one side of the auditorium and raucous jubilation from the other. The platform committee worked almost continuously for two days trying to find compromise between these two positions—it did not exist. Finally, William Jennings Bryan, after asking for God's intervention in prayer, found words that pledged "Constitutional freedoms"—absolute hokum in the South, where very few existed for Blacks—and made no mention of the Klan itself. The platform thus passed on that fiction.[4]

The utter disarray of the Democrats shocked Rogers. He tried to avoid the issue: his best efforts came in commenting on the "candidates' wives" in a piece printed as the deadlocked convention seemed on the verge of breaking up. Rogers found Mrs. Smith and Mrs. McAdoo to be charming and simply dressed. Others who gained mention included Mrs. Cordell Hull and Mrs. A. Michell Palmer. But the one leading light that impressed Rogers the most was "this Roosevelt woman." Eleanor, wife of Franklin D. Roosevelt who had nominated Al Smith, seemed a rising star. "If this Roosevelt Woman had been born a man we would not have to be worrying all this time over who would be one of our Presidents," Rogers quipped.

Discussing the contribution and speeches of the wives took attention away from the Klan. Despite being gone from Oklahoma for nearly two decades, Rogers still sensed a need to defend the home country, despite the activities of the Klan in it. By this time, however, the Klan's existence embarrassed Rogers.

---

[4]For a good discussion of the 1924 Democratic convention, see David M. Chambers, *Hooded Americanism: The History of the Ku Klux Klan* (Chicago: Quadrangle Books, 1965), 203–207.

He had learned much about the values of cultural diversity from his California friends, lessons that he still struggled with. Nevertheless, Will Rogers became sensitive to the lack of civil rights for colored people, Indian or Black. He came to abhor the lynching of Blacks that occurred frequently in the South during the 1920s. Fortunately, attention given to the Klan by the press declined by 1925, as its membership peaked and then fell precipitously, something that Rogers no doubt welcomed.

As Rogers left Madison Square Garden, William Jennings Bryan's speech remained as the only lasting impression. Bryan had brought some compromise to the Klan issue. While Rogers' opinion of Bryan would fade in a year or two, he had been one of Rogers' favorite politicians. Bryan, the Democrat and Populist, who had ran for President several times, had been very popular in the Midwest. He had retired to Florida by the 1920s but he reappeared regularly to voice his opinion on the issues of the day. Bryan was first and foremost a moralist, and he found compromise on some issues simply impossible. He also provided good copy for Rogers, who, while rejecting Bryan's idealism, still considered the man to be a powerful and fascinating politician.

Rogers frequently quoted William Jennings Bryan in his columns. "He preached Prohibition at a time when it meant political suicide for himself," Rogers wrote not long after their first meeting. "I bet the next Democratic candidate for President, no matter how strong he may think he is, would rather have the support of W. J. Bryan than any doubtful state in the Union." Rogers spent time with Bryan at the Republican National Convention, held in Cleveland a month before the Democrats gathered. As the convention turned to absolute boredom, Rogers and Bryan discussed a variety of issues. Bryan complimented Rogers on his weekly column, which everyone in the country seemed to be reading. In turn, Rogers sought ways to compliment Bryan, commenting positively on his strong stand regarding Prohibition. Despite Rogers' complete rejection of it and, to some degree, of organized religion, he had to admit that Bryan "brought more converts to Prohibition" than anyone else.

Other personalities parroted Bryan's stand on Prohibition, including especially Billy Sunday, a noted evangelist and former baseball player who would reach the height of his popularity in the early 1920s and Aimee Semple McPherson, the Los Angeles evangelist who built a religious empire at her massive million dollar temple. Sunday, according to Rogers, was Bryan's "accomplice." "Now Barnum invented the tent," Rogers exclaimed, "but Billy Sunday filled it." Sunday's two targets were liquor and the Devil, not necessarily in that order. As Rogers put it, "Billy Sunday picks his opponents with a carelessness that is almost reckless." Billy had "More mortal worldly combat with the Devil himself than any man living." And finally, "I don't know this Devil myself but if he heard Billy say these things and didn't come up and call him for it, I think less of him than Billy does." McPherson, on the other hand, received more charity from Rogers. The columnist was reticent to attack a woman, especially after she fell from grace in a sex scandal.

Rogers, who enjoyed poking fun of the Prohibition crowd—as well as religious fanatics—put Billy Sunday in the same tent as Bryan, despite his early adoration of Bryan. But unlike Bryan, Sunday apparently had a problem with drinking, despite his moral tone. Rogers once claimed to have seen Sunday—"who I discovered staggering from one of our local pulpits last Sunday"—preach on temperance. To Rogers delight, he reported:

> To some of you who can't or don't wish to remember, Billy passed out just as Andy Volstead [the Volstead Act] made his entrance . . . Billy used to lay all the drinking on this Devil, and claimed that if we had Prohibition, we could lick this Devil. Now we got Prohibition, [and] I don't think we can legitimately lay the present drinking onto the Devil.

Yet, as was commonly the case, Rogers then turned to saying something good about even Billy Sunday. "Billy sure did do some good in the old days, and no matter if you didn't like his style of sermon, you sure didn't get a chance to do any sleeping."

Rogers got fewer naps when Bryan became entangled in the most sensational trial of the 1920s—the Scopes "Monkey" Trial, which got underway in Dayton, Tennessee the next year. It was hot that summer in 1925, but William Jennings Bryan, then in his seventies, volunteered to help prosecute young John Thomas Scopes, a biology teacher who had dared suggest that Charles Darwin was correct when asserting in an 1871 book, entitled *The Descent of Man*, that humans shared common ancestors with primates. He had willingly violated the Butler Law, passed by the state of Tennessee, which made it unlawful to deny divine creation. The trial attracted such attention that Rogers' friend, Clarence Darrow, a member of the American Civil Liberties Union, rose to defend young Scopes. Darrow convinced Bryan to take the stand and defend the literal teachings of the Bible—that God had created man some six thousand years ago and that he had landed on earth in "God's image," that a whale had swallowed Jonah, and that Joshua had stopped the sun. With every statement, reported word for word in the daily newspapers, urban liberal intellectuals roared with laughter and rural traditionalists rose to defend their hero, Bryan. Rogers saw the trial as high drama with an abundance of humor. He especially lit into Bryan's blanket assertion that "Christianity is through" if Scopes were to win. As Rogers saw it, "No man should have to prove in court what he is, or what he come from." As for Bryan, Rogers asserted, "He ought to pay Scopes' fine." He was receiving more publicity from this trial than any other event. "It has been almost like a Democratic Convention year for Bryan. It's the most publicity any politician ever got in an off year."

After poking fun of the entire affair, Rogers got serious, a rarity at this time in his writing career. "Why don't Bryan and a lot of other people let the world alone?" "I can show you millions of people that think it is great, and are not worrying even if we arrived here from a tadpole." If the Lord had wanted us to know our origins, Rogers conceded, "he would have let us know in the first place." Ninety percent of the people on earth simply did not care about this issue, and the country should not push it. Such an argument was rather forward, especially for the usually careful Rogers. But Bryan's absolute moral tone seemed offensive, somewhat akin to those who preached "Americanism." Rogers' heroes of the past were suddenly out-of-date; the young man who departed Oklahoma in 1904 might have sided with Bryan, but not the seasoned comedian/journalist of 1925. Will Rogers' world-view had changed.

What was worse, Bryan intended to make the issue a national one. "Now personally, I like Bill," Rogers concluded, "He is a nice congenial old gentleman, and I can recall many happy chats with him. But when he says that he will make this his life's issue and . . . endeavor to get it into the Constitution . . . he is wrong." While Bryan had been wrong in the past, whatever he said "didn't do much harm." This, however, was different. "When those old Boys who blue-printed the first Constitution decided that a man can believe what he likes in regard to religion, that's one line that is going to stay."

Then Rogers became somewhat contrite, conceding that Bryan had a large following of "honest-to-goodness folk." But Bryan's role in America had been that of making an "example" for the rest of us, Rogers believed. He was a good man, a religious man. Nevertheless, he "wasn't put on earth as a leader," and Rogers intended to make up his own mind on such an issue as his own origins, and he felt that his readers should as well. Then, he conceded that he did not know where he came from. "I will just stay ignorant and take my chances at the end, rather than Bryan's chances if he willfully stirs up religious hatred."

As the trial loomed on and Darrow stepped to the defense of young Scopes, the situation became more absurd to Rogers. Both men, Bryan and Darrow, began using the newly introduced radio to voice their opinions on the issues, an event, Rogers noted, that at least allowed most Americans to tune them out. But America was not tuning out the trial, which had become a sensation. Rogers claimed in his column that he was about to travel to Dayton to see the affair firsthand, but he could not find his suspenders, as he said, "and I knew a man [who traveled to Tennessee] with a belt would be burned at the stake for being a Modernist."

While Darrow lost the verdict, and Scopes was fined $100, the sensational aspect of the trial came to a swift end when Bryan collapsed and died on July 25, 1925, just five days after the verdict had been read. Rogers, as always, offered a sympathetic eulogy. Harding's death had been a shock; the loss of Wilson had brought out the nation's sympathy; and Roosevelt's death seemed a great loss to the country. But Bryan, a man whose 40-year political career would likely be viewed as a failure, was, as Rogers noted, the "great commoner." Bryan had fought Tammany Hall—the political center for the New York Democratic bosses. Bryan "hated Bosses, Wall Street, Darrow and Darwin," Rogers concluded, "and who knows but what he may be even right.

None of them has ever been canonized by the Pope." Who now, Rogers asked, would fight for the "soul" of America? "Bryan had no Vice President!"

As Rogers' columns found their way into more and more newspapers across America, they attracted a readership that appreciated his humor. While cynical at times, the columns frequently exaggerated the truth, while based on events familiar to most people in the country. This made Will Rogers famous in the mid-1920s but it created difficulties for him later in his career when he wished to be seen as a serious columnist. On the other hand, the evolution of his column after 1925 from humorous social and political criticism, much of which skirted the truth, to a more serious tone in many ways was a reflection of the times. The early 1920s were an age of excess that avoided serious debate; this changed as the country engaged in world affairs in the late 1920s, faced economic disaster, and finally, depression.

But Will Rogers did not see these events coming in the mid-1920s. He had always contended that it was important not to take comedians too seriously. Any comedian who tried to be serious was bound to fail—they would simply not be funny. What had become so unusual about Rogers by 1925, however, was his apparent easy transition from being fundamentally a monologist, who did ten-minute bits for the *Follies*, to a satirist who composed weekly columns that often ran into two thousand words. And at times, he was serious!

There were some similarities between Rogers' humor and that of a vaudeville "ethnic" humorist, who was an "outsider" looking in. Perhaps he learned from those who commonly took that bent on the vaudeville circuit. Many of the comics who would follow Rogers—Mort Sahl, Woody Allen, Johnny Carson, Richard Pryor, Jay Leno, and David Letterman—present themselves as outside observers who have no axe to grind. Rogers may not have invented this genre of comedy, but he certainly excelled at it.

Part of Rogers' success at being an outsider came from his "cowboy" heritage and to some degree, from his identity as an Indian. He attended and fit-in well at high-brow affairs, such as dinner parties where the likes of Charlie Chaplin, Greta Garbo, and Mary Pickford rubbed shoulders with politicians and industrial leaders like Henry Ford and Bernard Baruch, yet he was just as at ease at a country picnic. He sensed the importance of the Progressive Movement and admired many of its leaders, but he often stood as well for traditional values, for small, let-alone government, defending feelings for the "old home," or the past.

Rogers was decidedly a Democrat who could and did speak well of Republicans. He actually liked them, despite his criticism of their wealth. In the end, he spoke mostly to middle America through his columns, and people liked what he said because he seldom lectured. "There's nothing as stupid as an educated man if you get him off the thing he was educated on," Rogers once said. It was an axiom that he practiced. He tried to write about events that he understood, but often admitted to knowing little about. This comedic humility carried him to the top as a newspaper columnist by the mid-1920s.

Rogers likely only recognized the impact of his success when he went home to Oklahoma to a hero's welcome in the late fall of 1925. He spent time as well in Arkansas with Betty's relatives. It was the first time Rogers had been home in years, given his hectic movie and *Follies* schedules. And to his surprise, the entire state of Oklahoma came out to see him as he played in most of the major towns—Oklahoma City, Ponca City, Bartlesville, and Tulsa. Will relished the notoriety. He ended his triumphant tour by attending a simple outdoor picnic in what he considered his home-town, Claremore.

Rogers' years in Hollywood, particularly those in the early 1920s, had taught him many lessons. He had learned tolerance of people who thought differently than he did, and an understanding of the contributions of others, some of whom had a far different appreciation of art and literature. He had learned much about politics and especially, about politicians. He had come a long distance from his days as a cowboy. He had gained a sense of security that few writers/entertainers ever experienced, especially those who had tried to continue on in vaudeville. He knew what his audience wanted, and he had demonstrated the ability to provide it.

A Liberal in an Illiberal Age

As strange as it sounds, the thought of appearing on an Oklahoma stage scared Will Rogers to death. Charles L. Wagner had recruited him for the tour, and offered Rogers the rather astonishing figure of $82,000 for a mere three-month stand, starting in October of 1925. Wagner later extended the contract for several more months, keeping Rogers on the road into April of 1926. Wagner wanted the tour to reach the heartland of America, where he had made his reputation putting on well-received concerts. It opened in Elmira, New York, not the entertainment center of the country, but where Mark Twain lived for a number of years. Wagner hoped that Rogers would imitate Twain, whose humor, while mostly recorded in books, captivated America.

Through November and December Wagner's troupe appeared at playhouses in the larger eastern and mid-western cities from Elmira to St. Louis. Rogers constituted the main act; a male quartet supported him. Will voiced some consternation when he signed the contract—his longest monologue when performing for the *Follies* never went more than fifteen minutes. The new tour forced him to be innovative; he needed more than a few "gags." He turned ferociously to the newspapers and built a longer, more detailed monologue.

The first few appearances nearly sank the production. Wagner failed to properly promote the show, but he soon fixed the problems—perhaps he picked Elmira for the initial shows to give him time for such a contingency. Within a few weeks, his gamble began to make money. Once the troupe entered Oklahoma, the act ran smoothly—indeed, Rogers could perform an hour or more if needed. During one night in which thousands of people showed up, some of whom stood in the rear of the theater, Rogers' monologue went on for over two hours. No one left. In the end, Will mused in his weekly article "Gee, I am lucky, I fooled 'em at home."

Rogers had "fooled them" to such an extent that the trip came to represent a turning point in his career. He continued to tour the heartland, and his efforts made him more popular in the country at large, which gave him a wider readership for his columns. Rogers had become famous in New York, and of course, he continued to do films in Hollywood, but he had never tested the waters of the mid-section of the country. In the age before television, these audiences were different, perhaps more appreciative than those on either coast.

Middle America embraced Will Rogers with an enthusiasm that surprised him. But the performances pushed his comedy to the edge. Rogers turned increasingly to the issues of the day, working them into his hour-long stands. He became a critic of American foreign policy, Republican politicians, the rich and well-off in America, Democrats who seemed disorganized, and he increasingly addressed a host of other social issues. The tours led to a more sophisticated comedy. What is more, the monologue soon represented what is best described as a liberal rhetoric in an "illiberal" age.

Rogers discovered that it took a more polished monologist to do sixty minutes in Peoria than it did to do fifteen minutes in front of a *Follies* crowd, especially one that had been preceded by scantily-clad chorus girls. This maturity led to a more worldly humor, something that Rogers had toyed with in the past. After trying it out, Rogers reached a momentous conclusion: if he were to continue in the new form of entertainment, he needed to broaden his understanding of important people, worldly leaders, worldly affairs, and especially world history. He had lived through the events surrounding World War I and its impact on American politics, but he knew little about how it changed the face of world affairs. He started reading a dozen different newspapers for material.

Rogers quickly understood that this larger world provided a fertile backdrop for comedy.

The need for new material led eventually to a strategic plan. Rogers would seek out important people and make friends with them. He also planned in the near future to tour Europe, meeting as many famous and interesting people as possible, including the likes of kings, or even such powerful leaders as Benito Mussolini, a man with whom Americans were fascinated. Rogers recognized that the stories of important people would lure readers. He included Betty and the kids on his travels, either in America or Europe, making the trips family affairs, often writing in his weekly columns about their experience as well as his own. But the European tour was not all that broadened his monologue. He knew that he must continue to intermix his columns with an understanding of the common man in America and Europe, his life and trials, as well as the rich and famous, especially the royalty of Europe, a particular group that continued to fascinate Americans.

Rogers' new "traveling education" mainly focused on meeting interesting people or covering interesting events. Along these lines, he embraced aviation, and the daring aviators who were then pioneering the field. While Rogers himself never flew a plane, he traveled in one whenever possible, even during his European trip. His interest developed quickly once he learned that he could fly from one show to another in government air-mail planes. Accordingly, Rogers went out of his way to meet famous pilots, some of whom were attempting to set new records for speed, others for altitude, and finally, a few for flight across the oceans.

This decision to tour Europe evolved from an expanding interest that Rogers slowly embraced in world affairs and the European countries that continually found their way into the news. Some years before Will saw the value of such material, the Senate, led mostly by resurgent Republicans, had refused to ratify the 1919 treaty of Versailles, which had ended World War I. With the treaty came an invitation for the United States to join the League of Nations, an organization that President Wilson had initially promoted. The treaty had blamed the war entirely on Germany, and created massive reparations that Germany had to pay. Congress finally passed a joint resolution ending the war during the summer of 1921. Yet the debate over the war, and who was responsible for it, led Congress to increasingly reject funding for the American military, which some congressmen believed, would lead America into another world war.

The key question considered by Congress became the defense of the Philippine and Hawaiian Islands, where the navy wanted to build bases and station a fleet. As congress balked, some politicians believed that negotiations could lead to "arms limitation" that might solve the problem over future war. Secretary of State Charles Evans Hughes, who was an internationalist, embraced the new view and became the chairman of the first conference held at Washington, D.C. during the fall of 1921 to limit arms internationally.

The urgency of the conference became clear when Great Britain announced that it intended to build four "super-Hoods," comparable to battleship *HMS Hood*, which was considered the best ship of its kind in the world.[1] Japan countered by announcing that it would build eight "super-dreadnought battleships," which were bigger. The Washington Naval Conference then addressed many difficult problems, including the belligerency Japan demonstrated over occupying islands to the north that the Soviet Union also claimed. Secretary Hughes finally offered a solution; he determined that the tonnage of all capital ships—or battleships—should be used as a foundation for a ratio, set at 5-5-3-1-1. Great Britain and the United States were at 5, while Japan accepted 3, and Italy and France were at 1. In reality, in the years to come, Japan virtually ignored its quota while the United States and Great Britain never reached the levels permitted.[2]

Will Rogers did not trust Japan—in general, he showed little sympathy for Asian people, including those in the United States—and whether from this bias against Japanese immigrants, or from the realization that Japan would be a power to reckon with, he ultimately lambasted the agreement, and he continued to make fun of other so-called "Peace Agreements" attempted in later years.

---

[1] *HMS Hood* was sunk in a few minutes by the German battleship *Bismarck* in a famous engagement in 1940.

[2] See Betty Glad, *Charles Evans Hughes and the Illusion of Innocence* (Urbana: University of Illinois Press, 1966).

As the conference in Washington came to a close in February 1922, Rogers penned what became one of his first comedic responses to a foreign policy issue, in a disapproving tone:

> Every man was allowed to keep the pen he signed with. England got six pens to our four . . . France received two pens and no submarines. . . . Japan got all the islands north of the equator, Siberia, Mongolia, Battleship Mutsu and three pens . . .

The references to "pens" reflected Rogers' disgust with the confusing formula for tonnage that Hughes had invented. It also reflected the opinions of most Americans who had come to dislike making any such agreements, since treaties of this sort had caused World War I.

The negative reaction of the American public to "European entanglement," as it was called, only increased after the conference, and Rogers led the criticism. His next foray into foreign affairs came when he learned, almost by accident, of a congressional debate regarding Turkey and Greece. While a few eastern newspapers carried short accounts of the debate, Will decided to get his own news by sitting in the Senate gallery on Capitol Hill. Modern Turkey, nationalistic and run by the dynamic Attaturk, had contested Greece for control of the Dardenelles, the waterway that separated the two nations. Secretary Hughes, ever the internationalist who also kept a close eye on the civil war in Russia—which the United States continued to meddle in—suggested using possible American forces to keep the narrow strait open, with the intent of aiding the so-called White Russians, or non-Communists. The debate increasingly centered on the modern United States navy, and whether it should be stationed in far-places and utilized to implement foreign policy, or not.

Rogers' reporting of the issue in one of his early weekly columns was bare-bones, and brief, almost a trial balloon of sorts, to gauge people's thoughts. His commentary, however, revealed his emerging isolationist political philosophy regarding foreign issues. This view came to dominate public opinion in the United States at the time, and unfortunately, would lead the country astray in the 1930s, as it failed to prepare the United States for World War II. Yet Rogers represented the average

American in his adherence to it. Taking on the Dardenelles issue, he wrote: "Years ago an American sailing ship came pretty near going through there [the Dardenelles]." It got within two hundred miles, the comic quipped with considerable sarcasm. Congressman Manuel Herrick from Oklahoma, who apparently supported the intervention, did not escape Rogers' banter. Twisting Herrick's language, Rogers proclaimed that he "said it was alright to keep them [the Dardenelles] open during the week but that he was for closing them on Sunday." This last stab was a reference to the religious conservatism of Rogers' home state and its blue laws, which forced retail stores to close on Sunday.

While Rogers timidly entered these debates regarding foreign affairs in the early 1920s, being somewhat unsure of himself, a unique opportunity appeared in 1924 to expand his worldly commentary. The Prince of Wales came to the United States. Edward Albert took the title upon the death of his grandfather in 1910, when he was just sixteen. Young and athletic, he was immensely popular in Great Britain and was one of the first royals to visit the United States since the American Revolution. In Washington, President Coolidge put on a grand affair, honoring his visit. While Albert would have a fairy-tale life for the next decade, when he ascended to the throne in 1936, he was forced to abdicate when it became known that he intended to marry an American divorcee, a decision that shook England.

Rogers met the young, dynamic Prince when he was yet single and just twenty-eight years old. The Prince had especially asked that Rogers be the keynote speaker at a dinner held in his honor on September 3, 1924, at the exclusive Piping Rock Country Club on Long Island. The table seated one hundred and fifty male guests, including a few dignitaries, the Prince, and Rogers. Apparently Albert had read Rogers' column, especially one or two comments about the Prince's falls from his horse during steeplechase competitions. Rogers had used a self-effacing approach, noting that he too had trouble staying on horses at times. "Are the Prince and I supposed to fall with the horse, or are we supposed to stay up there in the air until he gets up, and comes back under us?" In colorful form, Rogers blamed the horses for the falls, not the riders. The Prince got wind of his defender and quickly expressed a desire to meet Rogers.

At the dinner that evening Rogers talked for nearly an hour, moving from one "gag" to another. The Prince nearly fell from his chair with laughter when Rogers made some rather silly attempts to name the various titles that the Prince went by, using Rogers' own "cowboy" pronunciation. He then excused himself profusely for his ignorance, noting that he had only met royalty on one occasion, a man with the title "sir." But the Prince had, as Rogers described it, the "Ford [as in Henry Ford] of all Titles." As the banter went on, Albert at times grabbed Rogers' coattails, offering comments on his jokes. The next day the two played polo and had lunch, establishing a wonderful relationship that lasted for many years. Rogers was a frequent guest at the Prince's estate in England.

Rogers' decision to travel to Europe emerged for yet another reason. Will had made a momentous, and financially dangerous, decision in 1924 to purchased 159 acres of land in an undeveloped region just north of Los Angeles, later called Santa Monica. The land, with steep hills and canyons that sloped down to the sea, cost well over $100,000, which Will and Betty mostly financed at 6 percent interest. Rogers had signed on for a grueling 15-month stint with the *Follies* during the summer 1924, followed by another difficult tour with the Wagner show, starting in October 1925, in order to pay for the land. Rogers pocketed several hundred thousand dollars over these two years, money he desperately needed to finance his land deal. But his touring was difficult for the family, as Betty assumed the responsibility of rearing their three children while Will was on the road. Will and Betty kept in touch often by telegram, but when the tours ended, they both agreed that it was time for a family vacation.[3]

The opportunity to spend the summer in Europe also derived from a discussion that Rogers had with George Horace Lorimer, the editor of the *Saturday Evening Post*. Lorimer suggested that Rogers might use his connections with such people as the Prince of Wales to travel through Europe and meet various dignitaries.

---

[3]Some of the telegrams have survived in *The Papers of Will Rogers*, 5 vols., vols. 1 and 2, edited by Arthur Frank Wertheim and Barbara Blair, vols. 3–5, edited by Steven K. Gragert and M. Jane Johansson (Norman: University of Oklahoma Press, 1995–2005).

He could use the material to compose a number of columns for publication. Having put aside some money for the trip, Rogers jumped at the idea, getting letters of endorsements from the new Secretary of State Frank Kellogg and Senator William Borah, who Will often mentioned in his columns. He turned the trip into a five-month odyssey, which offered a wealth of information for his weekly columns.

Rogers left New York in May of 1926. His family followed a few weeks later after school got out. When everyone had reached England, the family moved over to the continent and traveled from country to country, mostly by train, tasting the foods and wine of Europe, seeing the sights, and being readily received by national leaders in many countries. The only exception came when Rogers flew alone from Germany into the Soviet Union, a rather hair-raising experience in which he sat alongside a very young and daring Russian pilot who spoke no English. Along the way, Rogers composed his weekly columns and contributed pieces for the *Saturday Evening Post,* all of which were addressed to President Coolidge under the by-line "Letters of a Self-made Diplomat to his President." Rogers gained insight into world affairs that few others, even state department officials, lacked—this was still a day and age when American politicians generally did not make junkets to Europe, or "fact-finding trips."

As Rogers traveled he constantly wrote, column after column. He commented on the massive labor strike in England, noting how "civil" it was, not like American labor conflicts, which often got ugly and violent. Rogers would draw on this experience during the 1930s, when labor in America struck. Rogers visited the English Parliament, where David Lloyd George, no longer Prime Minister, but rather a member, lambasted the conservative government for its failure to solve the strike. Winston Churchill rose to defend the government, and, as Rogers put it in a *Post* article, "that little E-flat Pamphlet that the Government had been putting out under the humorous name of a Newspaper." Churchill confessed that those publishing the paper—which was intended as a stand-in for the *London Times,* where workers were on strike—had never been in the newspaper business before. A Laborite then hollered, "Including the

Editor," who was of course Churchill. At the time, Rogers failed to see the pluck in this man Churchill, who would rise to defend the British nation and empire just 14 years later.

As Rogers looked on in delight, collecting material for his columns, Lady Astor came by to say hello. An American from Virginia, she had married Lord Waldorf Astor—one of if not the richest men in England—and in her 40s remained one of the most strikingly beautiful women in Europe. She and Lord Astor also held some of the most lavish parties in England at their estate, called Cliveden, on the Thames River. While Nancy Astor married into wealth, she was also the first female member of the House of Commons to take a seat, was well-known for her wit and charm, and generally supported social reform, including women's issues.

Perhaps the most enduring legacy of Lady Astor's life was the legendary dinner parties that she hosted at Cliveden. The most famous and powerful men and women in Europe attended, including Churchill, with whom she never got along, despite the fact that both were members of the Conservative Party. At dinner one evening, after a verbal scrape with Churchill, Lady Astor reputedly said: "Winston, if I was married to you I'd put poison in your coffee." Without a blink, Churchill replied: "Nancy, if I was married to you I'd drink it!" While Rogers missed this exchange, he was enthralled when this woman invited him to dinner. They became fast friends and Rogers often visited the Astor's thereafter.

The fact that Lady Astor extended an invitation to Will Rogers is indicative of his rising reputation as an entertainer and columnist. Chumming with the Astor crowd offered Rogers wonderful material for his column. True to form, Rogers avoided sarcastic exchanges with Nancy Astor—Churchill likely would have been disappointed in him. Indeed, at one dinner party, Will spent much of the night talking to Sir James Barrie, the author of *Peter Pan*. Rogers also attended parties at York House, the estate of the Prince of Wales. During a final evening with the Prince, just before Rogers and the family headed to the continent, Rogers and the Prince talked alone by a fire. The Prince spoke openly during the evening, somewhat of a tribute to Rogers' ability to interact with people, and

Rogers came away with a unique observation—"he don't care anymore about being King."

The trek to the continent began the next morning, as Rogers flew with the family to Paris and traveled to Italy by car. While Rogers correctly sensed the reticence of the Prince of Wales, he misjudged Benito Mussolini. After an hour-long interview—one in which Rogers suggested that he only wanted to have a friendly chat—Rogers came away believing that Mussolini had "done more for one race of people in three years than one man ever did." He compared him to Napoleon! Perhaps his enthusiasm for "Il Duce," as he was called, stemmed from Mussolini's popularity among Italian Americans, who were a strong readership of his columns. In the festive atmosphere, Rogers readily agreed to several photographs with Mussolini, some of which appeared in the *Saturday Evening Post*. The two did have a common love for horses, and several of the photos show Mussolini steeple-jumping.

While Il Duce had made the trains run on time since coming to power in 1922, he had also disbanded parliament and had made himself the chief executive of all governmental departments. Rogers struggled somewhat with Mussolini's penchant for power, as one of his columns clearly indicated:

> If he died tomorrow, Italy would always be indebted to him for practically four years of peace and prosperity. Not a bad record for a Guy to die on; but this Guy keeps getting better all the time. He is the only idealist that ever could make it work . . . Dictator form of Government is the greatest form of government there is, if you have the right dictator.

On the other hand, Mussolini's rise to power created rumors of torture, of using castor oil on opponents, much like trying to simulate drowning with water, a torture termed "waterboarding." He defended this practice to Rogers by arguing that it prevented "Bolsheviks" from coming to power, a common excuse for torture used by Fascists such as Mussolini. Since Will was on his way to the Soviet Union, Mussolini laughingly gave him some castor oil to take along, supposedly to use on the Bolsheviks there. In parting, according to Rogers, Il Duce laughed, looked "gay," and claimed to "like good times as everybody else, maybe more so."

After what Rogers described as a rather boring tour of north Italy's art and architecture—Lummis had not cured him of all his "cowboy" provincialism—Rogers flew into the Soviet Union, still in some political turmoil after years of revolutionary war. Just getting in took some effort as the United States had not recognized the new, communist government. Worse, the man who Rogers came to see—Leon Trotsky—was out of favor. Joseph Stalin increasingly consolidated power; Rogers described him as "the Borah [as in Senator William Borah of Idaho] of the Black Sea."

Rogers then went on to suggest that the interview with Trotsky might have had value. "I bet you if I had met him . . . I would have found him a very interesting human fellow, for I have never yet met a man that I dident like." The last quip would be used many times in the future, and become one of Will Rogers' many trademark sayings. Will's assessment of why Trotsky had lost power also came with a comedic twist. He was "too conservative" in comparison to those followers of Stalin. A conservative among Communists, Will concluded, "was a man with a Bomb in only one hand; A Radical is what you would call a two-Bomb man."

Despite his failure to meet Trotsky, Rogers did write several pieces on the Soviet Union, perhaps demythologizing it for many Americans. This may have helped a future president diplomatically recognize the Soviet Union in 1933, something that Rogers later supported. He thought the whole idea of Communism rested upon "propaganda and blood." "If Socialists worked as much as they talked, they would be the most prosperous style of government in the World." Despite the propaganda, communism had not really changed Russia. "There is as much class distinction in Russia today as there is in Charleston, South Carolina," Rogers concluded. Like Charleston, some "Comrades" ran the country, but most followed orders. Will rejected the notion that everyone remained somehow equal in the "workers'" paradise. Most of the people still lived in the countryside. Rogers concluded simply—"Russia hasent changed a bit."

Rogers' conclusions—read by millions of Americans in the *Post*—had important implications. The United States had been shocked by the "Red Scare" just a few years before—a fear that communism was invading America—and his discussion of the Soviet system likely mollified a large number of Americans who feared the spread of Communism. Both the Wilson and Harding Administrations had prosecuted a large number of newly arriving immigrants in 1919 to 1921 during the scare, who the Attorney General's office argued had Bolshevik leanings. A number had been deported, including the famous socialist Emma Goldman, who had once been a member of Mabel Dodge's New York circle. Rogers' trip, then, suggested that the United States had nothing to fear from the Soviet Union, a liberal view for the time of a changing world.

Readers back in America avidly read Rogers' articles in the *Post*. More significantly, Rogers found himself on the front page of the *New York Times*. *Times* editor Adolph Ochs, who had previously met Rogers, encouraged Will to send short pieces of interest while on his tour. One introduced Lady Astor, who intended to visit the United States. Rogers described her as "The Best Friend America has here . . . She is the only one over here that don't throw rocks at American tourists." Ochs decided to use the short piece on the front page, and Rogers had unknowingly created yet another venue for his quips. Dubbed "the Daily Telegram," Rogers composed over 2,000 of them in the next nine years. Syndicated by the *Times,* the telegrams were seldom more than a few lines long. They were found on the front pages of over 400 newspapers in America by the late 1920s.

The introduction to the Lummis circle in Los Angeles in 1919 to 1922 changed Rogers' views on America; his trip to Europe in 1926 expanded his knowledge of the world. Rogers returned from Europe that fall with a new world view that had been evolving in his mind since the early 1920s. His trip gave him confidence to report his findings. He put these views in simple language, using comparisons that the everyday reader in America fully understood. These simple statements ideally fit the short, 50-word daily telegrams that graced the front pages of many newspapers. "If a man's neighbors all hate him," he began in one such telegram, "and he is continually in trouble, and all his fights . . . are over in the other fellow's yard, he must be wrong." Rogers offered a simple solution: "If he won't stay at home what he needs is a good licking or a muzzle." The most simplistic reader could hardly miss the "isolationist" sentiment of such a view.

This stand regarding world affairs increased in popularity partly from America's involvement in World War I. An emerging isolationist belief convinced the Senate to reject membership in the League of Nations, one of the Fourteen Points that President Wilson had authored. The war and its baggage frequently became fodder for novelists by the mid-1920s, writers who lamented the death toll of the war, its failure to bring resolution to major problems in the world, and its general inhumanity. Writers lamented the "lost generation" of leadership, especially in Europe, as many young officers were gunned down by machine guns. Indeed, as a result of the war, world leaders considered schemes to "outlaw" war, including politicians in the United States.

Rogers sensed this attitude, although he quickly found the notion that war could be outlawed to be childish. This pessimism may have originated as a result of the awful mess known as the debt payment, which Europeans and Americans argued over throughout the 1920s. Germany owed the allies "reparations," totaling 33 billion dollars and tried to make a yearly payment. England, France, and Italy owed American banks and the United States Government some 22 billion dollars. They depended upon Germany's payments to cover their debt. This arrangement had hit a snag in 1923 when German currency collapsed. United States diplomats had to step in and shore up the German government.

Will Rogers believed, as did many other Americans, that all debts should be paid in full. "The whole problem in all these Countries," Rogers lamented, "reverts back to one thing and that is our coming into the war [World War I]." Europeans had concluded that we should have "declared war on Germany two days before they started to march into Belgium [1914]." Rogers strongly disagreed, and he put his sentiments in bold print in one telegram. "STAY AT HOME AND TEND TO OUR OWN BUSINESS! DON'T ATTEND A CONFERENCE! NOT EVEN A LUNCHEON!"

The discussion of the past war often led Rogers into speculation regarding a future war. Rogers commonly predicted such a struggle, in a humorous fashion on most occasions. He tied such discussion into his support for air supremacy, making a rather uncanny, and decidedly correct, observation by the late 1920s that it would determine the outcome of such a war—an argument that most generals and admirals in the War Department disagreed with. Rogers frequently mentioned the prospect, and he was more determined to press the idea after he met the famous flyer, General Billy Mitchell.

The meeting first came to light a year before Rogers' European trip, when he announced to his readers that Germany had just elected General Paul Ludwig von Hindenburg as President of the German Republic. Many writers in the American press assumed that this might mean another war, or that it might mean the return of Kaiser Wilhelm to power. Rogers expressed some uncertainty regarding such a view, but he used the occasion to note the difference in how the United States and Germany treated their war heroes. Hindenburg was rewarded with the Presidency, at the age of 77, while the United States Army forcefully retired General "Black Jack" Pershing, at age 66, though he had helped defeat Hindenburg. It proved one thing, "Germany is the only Nation that remembers the War," Will declared. Rogers had met Pershing at a dinner in Washington and praised his efforts, while he lambasted the army for retiring such a successful leader.

At the same dinner, Rogers met General Mitchell, a strong-minded military officer who overwhelmingly believed that air power would determine the winner in the next war. By noting the treatment of Pershing, Rogers easily moved on to his hero Mitchell, who was about to face a like circumstance. Rogers, who knew that Mitchell had commanded the entire American Air Force in France, some 1,500 planes, quickly took up his cause, devoting several columns to introducing Mitchell to his reading public. Indeed, to some extent, Rogers contributed to making Mitchell a household name in America.

Mitchell apparently knew Rogers' enthrallment with airplanes and on one occasion asked the comedian/writer if he might like to see the air field, just across the river from the Capital. Rogers agreed and discovered upon reaching the air field the next morning that Mitchell intended to take him flying. "It slowly began to dawn on me that at last there was going to be some flying done in the Army," a criticism of the military's failure to prepare its air crews, another Rogers gripe. Yet Rogers had his fears—"Congress was not in session and I didn't know whether there was enough hot air to keep us up or not!"

After several "gags" about how frightened he really was— written imitations of his standard monologue fright—Rogers got to the heart of the story. Once on the ground, Mitchell said, "You have been with me on the last flight I will ever make as Brigadier General. Tonight at 12 o'clock, I am to be demoted to a Colonel and sent to a far away post." Mitchell had been transferred to Texas, where the Army would train many of its pilots. But surely the top brass in the Army wanted Mitchell out of Washington. Rogers portrayed the demotion—which in fact many officers faced at the time who held "brevet" ranks—as a serious rebuff of an American hero, somewhat of an exaggeration. Mitchell, as Rogers put it in his column, "knows that someday America will have to have a tremendous Air Force, but he can't understand why we are not training it now."

A few months later, Billy Mitchell became embattled in a bitter struggle with the heads of the Army. He had demonstrated back in 1921 and again in 1923 that airplanes could sink unarmed, slowly moving battleships. Mitchell then lobbied for a bigger air force, one separate from the two services, Army and Navy. By fall 1925, his fight and his abrasive personality had led him to charge openly in the newspapers that the Army had been responsible for the crash of the dirigible Shenandoah and the loss of 14 men—clear insubordination. While the military might vanquish Mitchell to some forgotten outpost for his outspoken views, the generals found his charges unforgivable. Mitchell faced a court martial, a sad day for Rogers. The comedian/writer reported the trial in his column, disdainfully reporting that President Coolidge was simply going "to let nature take its course." Obviously on Mitchell's side, but reluctant to support such an abrasive man, Rogers let the issue drop. Mitchell later resigned from the Army.

While the issue of military preparedness became entangled with Rogers' personal relationship with Mitchell, in years to come, he did not drop the debate. And on air-power, Rogers proved an immensely accurate prophesier. A year after Mitchell's departure and not long after Rogers had returned from Europe, Rogers did a quick survey of military preparedness, visiting air fields and looking into the strength of "Coolidge's air corps." He found one particular field where some five "Pursuit Squadrons" were located with some 500 to 600 pilots. It all sounded impressive, but he wanted to see the planes, and he approached the "hangars" and "peeped inside." "I couldn't see even an old broken propeller." On further examination, he discovered that the entire corps of flyers had but six airplanes, likely a typical Rogers exaggeration: "six mind you, of the type we trained the boys in before we went into the War [1917]."

The story, which had many elements of fiction, grew more farcical in Rogers' hands when he "learned" of the training program. Each pilot got in about "15 minutes" of flying time every month, that is if "none of the planes were ever out of order, and they changed flyers in the air . . . When your 15 minutes was up you jumped out and another man jumped up in the air and took the wheel." The fuel situation was worse. The "gas shortage," Rogers concluded, cut flying time down to 2 and 3/4 minutes per month. Rogers put the blame where he felt it rested; "Mr Coolidge on account of his economy plan has suggested that they fly as high as they can on what little gas they have, and then coast down." That way, "they got twice the amount of distance out of the same amount of gas."

While it is difficult to say how many Americans believed such a yarn, certainly some did. And the story had at least one element of truth. The Army Air Corps had received little funding by 1926 with which to purchase modern planes. Over the years to come, Will Rogers continually pushed for more air power, both in the army and the navy. He hailed every advancement in aviation, as planes got bigger and flew farther. No journalist or politician in the 1920s did more to reveal the weaknesses of American air power than Will Rogers.

Rogers' nurturing of aviation led to a "hawkish" view regarding America's military preparedness. Nevertheless, in a contradictory sense, he became more isolationist when it came to world affairs. Isolationists within both political parties generally wished to cut military defense in the 1920s, out of fear that a large army would lead the country into another war.

Will Rogers had no such fears. He pushed for more battleships and especially airplanes at the same time that he continually lamented the involvement of the United States in the politics of other countries.

His views especially resonated with China, a country with a broken government and little hope of fixing it.

China had been in constant turmoil for years. All the countries of Europe, Rogers complained, had "grabbed off territory in China" for coaling stations to facilitate trade. "A Chinaman himself can't get into Hong Kong without a [British] passport." When Portugal landed troops at Canton, along the Chinese coast, Great Britain sent ships and men just to "protect their interests." The British contingent by 1926 consisted of a considerable force, including several battalions of Indian troops. They, at least for a time, brought the Chinese war lords in that section of China under some control.

Such actions led Rogers to discredit the new League of Nations and its attempt to prevent violent outbreaks in the world. It did nothing to solve the problems in China and was equally inept at stopping border disputes. When conflict started between Bulgaria and Greece, the League did intervene, but only half-heartedly. Rogers viewed the effort as typical: "Have you fellows got a permit for war?" Rogers' chimed in, as if speaking for the League. "We [the League] are just in the midst of trying to (unconsciously) show America that we are for Peace, and here you want to fight." It was unconscionable to Rogers that England and France, who wanted the United States to join the League, would interfere in the Bulgarian/Greek conflict and still press forward in dividing up modern Iraq, Syria, China, and Palestine, or, for that matter, support continued European imperialism in Africa. He believed that the League had become a mechanism for the big powers of Europe to work their will on smaller nations.

While the critique of European and American imperialism had its comedic side, there was a certain realpolitik to Rogers' columns, especially when he turned to Europe and war, topics that he commonly addressed after returning from his European trip. "No country has it in for Belgium personally," Rogers stated in one of his critiques, but somehow the country was "just a military highway." Given its earlier financial woes, Rogers suggested that it was best to rent the place to Germany and France for their next war: "They fight on schedule every 40 years." It could also be used by England, France, and Russia, during the intermediary years. Even Morocco, which had spawned a revolutionary movement struggling for independence from France, might be coaxed to come to Belgium. "Maybe France could find them if they contracted to meet in Belgium." The French army had considerable difficulty closing with the Moroccan rebels at the time.

Rogers' refreshing sense of isolationism appealed to most Americans. He proffered his criticism with a comparative fairness that hardly anyone could find distasteful. But his most straightforward discussions of the Coolidge years came in the President's dealings with Mexico, which escalated in late 1926 and threatened to burst into a serious conflict the next year. Rogers joined the fray when he noticed in the papers that several prohibitionist groups wanted the United States to close the borders at Tijuana and Mexicali, Mexico, or to invade Mexico and clean up these towns. It seemed that Americans were crossing into Mexico and buying drinks "right over the bar," a terrible violation, as Rogers jokingly viewed it, of the prohibition laws. Rogers, with his tongue-in-check tone, concluded that.

> It constituted a disgrace to have these things done right there in Mexico. And it was Mexico's fault. Americans don't want to drink and gamble. They simply went south to see the mountains, and these scheming Mexicans grab 'em and make 'em drink, and make 'em make bets, and make 'em watch the race horses run for money.

Then Rogers fictionalized the latest news from Washington. He suggested that Secretary of State Kellogg was about to send Mexico a strong "note" regarding the matter. "We come more near running Mexico than we do New York State," the latter reference likely being a barb at New York's committed "wet" governor, Al Smith, who did little to enforce Prohibition.

The gist of the entire argument had little to do with drinking in Mexican towns, and Rogers slowly moved from the increasingly target-prone prohibitionists to the real matter. The State Department at the time was in a dispute with Mexico over its attempts to nationalize the land leases of large American oil companies, who in turn, urged the American government to apply pressure, to invade Mexico in order to prevent nationalization. Mexico had adopted a constitution in 1917 that leaned toward socialism, and Mexican leaders were at times friendly with the Bolsheviks from the Soviet Union, granting diplomatic recognition to the Soviet Union in 1924. After bringing some stability to Mexico, the socialist government tried to recoup the natural resources that had been lost to foreign investors under a previous dictator. The American and European oil companies, which owned 90 percent of the best oil lease land in Mexico, had considerable influence in Washington, and the Coolidge Administration remained determined to prevent the confiscation of the leases. Indeed, as Rogers reported it in a January 1927 Daily Telegram, "Mr. Coolidge says he is not going to submit the Mexican trouble to arbitration. He says he feels so sure we are right that there is no one he would trust to decide it in our favor."

In a show of independent thinking, Rogers sided with Mexico in the dispute. He noted that in the past Mexico had been forced to accept the dictates of Washington politicians when it came to their own resources. "If they want to say that an American can own land down there but not the mineral rights, why we say its not constitutional." How did we get such a right? Rogers demanded to know. We can "say that Japs [a derogatory term for Japanese Americans] can't even own Land" here in the United States, a reference to the Alien Land Laws that western states had passed just a few years before. "Mind you, I am in favor of that law. We had a perfect right to say who can own land, and so does Mexico have the same right." To make his point stronger, Rogers denied civil rights to Japanese immigrants in the United States in order to make an argument for Mexican sovereignty. His final point, though, was prime Rogers—"For the love of Mike, why don't we let Mexico alone and let them run their country the way they want to!"

The crisis in Mexico grew into near conflict in March of 1927 when the Coolidge government announced that it planned to end the arms embargo on Mexico, allowing better-armed revolutionaries to attack the new government. Those revolutionaries were mostly *Christeros*, or Catholics, who had opposed the Mexican government's confiscation of church lands. Some Catholic groups in the United States openly supported the *Christero* movement with money, and lobbied in Washington for intervention. As a coalition of Catholic clerics (who emphasized the Communistic sympathies of the Mexican government), state department officials, and business leaders came together, it looked very much like the United States might send in the Marines to topple the new Mexican constitutional government.

Coming half-a-year after Rogers' return from Europe, the thought of destroying an elected government, even a socialistic one, seemed abhorrent to Rogers. In a surprising show of partisanship and independence, he lashed out at the Coolidge government in his weekly column:

> We are going to allow, and even encourage, all the bloodshed we can [by repealing the embargo], just because we are having an argument with them . . . Here we are the Nation that is always hollering for disarmament, and Peace, and just because we are not smart enough to settle our differences by diplomacy (because we have none) why we are going to make it possible for somebody else to exterminate the faction that we don't like . . . Here is the humanitarian nation of the world fixing it so more people can get shot!

What made such a policy more ludicrous, according to Rogers, was that American officials justified it by saying Mexico was acting against "Our Laws." "What's our laws got to do with Mexico?" Rogers noted, in a conclusion to one of his angriest columns of all times.

The outburst revealed Rogers' frustration with American foreign policy, one very much akin to that of England and France. But this time he was not alone; Walter Lippmann, an extremely respected journalist, joined him in calling for negotiation with Mexico, not war. The extent of the combined influence on that policy by these two men will never really be known. Rogers, however, likely had better political contacts in Washington than Lippmann.

Will had spent considerable time with the highly respected Charles Evans Hughes on the ocean liner that both returned from Europe on in late summer 1926. Hughes had been Coolidge's Secretary of State, leaving the post in 1925, and he would join the Supreme Court thereafter. Rogers and Hughes became close friends after working to raise $42,000 on board ship for victims of a hurricane in Florida. When they landed, Rogers and Hughes were seen walking arm and arm along the ship's gangways. While Hughes turned, to walk away, when photographers approached, sensing the disdain of Republicans in the White House for Rogers, Will convinced him to stay and allow the newsmen to take photos of the two men together. The photo appeared on the front page of many American newspapers. Hughes had influence with Republicans—he was known as a man who detested war—and there is no question that he listened to Rogers.

As opinion in the nation slowly shifted to one of negotiation—to the utter disdain of the *Christeros*—President Coolidge looked for a diplomatic solution. He removed the anti-Mexican, pro-American business ambassador Richard Sheffield and convinced Dwight Morrow, a well respected member of the J. P. Morgan Bank and a former classmate of Coolidge at Amherst College, to go to Mexico as an ambassador in 1927. Morrow started a dialogue that eventually led to compromise. The oil companies could keep much of the land where they had undertaken explorations, especially those lands developed before the Mexican Constitution of 1917, but other leases that were untouched would be given up. Perhaps Rogers said it best: "they [the big oil companies] have all the oil they need anyway." While only a partial solution, Rogers applauded it. Indeed, he felt duty-bound to see it work and put Mexico on his agenda for a future trip.[4]

Will Rogers, like all Americans, watched with great anticipation, as the news ticker followed the flight of young Charles Lindbergh, who set out to cross the Atlantic in a single engine plane on May 20, 1927. Six pilots had died trying to capture

---

[4]For the Mexican crisis, consult Daniela Spenser, *The Impossible Triangle: Mexico, Soviet Russia, and the United States in the 1920s* (Durham: Duke University Press, 1999).

the $25,000 prize that came with flying solo from New York to Paris. Two French aviators were missing at sea at the moment that Lindbergh's plane, heavy with fuel, took off from a rain-soaked field outside of New York. Most considered the adventure near-suicide. Rogers, who followed every pilot who sought a new record of any sort, published a sober announcement of the flight in his telegram, as he, like much of the nation, held their breath. "No attempt at jokes today . . . A slim, tall, bashful, smiling American boy is somewhere out over the middle of the Atlantic Ocean, where no one human being has ever ventured before. He is being prayed for to every kind of Supreme Being!"

Then the news came like a bolt of lightening. "Slim," as the "boy" was called, had landed in Paris. A crowd of over 100,000 Parisians swarmed his plane when he landed and police had to rescue him. While Rogers had ridden in an open cockpit with many different mail carriers by this time, he had never met Lindbergh, who himself had started out as an airmail pilot. Rogers gushed with joy in his weekly column: "It was the greatest wished-for, and prayed-for achievement that ever happened or ever will happen in our lifetime." While not a religious person, even Rogers had to thank the almighty—"Prayers was what he was sailing on."

Even the sedate Calvin Coolidge was ecstatic; the President ordered the cruiser *Memphis* to pick up Lindbergh and his plane in France and bring them home. As the *Memphis* carrying Lindbergh inched up Chesapeake Bay, a massive Navy armada escorted them into port. The army fired a 21-gun salute. After receiving the Distinguished Flying Cross from President Coolidge, Lindbergh got a ticker tape parade down New York's Broadway, as thousands jammed the street, literally shutting down the city. Lindbergh became *Time Magazine*'s very first "Man of the Year," and Lindbergh mania swept the country. He represented all that was good, pure and heroic, in an otherwise, decadent decade.

Given Rogers' love of flight and his efforts to push for more American air power, it certainly fit that he would search out young Slim. The two first met when Lindbergh flew his plane back to San Diego to thank the factory workers that had built

Charles Lindbergh and Will Rogers, November 1927. (Will Rogers Memorial Museum)

her just a few months before. "Maybe you think he dident sorter hurriedly pass us old reception committee by," Rogers lamented with considerable satisfaction in his column, "to grab these old boys [the factory workers] by the hand and tell them what the old boat had done." "You never saw such beams of happiness as was on the faces when they each felt that Slim had remembered them." The next afternoon the people of San Diego filled an athletic stadium just to see Slim. Rogers was there, next to him on the stage.

Henry Ford sent a new model of his Tri-motor passenger plane that he was just beginning to manufacture to San Diego to pick up Lindbergh. The plane, the largest built in America at the time, had a daring new design with three radial engines and a capacity to carry a dozen people. Built entirely of aluminum, also a first, it could reach speeds of well over a hundred knots.

Rogers joined the group that headed back to Los Angeles in the Tri-motor and sat next to Lindbergh in the "relief pilot's seat," and the two men chatted as the lights of the small towns below beamed upward. Slim was quiet and Rogers struggled to get him to talk. But Rogers came quickly to see what this new American hero deemed important. Lindbergh, Rogers concluded, "eats, sleeps, and drinks aviation."

Lindbergh, Rogers thought, epitomized the thousands of young men in America who wanted to fly. "All they need is the training and the proper financial backing." If we did train them, we would have "the greatest Air Force in the world," and it would guarantee our safety as a nation—unfortunately, Rogers never lived to see the Herculean effort of the United States to train some 500,000 pilots during World War II. "All we would have to do is sit here and take care of our own business, and you can bet no one would ever have any idea of coming over and pouncing on us."

Despite Rogers' defense of Mitchell—who still had supporters in the army—it took little time for the American military to exploit the good will of Will Rogers. Senior military brass often invited him to air shows where Rogers, along with the planes, became star attractions. He had access to the newest planes and technology, some of it considered secret. In 1927 he was piped aboard the USS Pennsylvania while sailing along the California coast. The captain allowed him to be catapulted off the deck in a biplane. "From a standing start, on a runway only sixty feet long, you are doing sixty miles an hour at the end of it." Three years later, Secretary of the Navy David Ingalls invited Rogers to inspect the American fleet of aircraft carriers near San Diego, which then included the old USS Langley, a converted coal steamer, and the new, sleek Lexington and Saratoga. Rogers, in the back seat of a Navy Hell Diver—the newest Navy plane then available, which Ingalls piloted—landed on the deck of the Langley—"you haven't had any landing in an airplane till you land on the deck of one of these things," he proudly proclaimed.

Rogers used his influence in the country to promote commercial air travel as well, often tying the argument into the Lindbergh story. "Lindbergh came from California to New York in 23 hours," he noted, "Why can't we go and get into a regular commercial air line that will take us out there in at least 30 or 40 hours." While Ford had built what Rogers thought was the plane to do it—the Tri-motor—it actually carried too few people to turn profits, despite its aviation success, and Ford tired of investing in planes. The Tri-motor was the last one he built until the federal government contracted him to mass-produce the B-24 during World War II.

Lindbergh's wonderful boyish appeal created a demand for his services as a foreign diplomat. Ambassador Morrow and members of the Coolidge administration asked him to join the American diplomatic corps in Mexico, to carry the flag and mend fences. Lindbergh readily agreed, as long as he could fly through all the Central and South American Republics that landed on the Caribbean. Henry Ford lent him a Tri-motor, and Lindbergh opened up the first commercial flight from the United States into the Caribbean and Central America. In Mexico City, throngs of people came to meet the boy-hero at the airport. Not surprisingly, Rogers too was on hand to greet Slim. "I saw over 200,000 people, including the President [of Mexico] and all his Cabinet, wait for eight hours to welcome him." The crowd simply "went Cuckoo," as Rogers described it, as Lindbergh stepped from his plane.

The trip south gave Rogers a chance to accomplish two important missions. He, too, would be a "good-will" ambassador—he was warmly received in Mexico City—and he would be able to praise the decision to negotiate an end to the so-called Mexican crisis. He did both with grace in the pages of his column, making lavish praise of young Lindbergh. Perhaps to gain back favor with Coolidge, Rogers then praised the president and the state department. Lindbergh's visit, the comic turned journalist retorted, "was a great stroke of diplomacy." For himself, Lindbergh had no wish to linger in the limelight; he was busy planning trips to other countries, carrying "aviation diplomacy" to the Third World. Rogers left him there, in Mexico City, studying a map.

After returning home, Rogers had high praise for ambassador Morrow. "They [Mexicans] like his style, and they are not turning his head by any flattery." Perhaps Morrow did not need to do much more than meet Mexico half-way since the Mexican government feared another American invasion and wanted a solution. Rogers helped immensely with his columns. After he had met the President of the Republic, Plutarco Calles, Rogers reported—and Americans came to believe—that Mexico wished to avoid at all costs conflict with the United States. "They have had fifteen years of it [war]," Rogers concluded, "and they are tired and want to be left alone in peace."

Rogers also put a human side on the struggle with Mexico. He went out of his way to meet the men who ran the government. They were not the "bandits" that members of Coolidge's State Department suggested early in the conflict. Morrow had developed a good relationship with Calles, and so did Will Rogers. And while Rogers lamented the so-called "religious problem," that pushed by the *Christeros,* Rogers felt that sooner or later Catholic priests would realize that the government would prevent church services as long as the violence continued. Rogers expected that these men of the cloth eventually would relent, and his sense of the struggle turned out to be correct.

In terms of diplomacy, Rogers made much of the Morrow mission, but he connected it to American foreign policy in general in Central and South America. He pointed to the Mexican opposition to the recent American invasion of Nicaragua. And he concluded that Mexico was correct. "Our original assertion, that it was only a few Rebels [in Nicaragua] that were dissatisfied had kinder been disapproved . . . The Rebels must have had a majority when they started out or else we couldent have killed as many as we have." In 1928, Rogers joined his old friend Charles Evans Hughes in traveling to Havana, Cuba, for a Central American conference where it became abundantly clear that Latin American nations remained quite outraged by American conduct in the region.

Little did Rogers realize that Lindbergh, for his part, did lift his eyes from the maps on at least one occasion. After Rogers had left for home, in December 1927, Lindbergh met the young and beautiful Anne Spencer Morrow, the daughter of the ambassador, and then a college student on break from Smith College. Charles and Anne married two years later in what became a storybook romance. In typical fashion, Rogers gushed at the news, "a fine match." But he felt such an affinity for "the boy" that he could not help himself—"We all felt like we ought to be the one to kinder pick out the girl!"

Rogers' trip to Mexico, and later Cuba, reinforced a consistent theme found in his weekly columns, of opposition to American involvement in world conflicts. His conversion to the cause of isolationism also reinforced his rejection of disarmament. The way Rogers saw it, the United States had been the loser in all of negotiations that had continued since the Washington Conference of 1921, and he feared that a new conference, scheduled for fall of 1927, might lead to more disarmament. "We offered to show them something that no nation had ever seen before, and that was a nation sinking its own ships," he lamented in open disgust. Worse, we followed through. "We just sunk till we had nothing else to sink." We also promised to scrap our massive building program, one that would have "made us the biggest navy in the world." Rogers was relieved to learn that England had refused to scuttle any more ships, at least in 1927. The American delegation, to his surprise, took the same stand.

Rogers' criticism, which generally reached every major newspaper in the land, may have influenced President Coolidge, who declined thereafter to scuttle any more ships. But Rogers remained pessimistic: "disarming is out now until we get enough ships ahead to start sinking again." War, Rogers concluded, "don't diminish our navy. It's peace that's so devastating." When we agreed to disarmament, "we had even our lifeboats shot from under us." Of course, such statements were gross exaggerations. The United States had nearly a dozen battleships on the seas, though many, like the USS Pennsylvania, had been commissioned before World War I. And, thanks to disarmament— which limited battleships—the country built two new aircraft carriers in the early 1920s. Many admirals still questioned their worth and wanted battleships. Of course, aircraft carriers would win the next war, then some 13 years off.

After what had been months of travel in Europe, the western states, and finally Central America, Rogers returned to California and re-embraced American politics in late fall of 1927.

The senate was investigating the circumstances surrounding a coal miners' strike that had hit the nation. Charles Schwab, an owner of several mines, became Rogers' main target, since he had recently cut wages of coal miners. "You can work for Charley cheaper than you can for anybody else because he is so congenial and nice about it," Rogers retorted. Like most of the other mine operators who testified, Schwab claimed that the industry was losing money. He claimed "he had never made a cent out of his Steel Company." Schwab, according to Rogers, "showed that money and humor could go together." This criticism of the rich in America—relatively new for a mainstream journalist—approached promoting class warfare, but Rogers always kept his quips humorous and non-threatening.

Rogers decried the cut of wages for coal miners and, just as frequently, he voiced strong support for farmers and farm legislation. Yet he frequently offered a stark distinction between the two different issues. Farmers were not wage earners but rather capitalists themselves. Rogers realized that farmers needed help but he also saw the farm legislation that passed Congress in 1927 and again in 1928 as being flawed, a position that was new in comparison to his views four years before. Rogers praised Coolidge for vetoing both bills; Democrats, including those from the South, had gone too far. Rogers concluded that the American farmer simply was too efficient, too productive for his own good. The key to a solution for farmers was limiting production, or so Rogers concluded—an idea that would become policy a decade later.

Rogers' rather gentle criticism of big business resulted in columns that slowly questioned the way capitalists operated in America. However, Rogers did not so much defend farmers or miners as he simply demonstrated sympathy for them. This compassion led to action on his part as he often used his name and abilities to raise money for the suffering and underprivileged. His favorite charity became the Red Cross, which he commonly supported both in his column and with his own funds. Will left the Wagoner Show in early 1926 to do a Red Cross benefit to help victims of the Mississippi River floods of that year. While Rogers had trouble with passing permanent laws to assist the underprivileged, he did believe that people with money had an obligation to assist them and so did the government during times of disaster.

A second, more devastating, hurricane hit Florida in September of 1928. The storm surpassed all previous ones with the exception of the Galveston hurricane in 1900. The winds came ashore as a category 5, the first ever recorded in history. It left 2,500 dead in south Florida, and thousands of homes washed away. Rogers spoke directly to the head of the Red Cross and promptly set out to organize fund-raisers. In a change from the past, he also lobbied the federal government for relief, urging Congress to give money directly to the Red Cross. In the end, Congress failed to act, but the event demonstrated yet again another transformation in Rogers' thinking. He slowly came to believe that government had a responsibility to help common folk in time of need, a view that mostly ran counter to political thinking in 1928.

Rogers had little time to castigate a reticent Congress for its failures at both farm and hurricane relief since 1928 was an election year and the country geared up for the event. Rogers' columns turned to outlining the issues at hand. He concluded that men like Henry Ford paid workers a decent wage, but others like Schwab, did not, a farm bill was necessary, but one that limited production. He asserted also that Prohibition had failed, that the foreign policies of the United States still needed correction, that legislation regarding flood control and hurricane relief should be supported, that both the Army and Navy needed more funding, and that the immigration issue should be reconsidered. In virtually every instance, these views were "liberal" at a time when America was electing "conservatives" to office. Yet the way in which Rogers introduced them, the "cowboy" logic that often put such issues in their simplest forms, made his columns and his views seem sensible to most of his readers.

Few Americans likely saw this political criticism as part of an overall agenda, primarily because Rogers always shrouded and intermixed the issues in a variety of stories and jokes about Hollywood figures, politicians being politicians, preachers, cowboy writers, and social reformers. The wonderfully interesting Judge Ben Lindsey of Denver, for example, who created the first Juvenile Court system in the country and promoted easy divorce and birth control, provided the classic sort of distraction that Rogers and his readers both enjoyed. The Judge, Rogers wrote, was coming to visit, with the intent "to explain to me his angle on all this marriage business he has caused so much talk about." But he prefaced his discussion of the judge's views with a classic admission that the friendly meeting came simply because little of importance was discussed in the newspapers. That all changed, however, when President Coolidge announced to the nation, with just six words and no explanation, that he "did not choose to run again."

Rogers found the speech unbelievable and concluded that Coolidge intended to trick the Republican convention into nominating him. Did "CHOOSE mean *won't* or *will?*" Complicating politics even more, William McAdoo, a Democratic frontrunner, followed Coolidge by bowing out. Rogers lamented that McAdoo had not acted first, and "put Cal in a hole." Coolidge, Rogers thought, "either does one or two things; he does what nobody thinks he will do [such as withdrawing], or he don't do nothing." Rogers thought it was "generally the latter." But Coolidge had fooled everyone. This early maneuvering left Al Smith the frontrunner for the Democrats, but his constant stand against Prohibition made his election an uphill battle. At first, the Republicans also seemed somewhat in disarray. According to Rogers, Coolidge had not even told his wife, Grace, before he announced his plans to retire!

Rogers took his well-known down-to-earth view on the upcoming election. He saw it purely as an issue of rain, yes rain. "Rain was with Cal instead of McNary-Haugen [the congressional authors of the farm bill] this last fall, and it is awful hard to beat for a farmers' 'relief measure' when the crops are good." The question, as Rogers saw it, evolved around whether the Republicans would continue to "have the Lord" pulling for them. The Bible, Rogers noted, says that the Lord "loveth the poor and down and out." The Democrats, he thought, generally fit this category. Unfortunately, the poor generally got little other than the "love" of the story. "If everybody instead of writing a poem about 'em [the poor] would have sent a dollar instead, there would have been no poor and needy." The Lord had certainly benefited "Calvin's gang" in the past, at least with rain.

After several paragraphs of "careful" political thought, Rogers concluded that most Americans were simply not interested in who ran, or who got elected. "Will the farmers get relief," Rogers asked, as well as "Can Al [Smith] hold New York, and not lose Alabama?" And what of the new Republican frontrunner,

Herbert Hoover? Many Republicans did not like him as he had worked for Democratic President Woodrow Wilson and was considered somewhat progressive. When these questions were hypothetically asked of supposed readers, Rogers found that most Americans voiced an interest only regarding whether "Ford's new car will be ready for delivery." Ford had completely redesigned his Model T, replacing it with the Model A, an inexpensive, assembly-line product that made its debut in 1927 to 1928. Everyone in America rushed to see the new product, which sold for well under a thousand dollars.

Despite the indifference, Rogers attended both political conventions in the early summer of 1928. The Republicans met first in Kansas City, where, as Rogers put it, "The Democrats watch the comedy in this one, and then they improve on it." Herbert Hoover had the nomination by the time the delegates met. Hoover had been in Coolidge's cabinet, "ever since Coolidge was old enough to have a cabinet." Hoover, Rogers noted, was known "wherever calamities are known." Among his important achievements were feeding refugees in Europe after World War I, and he had actively assisted victims of Florida hurricanes while in Coolidge's cabinet, though Congress had failed to fund the effort. Hoover had demonstrated some humanity. Rogers could see nothing wrong with the man.

Surprisingly, a few people in the country expressed a serious interest in Will Rogers running for president. One of *Life Magazine*'s writers, Robert Benchley, started the charade by claiming in a comical fashion that Rogers "Chews to Run" (Will was known for his gum chewing). A few campaign buttons were printed with the slogan that a much later candidate for president used successfully. It read "W is the man for the office." Benchley provided considerable dialogue, including a careful analysis of Rogers' many sensible political traits. Friend Judge Lindsey from Colorado quickly joined the chorus, endorsing Rogers, and then Henry Ford chimed in. Ford said Rogers' candidacy was "no joke," which of course it really was. Even so, Ford proclaimed Rogers' candidacy to be "a serious attempt to restore American common sense to American politics." Rogers, openly bashful over the idea when asked, ignored the pundits and went on to see what the Democrats were up to at their convention.

The Democrats had agreed to meet in Houston, after the party received $200,000 in cash from Texas millionaire Jesse Jones. One reporter thought it merely a good investment as Jones "owned the overcrowded hotels" where the delegates slept, "the theaters where they sought escape," "the banks where they cashed checks," and even the "laundry" where hopeful politicians often "lost their shirts!" Above all, Jones owned newspapers, oil wells, and a considerable portion of downtown Houston, and he later became a major figure in Democratic politics, his bequeath of 1928 doing much to help his reputation.

While few Texans could match Jones' wealth, at least one, Amon Carter from Fort Worth, had as much influence in the state. Carter, who owned the Fort Worth *Star-Telegram*, proudly proclaimed that the "West" began at Fort Worth, and he lived the part, often calling himself a "simple cowboy." In reality, Carter was larger than life, vain in the extreme, confident, sacrilegious, and at times insufferable. Carter thought Prohibition was "insanity," as he put it, and as it went into effect, he purchased an entire warehouse of liquor, and stored it in various places, burying ten barrels of whiskey for emergency purposes. With such characters running the Democratic Convention, it was expected to be interesting.

Rogers had met Carter some years before in New York City when both attended a party at John McGraw's house, the then manager of the New York Giants baseball team. The two became the closest of friends, as Carter often wined and dined Rogers, providing a free hotel suite for him to use in Fort Worth, and the latter reciprocating by inviting Carter along on various trips. Accordingly, in 1928, Rogers, who intended to cover the convention, flew directly to Fort Worth, where Carter awaited him. Carter had invited other dignitaries. Among the important men who joined the group at Carter's marvelous Shady Oak Farm were Paul Patterson, publisher of the Baltimore *Sun*, and his famous writer, H. L. Mencken. Carter forced all his guests to don one of his signature cowboy hats that he specially purchased for visitors (others to get a hat in later years included President Harry Truman and General Douglas MacArthur). The hats were wide-brimmed with a huge crown, but ironically, were made in Italy. This changed after Mussolini attacked Ethiopia some years later. Carter then bought his own hat company and produced hats similar to the "Stetson" that singing cowboys made famous in the movies.[5]

With friends in hand, Carter chartered a train to Houston where he put everyone up on the top floor of the Rice Hotel, the convention headquarters. But Carter became distraught as his hand-picked candidate, John Nance Garner from Texas, faded. Rogers, too, seemed miffed. Democratic delegates continued old feuds, the smallish Rice Hotel was packed with people, making it impossible to get around, and the weather turned awfully hot. Rogers wrote that the "lobby was so packed . . . that I reached up and mopped three brows before I could find my own." As tempers flared, and Carter tried his hand at lobbying, he discovered that it was nearly impossible to get from floor to floor in the hotel as the one elevator could not handle the job. While standing next to Sheriff Carl Smith of Fort Worth—Carter's supposed bodyguard—Carter pulled out the sheriff's revolver and shot three times into the glass elevator door. The wire mesh in the door kept it from shattering and fortunately, no one was hurt.

Nearly every newspaper in the country began reporting on the "Houston Incident." But Rogers remained calm, hardly mentioning the event, no doubt out of respect for his friend, Carter. Mencken, too, took the gun-play in stride, at least until he too became a victim. After Mencken encouraged the pestering Carter to leave his room so he could complete his column, and then turned his back, Carter pulled out Smith's pistol a second time and fired three shots out the window. "The aim of his volley," as Mencken later calmly put it, "was simply to entertain me pleasantly in the Texas fashion." The local police agreed, as they concluded that Carter's antics were simply "a natural sign of discontent in Texas." After returning to Baltimore, Mencken's publisher, Paul Patterson, got his hands on the bullet-holed glass door, which he framed and put on his wall! Much later, a retrospective Mencken wrote that Carter believed himself to be

---

[5]The hats became collectors' items which famous actors and politicians alike gladly accepted. Inside the band, the citation read "Shady Oak Farm, Fort Worth, Texas, Where the West Begins, The Latch String Always Hangs Outside. Amon Carter."

"a West Texan, which connoted a familiarity with firearms and a willingness to use them."

Rogers, who concluded that it was simply his friend Carter being Carter, suspected that his antics somehow mimicked the Democrats, who were ready for, as Rogers put it, a "dog fight." And the fighting went on for several days. When it subsided, the party endorsed Al Smith of New York. Being a wet and a Catholic, Rogers had once thought he would have been the ideal man to settle the Mexican crisis. But as a presidential candidate, Rogers thought he would lose badly. Indeed, outside the convention center, protestors marched with signs that read "Democratic Drinking Devils." Other women prayed in a nearby church, chanting out-loud, invoking God to strike down Al Smith. The convention, then, won by a wet from the north, was held in the heart of the Bible belt, where many considered alcohol consumption a sin.

By the summer 1928, Rogers tried to put the best face on the events. He wrote that either man would do—"They will all do the best they can." Republicans would likely win, however, "if weather and crops," are good, and "no wars, and a fair share of prosperity is with them." But the Democratic convention, with its anger and conflict, seemed ominous.

There were a few signs that the prosperity that Rogers hoped for might not continue. Factory production had declined by the fall and some important industry leaders had cut wages, the real estate boom in Florida had ended with the hurricane, and coal-mine owners were reducing wages, again. Rogers did not sense economic troubles. Yet he questioned the prosperity theme that Republican candidates espoused. Andrew Mellon, Coolidge's Secretary of the Treasury, assured America that "the majority of the Country is prosperous." Rogers treated the statement with some sarcasm: "Mellon kinder insinuates that if a man don't know enough to be a Republican than how can he expect to know enough to be prosperous."

The election proved another disaster for the Democratic Party. Hoover won nearly every northern state and took Texas and Florida in the South. Smith lost his home state, New York. The only real gains by Democrats came in northeastern cities, where Democrats began to slowly build support thereafter. Smith did well in them, especially ethnic communities. In the months afterward, Rogers' column turned to what had become regular banter—discussions with everyone from Lady Astor to the famous baseball player, an American Indian, Chief Bender, a star with the Philadelphia Athletics. One of Rogers' columns revealed that the newly elected Governor of Oklahoma, Henry S. Johnston, consulted the Zodiac before making decisions. "Ain't the old State of Oklahoma just taking the prize for continuous humor?"

In some ways, this rather senseless dialogue reveals a Will Rogers who was becoming more skeptical of America's ability to improve itself. The populist liberal who had emerged by 1926 was becoming more pessimistic. Congress seemed hopeless, the presidents of the 1920s were good men but they did little to move the country forward, the farmers suffered, and Prohibition—a stupid experiment as far as Rogers was concerned—remained the law of the land. As for religion, Rogers moved farther and farther away from it as he grew older. One of his biographers, Ben Yagoda, suggests that he had become a Nihilist, one who rejected most attempts to implant a morality upon society and one who scorned virtually every organized religion. In a sense, Will Rogers had immersed himself increasingly in travel, to various states and countries that he had not seen, but these visits offered few better answers to his concern as to where America was headed.

While the travel may have put some strains on Rogers' family life, Betty and the children seemed no worse for it. Nevertheless, after the Rogers family had returned from Europe, Will and Betty made one important decision—they would return to California and stay there as the children finished school. And try as he might in later months, Ziegfeld never again was able to entice Rogers to go on the road. Will and Betty had paid off the land in Santa Monica. The two columns returned a handsome profit—Rogers received $10,000 a month for the weekly column alone by 1928. And Will devoted more time to motion pictures, a media that changed dramatically when "talking" was added to films. The invention of "talkies," as they were called, benefited "talkers" like Will Rogers and his acting jobs increased after 1929. Talking pictures also offered a new form of social criticism that Rogers would employ some years later.

The land at Santa Monica allowed Will to renew his love for horses. One of the first structures to appear was a small barn for horses, and then a fenced ring for roping cattle. Then a small house was added. By the late 1920s, Rogers could no longer handle large cattle and turned instead to practicing on calves. His youngest son Jim often joined him in hour after hour of riding and roping. Visitors who came by to see the operation discovered that Will would not stop and ultimately gave up ever talking with him. He became so obsessed with roping that he wore out the calves; they would not run any more. He then sold them and bought another group. The ranch, as it slowly took shape, gave Rogers an opportunity to escape back to his youth, and he dearly loved it.

Rogers fully realized in 1928 that journalistic success depended upon a readership; that translated into restraint in his criticism of American politics. The majority of Americans belonged to the Republican Party in 1928, and the party, at times, appeared more progressive than the Democrats—who had a serious problem in defending segregation in the South—something that Rogers occasionally admitted. The election of 1928 had demonstrated to Rogers and to the nation that the Democrats would remain a decided minority for years to come. They were terribly divided and disorganized. Republicans believed in a strong work ethic and the profit motive. Will Rogers had no difficulty with this. And parts of the Old South seemed to be on the verge of converting to Republican politics, breaking up what had been the so-called "solid Democratic South."

This left Will Rogers, a man with a considerable knowledge of world affairs and an opportunity to voice them, as someone who embraced a number of liberal ideas in an age that remained mostly illiberal. In reality, in the older Democratic tradition, he trusted people who lived off the land more than people who lived in cities, despite the fact that he often lived in either New York or Beverly Hills. Such people, he believed, were the heart and soul of America and should be helped when they needed help. Rogers recognized that many rural Americans were suffering, especially in the South. The Democratic Party that he supported was making inroads only in urban environments, and it was terribly divided between the urban, ethnic masses and southern "Bible-belt" rural communities, regions of the country that he knew intimately, regions that put Prohibition ahead of their own political self-interest. Such a division would only lead to complete Republican hegemony, a notion that anguished Will Rogers.

Yet in a somewhat contradictory sense, Rogers remained a staunch capitalist, but one who avoided dealings with big bankers or the stock market, both of which he believed to be sinister. He mostly trusted his instincts in real estate investment, and he had made many good decisions in purchasing land. Above all, his socio-political beliefs held a compassion for the underdog. He, unlike most Americans, believed that government could do good things for the public at large, particularly those who were suffering. Individual Americans certainly possessed the heart and ambition necessary to take care of themselves, but when they could not do so, the government needed to step in and help. Just as clearly, Rogers believed that government should stay out of the lives of people; religion—or in his case lack of it—was up to the individual, and so was the consumption of alcohol.

Republicans of the age rejected most of these views and a number of Democrats gave them little support. Congress generally refused to help individuals, most members citing their principles. They voted down legislation designed to support the efforts of the Red Cross. Republicans supported Prohibition—as did many Democrats—and pandered to the church groups who wanted it. Republicans generally catered to the rich and business elite; they refused to help the struggling farmer or the homeless hurricane victim and viewed the powerful industrial elites of America, who Rogers believed sometimes exploited people, as heroes. And they believed that the military should be used to protect American commerce if it meant violating another country's sovereignty.

This kind of hands-off government that favored big business was clearly what the majority of the American voting public wanted. This left Will Rogers somewhat bewildered in 1928—a man who took out his frustrations by roping calves. Yet he was still a man with incredible influence in the political life of America and he had learned so much in such a short time. His opportunity to help re-shape the muddled beliefs of many Americans was not far distant.

April 1930. Will Rogers delivers a radio address at KHJ, an early radio station in Los Angeles and one of the first affiliates of the Columbia Broadcasting System. (Will Rogers Memorial Museum)

5

Will Rogers, the Journalist

Will Rogers knew Al Smith as a friend. As the Democratic Party readied to nominate Smith (a Catholic and a wet from New York), for president in 1928, Rogers tried in vain to talk him out of running. The stock market was booming, and a Democrat had little chance to unseat the Republican Herbert Hoover. Rogers proved correct. Smith went down in a crushing defeat. Rogers' advice was indicative of his new role as a political pundit. Indeed, by 1928 Will preferred to think of himself as a journalist, not just a comedian. The transition came slowly, almost naturally, as the performer traveled the world, looking for stories. Will Rogers began to take his new job as a journalist more seriously than any other aspect of his career. His refusal to rejoin the *Follies* in fall of 1926 marked this turning point in his life.

Will's journalistic skills improved dramatically after he returned from Europe. A strong indication of this was apparent when well-known journalists such as Arthur Brisbane, Walter Lippmann, and H. L. Mencken took note of his success at attracting readers. The invention of the "Daily Telegram," a short piece that averaged fewer than a hundred words, was crucial to Rogers' journalistic success. Given its length, the Daily Telegram usually graced the front page of the newspapers it appeared in, and it was often the first item readers read. Rogers continued to write his weekly column, which by contrast increasingly reported Hollywood gossip or gave in-depth discussions of important personalities. The Daily Telegram hit hard—in a very brief sense—at some of the most important issues of the day.

By fall of 1926, some 91 newspapers carried the daily telegram, including the *Times,* which syndicated the piece. The number doubled and then doubled again, thereafter. The *Times* was slowly becoming America's leading newspaper, and the editors there struggled with Will's "ain't's." But the paper's senior editor sent out a memo suggesting that Rogers' language was "unique because he makes his own English." The paper changed very little of what Rogers wrote—at least at first—leading the piece with a simple "WILL ROGERS SAYS." The Daily Telegram often resembled the lead piece in what later became the evening news on television—a hard-hitting fact followed by a brief analysis of the meaning of the event. A case in point came when Coolidge announced that he did not "choose to run"—clearly front-page news. Rogers wondered in his daily column how many hours Coolidge had spent in the dictionary "looking for the word 'choose,' instead of 'I will not.'"

Life for the Rogers family remained stable despite Will's travels, his speaking tours for which he was handsomely paid, and his continued work on various motion pictures. Will's film career increased dramatically in 1929 when "talkies" came to dominate the business, but some silent screen actors could not make the transition. Performing in talkies came naturally for Rogers; indeed, they enhanced his movie career, given his comedic experience. When it came to reading lines, Rogers understood timing, and he had mastered facial expression. He signed a lucrative contract with Fox Studios that year and did 22 films with them over the next six-year period, averaging three a year.

The money that came in from all these efforts—writing, performing, and acting—allowed him to add to the land he had acquired in Santa Monica. Will and Betty bought another 84 acres in what would become Pacific Palisades, most of it hilly and almost inaccessible by automobile. Here in 1927, they constructed a small "ranch house," used at first only as a summer retreat. Will's concern was with stabling his horses, the housing that consumed his time in the years that followed. He rode his horses frequently; on occasion down to the ocean. The rides he and Betty had down to the beaches convinced them both to buy more land by the ocean. By 1928, Will mused that his real estate investments were worth four million dollars, but he still owed on the new land purchases and looked for ways to pay off the debt.

Ironically, Rogers, who always avoided putting money into stocks, strongly considered doing so with the roughly $900,000 that he had accumulated over 1928. Many of his friends were making fortunes in the stock market. Before doing so, however, he invited Bernard Baruch out to his summer ranch, and asked him for advice. Baruch, a banker and financier as well as a Democratic politician, strongly advised against it. Other smart investors, including Joseph P. Kennedy from Massachusetts, another leading Democratic supporter, had started to slowly pull out of the market, suspecting that stocks had to take a correction in the near future. Rogers took Baruch's advice and used the money to consolidate and pay off various mortgages on his ranch and new beach-front property, avoiding what might have been a disaster. Baruch, who often offered Rogers advice for his column on the state of the national economy, later reminded Will of this timely advice.

Financially secure and blessed with an abundance of friends, the Rogers ranch became a Mecca for many of America's elite performers, writers, and politicians—not unlike the Lummis home some years before. Young Joel McCrea stayed often, as did Charlie Chaplin (who often had a young, budding actress on his arm), W. C. Fields, Jack Benny, and a very independent 21-year-old Katharine Hepburn, who would win more Academy Awards than any other actor. Others within his circle of Hollywood friends included Ray Milland, Alice Faye, and a young actor whose first name was "Leroy." Out of admiration for Will, Leroy changed his last name to "Rogers," becoming Roy Rogers.

Will Rogers' fame reached such proportions that the social and political elite of America went out of their way to make friends with him. Besides Baruch, Franklin Delano Roosevelt, who had nominated Al Smith for the Presidency for the second time in 1928, kept up a fairly consistent correspondence with Rogers. Roosevelt particularly liked the fact that Rogers had contributed liberally to a fund set up at Hot Springs, Georgia, where Roosevelt supported a special hospital to help young people in their struggles with polio. Columnist Arthur Brisbane developed a friendship with Rogers and continued a constant correspondence, albeit with a somewhat competitive bent. William Randolph Hearst, the New York newspaperman who built a publishing empire as well as a lavish palace along the California coast, became a close friend. Rogers relied on Hearst to distribute money to several children's charities, one check that Will sent him being for $5,000. Rogers even developed a close relationship with Charles Schwab after 1928—suggesting, given the content of his earlier columns that Rogers could pick on powerful men, meet them, and win them over as friends.

As his fame and political influence grew, virtually every American politician listened to Rogers by the late 1920s. His pen did attract some criticism from those who considered themselves to be "serious" journalists. H. L. Mencken, whose experience with cowboys had been less than favorable, found Rogers unbearable at times. Mencken had made a living off of criticism—so different in approach to Rogers—nick-naming the Scopes Trial the "Monkey Trial;" he also attacked organized religion. Mencken once defined a Puritan as someone who had "the haunting fear that someone, somewhere, may be happy." When it came to religion, he and Rogers agreed, but they had little else in common and they were both competitive people. Meeting first in Mexico when Rogers traveled with Charles Lindbergh, and then rooming together at the 1928 Democratic Convention, the two men quickly recognized that their views of the world differed.

Mencken, an elite eastern journalist, could not understand the popularity of Will Rogers—the fact that Rogers was syndicated in over 400 newspapers literally disturbed Mencken. Further, these two men came from decidedly different backgrounds—Mencken knew little about the South or the West. While traveling with Rogers through Texas in 1928, Mencken saw southern poverty for the first time. Rogers noted the shock on his face: "Mencken says after seeing the South he is going to start picking on the North." At times, the two men scuffled intellectually. Another reporter overheard the rather obnoxious Mencken mock Rogers one evening while Will stood quietly by. Mencken retorted: "Millions of Americans read his words daily, and those who are unable to read, listen to him over the radio." Rogers was, Mencken believed, "the most dangerous writer alive today." Rogers remonstrated that his gags were never taken seriously, to which Mencken replied, "they are taken seriously by nobody except half-wits, in other words, by approximately 85 percent of the voting population."

Some newspaper editors agreed with Mencken, occasionally scrapping Rogers' column. Adolph Ochs, the publisher of the *Times*, tried on several occasions to tone down Rogers' "political" wit, believing that true journalists had an obligation to report facts, not to offer political judgments. The two came to loggerheads on several occasions, once when Rogers used characteristic sarcasm regarding the 1930 disarmament conference in London, the last one before Japan started its aggression in Asia. Ochs believed that the conference held some future benefit for the nation and that Rogers should remove his criticism of it from his column. On yet another occasion, the two tangled over the issue of the European debts. The *Times* had written an editorial opinion suggesting that all or portions of the debt should be canceled. Rogers' column strongly disagreed, prompting Ochs to edit his commentary. Columnist Walter Lippman, one of the most respected writers of the age, agreed with the *Times'* editorial.

As Rogers sought more and more recognition as a journalist, he found himself occasionally in a conundrum, defending his work, which often approached comedic satire, though he wanted to be taken seriously as a journalist. When the two concepts clashed, or when he contradicted the *Times'* editorial page, Ochs argued with him and demanded changes.

While censored occasionally by the *Times*, Rogers had a free hand on most of the issues of the day. A May 1930 memorandum, found in the executive correspondence of the *Times*, indicates that while some senior editors considered Rogers' pieces to be below the standards of the *Times*, they all agreed that his columns, which originated at the newspaper, attracted more income to the newspaper than any other. The *Boston Globe*, for example, paid the *Times* $250 a week to print Rogers' pieces, the going rate. When multiplied by several hundred newspapers, the sum suggested that even the mighty *New York Times* could ill afford to antagonize Rogers, despite the contempt of some of its editors.

During the early days of the new Hoover Administration, Rogers found plenty on which to comment. At times, the new President appeared progressive, appointing, for example, a woman, Mabel W. Willebrandt, to be Assistant Attorney General. Rogers reported that Willebrandt, while at the Justice Department in the mid-1920s, had prosecuted violators of the Prohibition laws. That, in itself, might have set Rogers off, but in this case it was her gender that attracted him to the issue and he came out strongly in favor of her appointment. Will posed a question of whether she could handle a job that a man usually did, and he wondered how men would react to the appointment. "It was all right with the men when the women took the little Committee assignments where there was no salary," Will concluded, but when women "put their powdered nose into the feed trough, why that brought on complications." There was one final benefit: "Every job a Woman can grab off it just drives another politician to either work or the poor house."

Hoover got similar praise for the hospitality that his wife offered at a tea party in a piece that demonstrated the long way that Rogers had come in dealing with the race issue. In November 1928, Chicago elected the Black politician Oscar Stanton De Priest to the House of Representatives. He was the first African American to serve in the House since the 1880s. Rather than stay in the shadows, his wife, Jessie, showed up at the inaugural White House tea hosted by Mrs. Hoover. Needless to say, this raised eyebrows, especially among southern congressman and their wives—indeed, it later hurt President Hoover politically. Rogers, who hailed from the South, met the issue head-on. "Now Mrs. Hoover knows what she is doing," he started in a two-paragraph assessment. "If it was custom for the first Lady . . . to entertain all the Congressman's wives, then when a colored one come along there was nothing else to do." Both parties willingly accepted the congressman's vote, Rogers noted, and it was high time "to give 'em [Black Americans in general?] a little consideration."

The commentary suggested considerable maturity regarding Rogers' views on race. While most liberals of the age agreed that the mistreatment of Blacks in the South was unacceptable— as increasingly did Will Rogers—and lynching did begin to decline after 1930, precipitously, there was still little support for integration, even in liberal circles in America. To some degree, Rogers had moved ahead on this issue, suggesting that a Black congressman's wife should be "integrated" into the circle of wives that attended functions. He fully realized that if Mrs. Hoover accepted the woman, that she would also be included at the various balls and celebrations that went on each year in the capital, a dramatic change that many in Washington did not support.

Neither of these positions, supporting a woman's right to a job generally held by a man as well as the right of a Black woman to come to tea in the White House, was popular in the America of 1929. Likely, neither idea went down well with Will's readership in Oklahoma. His views, then, demonstrated just how far he had come in escaping the provincialism of the South. Rogers' espoused liberal views on both gender and race issues at a time when neither was popular.

Rogers displayed similar logic when the press began attacking young Charles Lindbergh, who had wanted a private wedding and honeymoon in 1929. Some editors claimed that the press had made Lindbergh, and he had an obligation to let them attend the affairs. Rogers found the attacks appalling:

> Lindbergh was made by just two things. The Lord and a Wright Whirlwind motor. Newspapers couldn't have flew him from one side of a razor blade to another. They reported the fact that he arrived there . . . but don't you think the French would have found it out sooner or later, and eventually have got the news back over here to us?

Rogers implored the press to leave the couple alone.

Unfortunately, the Lord failed to protect the young flyer against a ghastly crime. Nearly three years later, Rogers took a middle-of-the-night phone call from young Bill Hearst, William Randolph Hearst's oldest son, who ran his father's paper in New York. The Lindbergh's 20-month old baby had been kidnapped. After the family had paid the ransom, the baby was found dead. "It was just one of those things that hit you right between the eyes," was about all that Will Rogers could muster for what some considered the "crime of the century." He had been with the Lindbergh's just days before and witnessed their adoration for the child. The nation, which waited in vain for a rescue, was shocked at the outcome. The famed flyer was never the same again—even his marriage would fall apart in later years—and he embraced a secluded life for some years thereafter, at times moving into the Rogers' ranch at Pacific Palisades to hide out from the press while Will and Betty were traveling.

Much less shock came over the escalating debate regarding Prohibition. Most of the nation wanted the Eighteenth Amendment to the Constitution, which prohibited the sale, transportation, or consumption of alcohol, repealed. The actual amendment did have a confusing "out" clause. The language read: "The Congress and the several states shall have concurrent power to enforce this article by appropriate legislation." By the time Hoover took office, some states—especially New York— had become openly lax in enforcing the law and the federal courts refused to intervene. While Congress could have turned enforcement over to the states entirely—a decision lobbied for by many Americans—the votes necessary to pass such legislation were not yet there. Indeed, Prohibition remained unenforceable and hopelessly bogged down in politics.

The silliness associated with Prohibition offered much grist for Rogers' columns. It became a class issue for him, as he often noted that the rich had no difficulty in getting and consuming liquor. The issue became especially farcical after Senator Tom Heflin from Alabama charged the Roman Catholic Church with making his son into a drunk. "It was the Son of a Roman Catholic that give my Boy the drink," Heflin reputedly said, "and then insisted that he [his son] take another." Rogers could hardly believe the charge. Despite no real appreciation of the Catholic Church, Heflin became the target of a merciless Rogers' pen.

Unlike Rogers, President Hoover considered the issue to be so important that he had to do something about it. He created a commission to investigate liquor consumption and offer suggestions on how to bring about compliance with the law. The President selected George Wickersham, a very respected former attorney general, to head the group, though it had little power other than to make recommendations. Wickersham was a close friend of Charles Evans Hughes, who Rogers had grown to appreciate, but Rogers likely disagreed with some of Wickersham's views, especially on foreign policy. Both Wickersham and Hughes had signed the *Manifesto of the Thirty-One* back in 1920, a document that called for the United States to join the League of Nations. Wickersham was a well-known internationalist, similar to many other cabinet-level officials who went to work in the Hoover Administration, including his Secretary of State, Henry Stimson.

Wickersham quickly called a meeting of America's governors. He wanted their help in enforcing Prohibition. This, according to Rogers, was not well received: "New York and a lot of others got their annual laugh." Wickersham made matters worse by releasing to the press the letter that he sent to the various governors, which left many options open. "They don't know from it," Rogers reported, "if he is wet, dry, damp, repeal, enforce, endure, modify, or let bad enough alone." Given the general lack of agreement among the governors, most, according to Rogers, "agree that Wickersham is all wet!"

Over the next two years, the commission accomplished little. Rogers assumed that sometime in the future, they would issue a "Joint Report," followed by each member telling "their own story," or a "Minority Report"—this allowed members to deny what was in the Joint Report. "Its kinder like Double Entry Bookkeeping," Rogers suggested. The red ink, as he said, would counter the black ink. Wickersham's final report, which did not appear until 1931, proved Rogers correct: there was no consensus, though the report did confirm that Prohibition promoted disrespect for law and order and also corrupted police departments. Hoover likely realized this from the start and thus ignored the entire process. Rogers thought that was only proper. "He shouldent be asked to settle prohibition any more than he should the short dress problem [the mini-skirts that so-called 'flappers' wore in the 1920s]."

News of the Wickersham Commission suddenly disappeared from the front pages when, on October 23, 1929, news came over the radio of a vast sell-off in stocks on Wall Street. In the preceding years, Rogers had watched with astonishment—as did the nation—as the market dramatically rose. The market value of all stock on the New York Stock Exchange increased from $27 billion to $67 billion just in the mid-1920s. The sell-off erased this "paper wealth" and was soon dubbed a "crash."

During the boom years, banks and corporations found their bottom lines increased by as much as 150 percent, simply by issuing stock. Corporations saw a golden opportunity. They issued more stock, well beyond the value of their companies, which in turn provided interest-free capital in order to build more factories.

With massive amounts of "paper" capital pervading the market, investors grabbed the stock, buying it on margin through bank loans, sometimes putting down only 10 percent of the value of the stock. It was then an age where banks and corporations both wildly speculated and chased what can only be called "bad debts," which encouraged more lending on investments for which lenders lacked knowledge of the prospects for a return.

Making matters worse, what most economists and government officials failed to see was that by 1929 a middle class did not yet exist that could support the increased industrial production of the 1920s. Indeed, roughly 2.3 percent of the population held half of the savings in the nation. As the economy worsened over the summer 1929, tell-tale signs of trouble included a serious decline in new car sales, followed by a dramatic drop in construction. The Republican Secretary of the Treasury, Andrew Mellon, adopted a policy of cutting taxes for the rich rather than for consumers, who were unable to buy goods being mass produced. A week after the first frantic selling—on October 30—it resumed again, and all hope of stopping it vanished. General Motors lost over $2 billion in value in one day; other corporations, including those with strong production capabilities, suffered along with those that had inflated their bottom lines, and some faced bankruptcy—if not in the fall of 1929, in the three years that followed.

Rogers, who happened to be in New York, watched the market crash on October 23. The next day his daily column addressed the issue. It was, he announced, "wailing day." You had to "stand in line to get a window to jump out of." Despite the "dark" comedy, it is uncertain whether Rogers was responsible for starting the common myth that stock holders, bankers, and brokers jumped out of windows in New York. For certain, the CEO of the Union Cigar Company, whose stock fell 100 points that day, did take a room at the Beverly Hotel in Manhattan and jumped out the window. Other bankers were revealed as manipulators who had deceived countless investors. The most famous was Charles Ponzi of Boston, who promised investors a 50 percent return on money that he would use to buy and sell foreign currency. Ponzi made millions in what became a typical "pryamid" scheme, where investors gave money to a trusted broker who simply purchased nothing with it, reporting false profits to the investors. The "Ponzi Scheme" was thus born, a manipulative practice that continues to plague the stock market.

Investment schemes attracted the most respected bankers and brokers. They often quietly bought and sold each other's stock, driving up values to unsustainable highs, and then quickly sold everything, leaving the unsuspecting outsiders to watch their stock tumble. While the Federal Reserve tried to rein in speculation by raising interest rates in 1928, the CEOs of major corporations, such as Bethlehem Steel, Standard Oil, and Chrysler replaced declining bank capital with loans to brokers, who in turn, sold stock on margin to eager investors. The stock market had become a house of cards by late 1929, with stocks vastly over-valued and instability associated with bad investment. Government regulation, which might have prevented some of the excesses, did not exist.

Will Rogers certainly did not see the October 23 "crash" as a devastating economic blow. Indeed, hardly anyone in the country did believe that the crash would lead to worse economic times since the market affected so few people. "There is nothing that hollers as quick and as loud as a gambler," Rogers concluded. The "crash," Will assumed, only affected speculators. Life in the rest of the country was little changed by the event, at least in late October of 1929.

Rogers left New York on October 25 for California. The stock market was a long way from Los Angeles. The week after the crash, Rogers ignored it in his weekly column and wrote a whimsical piece on the huge party that Henry Ford put on for Thomas Edison at his Dearborn, Michigan estate. Rogers received an engraved invitation that thrilled him to no end. President Hoover attended, as did Charles Schwab and young John D. Rockefeller. Ford had created an historic village complete with old cars, railroad locomotives, and completely stocked nineteenth-century stores. He had even moved Edison's old laboratory from Menlo Park, New Jersey. Rogers thought it a joy to "see just hundreds of the men that we read about all the time . . . just bumming around."

Within a week of the celebration, President Hoover called in several of these dynamos of industry to discuss the market crash. After many meetings, he offered the nation a simple solution. He called upon Americans to spend money by purchasing goods.

Ford accommodated him by raising the salaries of some of his workers. Rogers mentioned the irony of it all: Coolidge had always advocated saving; now, the Republican President wanted spending. "So that makes a splendid arrangement," Rogers quipped, "have everybody save during one administration, and spend during the next." Will thought perhaps Wall Street had done America a favor. "It's going to be a great year," Rogers predicted, "and we will have plenty of prosperity . . . Course it may not reach everybody, the Prosperity." These words proved prophetic.

As months went by, some saw recovery around the corner. The market had finally stabilized—it had been worth $87 billion in the summer of 1929, and had fallen to roughly $55 billion by the end of the year. There was good reason to believe that this "paper loss," as Rogers called it, was over and had been temporary. When President Hoover spoke of "restoring confidence," Rogers agreed and joked about it in his usual fashion: "But you will have to give me some idea of where 'confidence' is. And just who you want it restored to." Rogers then reiterated the theme of a few weeks before, blaming speculators: "Confidence hasn't left this country," he wrote in late November. "Confidence has just got wise, and the guys that it got wise to are wondering where it has gone."

Rogers seemed unaware, however, that in the eastern industrial belt some factory owners were cutting jobs and others were closing their doors. At the time, reliable unemployment statistics did not exist. The economic decline in the country continued over the next two years, culminating in the "Great Depression." While the stock market would be worth $55 billion in early 1930, it fell to just $18 billion by summer 1932, in what was a continuing spiraling decline. But no one sensed any urgency as the spring of 1930 dragged on. Signs suggested that recovery lay ahead. Given the uncertainly, but the general belief that all would work out in a few months, Will Rogers turned once again to foreign policy. The disarmament conference was scheduled to open in London in January 1930. Will intended to be there.

Rogers had been following the diplomacy of the last year of the Coolidge Administration with considerable interest, given its efforts to outlaw war. Secretary of State Frank Kellogg had been approached by France to sign a simple agreement in 1928, the French believing that a treaty of peace would bring the

United States more closely into their European alliance system. Kellogg shrewdly opposed a simple two-party agreement with France—which resembled the sort of alliances that had led to World War I—and discussions involved many other nations. The leading nations of the world, including the United States, most European nations and Japan, finally signed a simple pledge to end war in August. The Senate ratified the treaty a few months later, though the article defining "self-defense" was ill-defined.

Rogers had much to say about the agreement in his column, mostly disagreeing with it. "A lot of folks don't seem to be enthusiastic about it," he vented. A particular critic was the sage of the Senate from Massachusetts, Henry Cabot Lodge, who simply noted that the Kellogg-Briand Pact, as it was called, "only thickens the haze, deepens the pitfalls." Yet the editors of the *Times* made it clear that the paper supported the idea, at least in principle, and Rogers, while not muted, blunted his criticism considerably. Given the goals of the Kellogg-Briand Pact, further discussion continued in Europe in 1930, regarding disarmament, a key ingredient to making the pact work.

Before Rogers left for Europe in January, several of Rogers' columns addressed the expanding conflict between the Soviet Union (which he always referred to as Russia) and China over the Trans-Siberian railroad. The road traversed northern China. Politically, China was in shambles and the Soviets had a special interest in running the railroad. Worse, as Rogers noted, Japan, which had troops in Korea, was "watching to see if she can dip in to the best advantage." Japan had already occupied some of the "best parts" of the northern coastal towns of China and appeared bent on seizing more. But in all fairness, Japan simply had mimicked what other European powers had done for years. Rogers feared that the "first thing you know we will all be lining up and forming little alliances [much like what happened before World War I] and the same old combinations will get together again." While not a direct criticism of Kellogg-Briand, it was as close as Rogers dared come without distressing his New York editors—entangling alliances was exactly what the French Foreign Minister Briand had hoped to establish.

A new factor in this debate emerged in the form of the Chinese Nationalist Government under Chiang Kai-Shek, who intended to enter the fray. Rogers knew little about Chiang, as did most Americans, but he was a Christian and he had thrown all Communists out of his party in 1927, worsening the rift with the Soviet Union. Chang opened up an onslaught against the Soviets in 1929, and pitched battles occurred that the western world only learned about well after they occurred. The Chinese Nationalists, poorly armed and equipped, suffered several humiliating defeats. The conflict did constitute the first test for the so-called Kellogg-Briand pact, which had outlawed war. When the new Secretary of State under President Hoover, Henry Stimson, tried to convince both the Soviets and the Chinese to stand down and negotiate, the Chinese blamed the Russians, and the Soviets simply reminded Stimson that the United States had no diplomatic relations with the Soviet Union. The Soviets had not been invited to France to sign the Kellogg-Briand Pact.

Rogers wanted to be in London in January 1930 to see what, if anything, the nations of the world would do. The trip over went as planned and Rogers reunited with many of his old friends, including Lady Astor. While on board ship, he learned that one of the goals of the London Conference, to reduce the number of submarines built by the major powers, had already failed. Japan demanded, and got the right to build on an equal footing with the United States and England. This failure to rein in the Japanese only escalated in years to come.

Rogers concluded that the failure of the disarmament effort was best noted by the venues where the meetings were held. The King of England addressed the group at Parliament, in a room where above him was a huge naval battle scene depicting Lord Nelson's victory in 1805. Across the room was another naval battle scene where the British, had, according to Rogers

> sunk somebody else. You would have thought their sense of humor would have made them change these things and get them out of there while this great effort to abolish ships was on. It would be just like the Anti-Saloon League holding their convention in a Speakeasy.

The seriousness of the endeavor also seemed questionable. As Rogers watched the debates over the number of battleships, cruisers, and submarines that each nation in the world could supposedly possess, it occurred to him that the discussions were not so much about numbers, but rather the prestige of nations. Will elaborated in a long column: "The minute you rate a nation, they naturally think you are establishing their importance in comparison to everybody else." Nations did not mind "being small . . . but they don't want it advertised to the world." If the politicians only had to "divide up ships" they "would be done in a day." The decline in prestige, associated with giving up ships, whether a country could afford to make them or not, bothered smaller nations.

As the conference slipped into a series of unsolvable discussions, Rogers turned to other column-filling issues. He had learned from Ambassador to England Charles G. Dawes—the former Vice-President of the United States under Coolidge—that there were many wealthy American families in London who were trying desperately to get their young daughters presented to the Queen. Dawes found, to his dismay, that much of his time was taken trying to satisfy the mothers of these young debutants. "A girl comes back home and lives on that 'Presentation' like a Channel Swimmer [an athlete who swam the English Channel]," Rogers quipped. "The folks at home want to meet the girls that took the bow in front of the Queen."

As Rogers headed home, his columns returned to his European discoveries, and he ignored a discussion of disarmament that he saw as a total failure—any attempt to proclaim its lack of success would also have irritated his New York editors. He had gathered considerable information about a dynamic new leader who had emerged in Germany. Adolf Hitler headed a new German political party with strong nationalist tendencies. Hitler had gained enough support within the Germany parliamentary system to have a say on some issues by summer 1930. One that he spoke of frequently was the Versailles Treaty of 1918.

Rogers focused on Hitler's new arguments in his weekly column, quoting from one of his new, fiery speeches, which had been broadcast in England:

> he [Hitler] advocated the breaking of the Versailles Treaty, he
> said that it was made by a lot of old men, who . . . were about
> ready to die, and now here was a lot of young men grown up

and they had to carry all this [financial] burden . . . that it was
only a matter of time till they just wouldent do it. They would
say, 'Well come on France, what are you going to do about it?
We cant be any worse off if you come in and take over our
Country than we are now.'

Hitler represented the new Germany, or so Will thought, as
early as 1930. Hitler advocated rearming his country, which
Rogers correctly saw as posing a threat of a new war in Europe.
Rogers' description of this new, rising politician also reinforced
his views regarding the frivolity of more disarmament confer-
ences. And again, by discussing Hitler, Rogers avoided clashing
with the *Times'* editors who wanted disarmament to work.

Trouble existed elsewhere, in the Balkans, Bulgaria, Romania,
and Asia. Worse, Will thought, "Russia and Poland are always
on the verge of war." They were "growling at each other like a
couple of Fat Prima Donas on the same Opera bill." Rogers worried increasingly about Mussolini, who he had once admired,
now intent on finding new lands to conquer. "All this whole mess
[of countries]," Rogers concluded, "have no more love for each
other than a litter of Hyenas."

Yet another trouble spot was the Soviet Union, which had
created an international organization to spread communism
around the world. Rogers had generally depicted Russia, as he
called it, as a backward country, based upon his trip to Moscow
in 1926, and his views had not changed appreciably by 1930.
Columnist Arthur Brisbane, whom Rogers liked and respected,
considered the issue to be more serious than Rogers did.
Brisbane wrote an open letter to Rogers challenging his views on
the issue, which Rogers promptly published. In it, Brisbane
noted the tremendous development in the Soviet Union that
occurred in just a decade. It had adopted five-year economic
plans that propelled the once backward nation into the industrial age. Brisbane suggested that the United States should recognize the Soviet Union, trade with it, bring it into the western
world, and thus defuse its aggressiveness.

Rogers pleasantly brushed off his friend Brisbane's criticism.
"Any man as high salaried and busy as he is, that will sit down
and take his valuable time to write my Sunday article for me,

I am not going to find any fault with." Rogers enjoyed the banter with Brisbane, which continued through the years, as it gave him a sense of legitimacy as a journalist. Brisbane was well-known—syndicated in over 200 newspapers—and intelligent. The two men exchanged many letters thereafter, cementing a friendship that grew over the years. Unlike columnists Lippmann and Mencken, who tried to mostly ignore Rogers, Brisbane kidded Will about using his material in a column, and vice-versa.

As a result of Brisbane's critique, Rogers did promise to look more carefully at the Soviet Union. His first opportunity came when aviator Wiley Post, a fellow Oklahoman, flew with a small crew around the world in 1931, leaving Alaska on a route over Siberia. The Soviets greeted Post and his fellow crewman with lavish dinners. This stocky man Post, who had a patch over one eye from an earlier accident, lacked Lindbergh's star power. Rogers embraced him anyway, having met Post years before. Post's 1931 flight in the newly built Lockheed Vega set a world record, and Post broke that record again two years later. It stood for several years at seven days and 19 hours. Eddie Rickenbacker, the famous World War I fighter ace, said of Post that he had the most "sensitive touch" of any aviator in the world. Such comments only reinforced Rogers' affection and trust of Wiley Post.

Post gave Rogers the columnist a careful rundown on the trip into the Soviet Union, which Rogers published. They spoke for some time, not just about Russia but also about their common interest in aviation. Post indicated that the Soviets might actually be ahead of the United States in the field. Rogers was unconcerned, almost questioning Post's assessment. But with both Brisbane and Post suggesting that the Soviets were making advancements, Rogers could hardly ignore such evidence. Unlike in the past, he gave Russia modest credit: "You know those rascals along with all their cookee [crazy] stuff, have got some mighty good ideas."

Other friends of Will Rogers remained more impressed with the progress of the new Soviet political and economic systems. Many articles in respected magazines were praising the Soviets' attempt at implementing government-designed economic plans, which seemed to propel them forward, while in the United States, the Depression only worsened. In a controversial piece published in late fall of 1931, Rogers took yet another look at the Soviet system of planned government through the lenses of Bernard Shaw, a Nobel Prize–winning British playwright whom Rogers had met in England, and Lady Astor and her husband, who had traveled to the Soviet Union with Shaw earlier that summer. Shaw, a committed socialist, might be expected to have leftist leanings at a time when many leftists were praising the Soviet Union. But the Astors were hardly of that vein.

The commentary from Shaw, Lady Astor, and Brisbane slowly won Rogers over. "Bernard told 'em [the Soviets] if he was a young man he would stick with 'em," Rogers noted in his column. Shaw was immeasurably impressed with the large, well-equipped, state farms and the massive industrial growth underway in Russia. Suddenly Rogers thought the "advantages" of such a system made some sense: "it sounds so big it almost scares you, a whole nation of 150 million people all working, no profit, no board of Directors, No Dividends, No Wall Street to support." And profits supposedly went directly to the producer. "Look what a Farmer would get if he got all that the Consumer paid. Then all the Big Industries being run with no profit, turning everything out at cost." Such comments were, of course, nonsense, as the Soviet government did not allow Russian farmers on collectives to divide up the profits. Had Shaw been the only source of this comedic admiration, Rogers might have been suspicious. But the Astors were just as impressed. "Cause if Nancy don't think it's working, why she will sure blat it out."

Carrying the comparison further, Rogers next considered productivity. "Look at what we produce," he wrote, "there is only about one third of us producing anything." The two-thirds who were producing nothing were living off the others, and by contrast, "They [the Soviets] have got some ideas that if carried out properly is bound to make the world do some changing in this unequal division of wealth." While Rogers did not believe that Americans would be inclined to take up the Soviet system, the Soviet story convinced him that the federal government could be more active in helping move the economy along. Rogers no longer saw the Soviet Union as a country of backward peasants, but as a country that we should study and learn from. There could be no doubt that studying the Soviet system did highlight the unequal distribution of wealth in the United States.

Yet another topic that Rogers explored splashed across the front pages of newspapers in August 1931, when Japan invaded Manchuria, seizing the central Manchurian city of Mukden. It was a key route along the Manchurian Railroad. The conflict suggested simple Japanese aggression, the sort of which the League of Nations and the Kellogg-Briand Pact might readily condemn. But beyond the basic invasion other issues existed. Chinese Nationalists, under Chiang Kai-Shek, had broken into factions. Many had attacked American, European, and Japanese citizens in many major cities between 1928 and 1931. Chiang's nationalists believed that foreign influence had weakened China. Indeed, European nations as well as Japan had extraterritorial rights in many Chinese cities, and they paid no import or export taxes. China lacked a government strong enough to control the violence, which reached Manchuria. To some, the Manchurian situation appeared to be an extension of the violence that existed across China, justifying Japan's invasion. To others, Japan was a blatant aggressor.

Getting accurate news out of the region remained difficult, prompting Rogers to leave for the Orient in December. Rogers realized that some editors at the *New York Times* wished to drop his column. It came across as anti-intellectual, and it dabbled more and more in foreign policy, a discipline that some critics thought Rogers ill-suited to write about. Before he left, Rogers cabled *New York Times* publisher Adoph Ochs and asked for a letter of credentials indicating that he was a bona fide *Times* correspondent. Ochs, who had angrily argued with Rogers over his pessimism toward the London Conference, refused. The sense at the newspaper was that a good correspondent on Asian affairs required years of study and training, which Rogers lacked. Rogers ignored the criticism and went to the Far East anyway.

Leaving Tokyo by air in early December 1931, Rogers landed in Korea and proceeded via the Manchurian Railroad all the way to Mukden. After being in the Orient a month, Rogers concluded that the Manchurian invasion was much to-do about very little. Spending several weeks with about 20 correspondents in the local hotel, he discovered that most simply wanted to go home for Christmas. The battle for Manchuria they all hoped to report on never occurred. The Chinese evacuated Mukden well before the Japanese arrived in force. Most reporters indeed left by Christmas, including Rogers. Rather than returning home, Rogers proceeded to Peking, Shanghai (where the British had a protectorate), Nanking, and Canton. Rogers' columns back home became nothing more than a travelogue—these, at least, did not cause trouble at the *Times*. His "news" turned to descriptions of curio shops, "coolies," including the sleeping arrangements in Chinese homes, hardly the stuff of a seasoned foreign correspondent but typical Rogers' material that his readers loved.

As he left for home, Rogers concluded: "The war in Manchuria is over, Japan has already got all she wants and more." Back in Tokyo, Rogers had tea with Japan's Minister of War and the newly installed Japanese emperor of Manchuria. They solidified Rogers' isolationist views of the world, which he made abundantly clear in his column: "America could hunt all over the world and not find a better fight to keep out of." Most Americans agreed with him. Three days after Christmas, Rogers offered his obituary on the Manchurian invasion. Japan was marching on Chinchow, China, virtually unopposed. "When these Japanese run a war they run it on schedule." As for the League: "This washes your League of Nations up. This slapped them right in the face." Editor Ochs let the comments slide, as he too undoubtedly realized that the conflict in Asia could not be contained. Having traveled halfway around the world to see a war, Rogers decided to return via India, Iraq, Greece, Italy, and London. There, Betty joined him for a bit of rest, some socializing with friends, and sight-seeing before they returned home.

Despite Rogers' obituary, Washington diplomats had not given up on forcing Japan out of Manchuria. While President Hoover said little publicly about the problem, Secretary Henry Stimson remained a committed internationalist, determined to force the Japanese to leave. He first assured the members of the League that the United States would cooperate with any of their efforts for peace, and he convinced Hoover to allow American participation in League discussions regarding the issue. He then called in the Japanese ambassador and urged an end to hostilities, and sent notes to both the Chinese and Japanese, in which he applied the "non-recognition" doctrine—a policy that would lead eventually to World War II. The United States would simply not recognize Japanese aggression in China. Over the next year, the issue festered while Japan consolidated its rule in Manchuria, creating a puppet state. Ultimately, the League, backed by the United States, demanded Japanese withdrawal. Japanese diplomats, then being directed by the Japanese Army, which had seized power from moderates in Tokyo, walked out of the conference on February 4, 1933, ending what little influence the League of Nations might still have possessed.

By this late date, the Manchurian issue had been moved well off the front pages of all American newspapers, though many commentators would later suggest that this aggression constituted the starting point in the Far East for World War II. In time, Japan would be knocking on the gates of Peking, the Chinese capital. Nevertheless, Rogers' trip to Manchuria had provided a new perspective. In the end, he agreed with most learned Americans that we as a nation had no business involving ourselves in "Far East wars."

At the same time, Rogers' commentary possessed a slight contradiction. He understood that the world was getting smaller, that aviation would be a powerful weapon of the future that transcended boundaries, and that perhaps the United States should be more actively involved in foreign policy. He sensed that Hoover's Administration held different views regarding foreign policy than had Coolidge's. Regarding the League, Rogers noted that "everybody agreed that we had no business in it, but the first thing you know we were 'advising' with it." The same was true in relation to the World Court, where Rogers sarcastically noted that "we wouldent put on a cap and gown, but we would sit on the bench with 'em." Did this constitute "entanglement?" Rogers thought that it did, but he did not really condemn it.

Rogers did come to a better understanding of American presence in the Pacific as a result of his trip. He noted that the Navy had once advocated building large bases in the Philippine Islands, Guam, and in Hawaii. Complicating this option were rumblings about independence in both the Philippines and Hawaii. It looked to Rogers that "we are going to get in a war someday either over Honolulu or the Philippines." In other words, these islands did not want an American presence; while he never openly concluded that the United States should grant the Philippines its independence, such a conclusion was consistent with his views regarding Central and Latin America. Every nation, he concluded, should be allowed to "ride its own surfboard."

To some degree, discussing world issues offered a respite from what remained on nearly everyone's mind by the summer of 1930: the economy. Factories continued to put men out of work. The Hoover Administration assumed that the collapse had bottomed out; the President appealed to people to spend money that many—in particular the far too small and declining middle class—did not have. Rogers saw the irony: "Course I haven't been buying anything myself," Rogers quipped. "I wanted to give all the other folks a chance to have confidence first." Nevertheless, Rogers remained optimistic. "The Country as a whole is 'Sound,' and . . . all those who's heads are solid are bound to get back into the market again. I tell 'em that this Country is bigger than Wall Street."

This argument appeared again and again in the press, offered up by the President and many other commentators, as well as Rogers. President Hoover declared that unemployment existed in only 12 states, and even there, employment was on the rise. "All the evidence," the President said, "indicates that the worst effects of the crash upon unemployment will have passed" within the next two months. And Hoover, to his credit, did offer some new programs to get the economy moving again. He encouraged the new Division of Public Construction, a government agency, to speed up government-financed construction contracts—a modest "stimulus" package of sorts. He requested and got from Congress a temporary tax cut, which naturally drove up the federal debt, but did nothing to quell unemployment. The major problem was that factories could not sell their goods. By fall of 1930, Rogers' column reflected this reality and it voiced some real concern; "There has been more 'optimism' talked and less practiced than at any time during our history."

Some hope rested on revisiting the tariff issue, since Congress had failed to act on it in 1929. The two largest supporters of a high tax on imported goods were Republicans Reed Smoot of Utah and Congressman Willis C. Hawley of Oregon. They proposed increasing the tax on many imported manufactured items and food products. Big industry had generally demanded such high tariffs in this day and age, or what opponents called "protectionism."

Nevertheless, it was western senators, such as Smoot, and some who came from agricultural states, who helped pass a new bill. They generally feared that other countries would dump cheap agricultural products on the American market. President Hoover signed the Hawley-Smoot Tariff into law in the summer of 1930. Many of his supporters announced that it would save the country. One, Senator Jim Watson of Indiana, believed it would lead to economic and commercial recovery "within thirty days."

The Hawley-Smoot Tariff became a highly discussed issue, one that Rogers had in the past commented on. He opposed high tariffs and ridiculed all involved with the bill, especially Smoot, who was "born, weaned, brought up, and turned loose just with one sole purpose . . . that was to get a higher Tariff on Sugar." Seven Democrats "sold out" on the issue, or so Rogers felt, and joined the Republicans. To his credit, Henry Ford came out against the measure. Obviously, as Ford and Rogers both correctly noted, other countries would retaliate. "You can't stop the other fellow from shipping his goods to us without him doing something to get even," Rogers concluded. The high tariff bill— the only Republican policy enacted during 1930 to stem the economic slide—actually hurt the American economy as it brought foreign trade to a virtual halt.

Despite President Hoover's claim that prosperity was "right around the corner," many Americans expressed doubts. Rogers tried to put a comedic face on the disgruntlement of many Americans. In one column, he offered up a parody from the immensely popular radio comedy "Amos 'n' Andy." The show chronicled the exploits of two Black cab drivers in Harlem. Rogers gave his rendition of Amos' discussion of the President's optimism; "Well de paper says dat Mr. Hoover has jes talked with Mr. Mellon and Mr. Ford . . . and dat means dat de good times is right round de corner." Andy followed: "Well why don't they tell us what corner, so we can go round there. If we can get some of dis resiprocity [prosperity] by jes going round de corner, I is a man dats going to start turning right now."

The economic collapse worsened over the winter of 1930 to 31. Increasingly, hundreds of men rode freight trains from one destination to the next, looking for work. A *New York Times* article suggested that 100,000 men had applied for jobs in the

Soviet Union! In his column, Will Rogers searched for serious answers. While he believed that the United States was "the wealthiest Nation of all time," he concluded that its wealth was unevenly distributed "between rich and poor." Too many millionaires paid too little in income tax. And then Rogers returned to a central theme of his critique of America: "You can't get money without taking it from somebody." The lesson was simple: as the rich got richer, they took more and more money from middle class and poor Americans, who were "not eating regularly." The reverse had to happen before recovery would occur.

Despite this populist assessment, Rogers had yet to use the word "depression" in his column. This changed, too, after President Hoover's speech of early December of 1930. The President finally admitted that "during the last 12 months we have suffered with other Nations from economic depression." Rogers bristled with anger over the speech. He saw it as an attempt to offer "excuses," blaming the world economic downturn for failed Washington policy. Rogers then reiterated an argument that became central to his criticism of the Republican Administration. While Hoover claimed that we still had plenty of wealth left, he failed to tell, as Rogers saw it, "what's the matter with us." Rogers knew: "Our rich is getting richer, and our poor is getting poorer all the time." And then Rogers spoke directly to America's corporate and political elite. "I got a wish," he began, "It's to leaders of industry prominent men and even dear old Charley Schwab. Please on New Year's, don't predict prosperity . . . don't predict anything . . . You have had one solid year of being 100 per cent wrong, and we just kinder lost our tastes for your predictions."

Prosperity looked ever more distant when the news surfaced that between November 1 and December 31, 1930, some 609 banks closed their doors in the United States; during the next year, 2,293 also went under. Banking in America, and virtually the capitalization of the country, was in a state of collapse. With them went billions of dollars in assets, liquid money that the economy needed. Then in May of 1931, the crisis hit Europe. It started in Austria, spread rapidly to Germany and then England and France. Banks closed, reneging on debts and leaving investors poor in the wake. By the summer of 1932, the European economic community was in shambles and unemployment soared.

Worse, leadership at the United States Federal Reserve, which determined interest rates and judged economic growth, utterly failed to understand the needs of the economy. The Fed, as it was called, had actually increased interest rates in 1929 when the economy was slowing down, in the hopes of curbing speculation, and it continued to keep the rates at high levels into the next three years. This became necessary because the Hoover Administration refused to leave the Gold Standard, a condition whereby American currency was backed up with gold. Theoretically, an investor could not get interest on gold, which sat in a safe or vault. With higher interest returns, protected by the Fed's rates, Hoover's government assumed that investors would want paper money, which in turn made interest, money that protected the gold supply. High interest did prevent a complete run on the American gold supply, but most European countries dealt with the problem by abandoning the standard, and it came as a shock to the Hoover Administration when England, which had remained solidly in the gold camp, joined them in September of 1931.

Rogers found it difficult to follow this monetary argument, which appeared on the front pages of newspapers after England made its decision. "I don't know any more about it than a prominent man knows about relieving depression . . . [but] I do know you can't get any gold out of the Bank of England even with a check from the King." The columnist had a better understanding of these issues a few months later after returning from China. Along the China coast, European goods were selling at much lower prices than American-made goods. "Our salesmen say they haven't sold anything out here since other nations' stuff went off the gold, and got cheaper." Yet President Hoover remained firmly in the gold camp. He fought vigorously for a restoration of the Gold Standard in Europe, defended the Tariff of 1930, and accordingly, drove the American economy into further decline. Ironically, he incurred the wrath of Will Rogers further when, after staying rigid on monetary policies, Hoover suddenly offered a one-year moratorium on European war debts. Rogers was incensed.

Rogers quickly charged Hoover with agreeing to the moratorium because it allowed Wall Street bankers to collect private loans, rather than the public ones that were owed the American taxpayer. Those "old big boys work fast and away ahead of time," Rogers concluded. "Big bankers are coming down from New York daily to show President Hoover that the debt moratorium [on government loans] should be extended maybe a year, maybe five years." This failed to help the American people. "Its individual debts that's got the 119 million [Americans] by the nape of the neck." Hoover remained completely frozen by a rigid ideology that prevented helping the common man in America by either distributing food or offering loans. Rogers had little hope that anything would be accomplished, by either Congress or the president, and he proved right. "I believe the Rascals meant well," he concluded. "They really wanted to help the people, but as usual dident know how."

"How" became an increasingly obvious question to Rogers. While a capitalist at heart, he finally concluded that massive government action was necessary. The private market was incapable of bringing recovery. Rogers used the thousands of poor "sharecroppers" in a March 1931 column to make his point. As a class, they constituted fully half the farmers of Texas as well as a large percentage in Oklahoma, Louisiana, and the Deep South. These people suffered from two major blows; drought had destroyed their crops, and the price of cotton had fallen for several years, bottoming out in 1931. Rogers speculated that very few people in the country knew that these farm families, who did not own the land they farmed, literally faced starvation.

Rogers set out to publicize the issue by doing charity shows across the South. He enlisted his friend Amon Carter in the effort, urging him to recruit the various "women's clubs" in southwestern towns to plan the shows. Will flew to Fort Worth in late January 1931 and started doing two, sometimes three shows a day. While Rogers attracted huge crowds, one afternoon while checking into an hotel, a Black porter approached him and simply said he wished the African-American community could see his act and contribute. Segregation prevented Blacks from attending the shows. Both Carter and Rogers realized that while the Black community lacked the funds to really help, a show for them would at least boost morale. Carter recruited a venue, the Mt. Gilead Baptist Church, and Rogers went on stage in front of a mostly Black audience at 6:30 that evening.

The performance was hurriedly put together, and some confusion existed as to who should introduce Will Rogers. When Carter's name came up, Rogers said no and instead approached the blind, Black pastor of the congregation and asked him for an introduction: It was his church! The pastor hesitantly agreed, praising Rogers for his attention to the needs of all people, of all races. When finished, Rogers rushed to grasp the pastor's hand and vigorously shook it, telling the audience "I've been repaid," even if "I make my talk and not a person laughs." Will then went on to pay tribute to African Americans, praising their talents and perseverance. Carter reported the wonderful exchange and Rogers' address in his newspaper.

The next day, the group headed out into the neighboring states, touring by plane drought-ravaged Oklahoma, Arkansas, and Texas. Along with Carter, the show included the young country western singer Jimmy Rogers. At the end of the tour, Rogers handed over $221,000 to local agencies for relief, in particular those run by women's organizations. Given the fact that southern states and towns had little institutional help of this sort, the money went directly to people in need. Having seen the devastation firsthand, Will turned to educating his reading public through his column.

"Now take this drought affair down south," he began in his column. The farmers caught up in it "made what little living they ever got out of the soil, so they are certainly entitled to be called Farmers." But they were not "the farmers" that most eastern politicians knew of—self-sufficient individuals, who owned their lands and had "big red barns, the cows, the Pigs, the Chickens, [and] the big fat work horses." Sharecroppers were "Renter farmers," who tend "ten acres, that is if he uses one Mule." These were called "One Mule cropers." Such a man lived in a "little box house, generally two rooms and a lean too. They are eternally in debt to the Land Owner who generally owns the store," where the cropper attempts to buy food. But with the drought, there were no crops, "no food to be bought, no seed to plant." The sharecropper was, according to Rogers, "the poorest and least provided for man in this or any other country."

In what was literally becoming a crusade, Rogers took his argument directly to President Hoover. He revealed in a column that the federal government had created a "farm board," the year before, under the Agricultural Marketing Act, which had purchased some surplus food. The board's real purpose was to stem the price decline, especially in grain. Some in Congress, including Senator Borah, believed that this food should be dumped on the world market. They, Rogers believed, apparently had no idea how bad the drought and suffering had been, especially in the South. Rogers strongly opposed this proposal, suggesting that the President authorize the board to give the grain to "renter farmers" so their families could have bread. Congress and the President both ignored the idea.

Ironically, Hoover had helped feed millions of people in Europe after the war, but never had the United States federal government fed its own people. Many conservatives, such as Hoover, feared that doing so would lead to socialism, or create an obligation on the part of the federal government to continually help individuals. Rogers addressed this issue in a column a few weeks later, entitled "Let's Give every Man a Job!" He started by insisting that the people of the southern Plains and the South, who were suffering terribly, detested taking "charity." Yet government charity was offered in many countries of the world, including England, where it was called the "Dole." "When you can't get work, they give you a certain weekly allowance."

Rogers understood that some critics in England thought the dole a failure. "But," he countered in his sarcastic manner, "I guess the ones that have been receiving it and buying their bread, don't think that it is such a terrible blunder." Rogers then composed an editorial that shocked many of his readers:

> If you live under a Government and it don't provide some means of you getting work when you really want it and will do it, why then there is something wrong. . . . [The government] simply cannot standby and let the people starve. . . . So if you don't give 'em work, and you don't give 'em food, or money to buy it, why what are they to do? . . . Millions of bushels of wheat are in Granaries at the lowest price in twenty years. Why can't there be some means of at least giving everybody all the bread they wanted anyhow? What is the matter with our country?

Indeed, what was the matter with the country? Will Rogers offered a solution, one that would reoccur again and again in his column throughout 1931 and 1932. The problems were all caused by the "unequal distribution of wealth." How, he then asked, can wealth be "equalized?" "By putting a higher surtax on large incomes, and that money goes to provide some public work, at a livable wage." Such a program could be administered by local governments, the states or the national government. Rogers called this "honest work," so much so that it needed to be funded "at a wage that is maintained in other lines [minimum wage?]." He then challenged Congress to "see if the Republicans will vote a higher income tax on the rich babies. It might not be a great plan, but it will DAM sure beat the one we got now."

Such legislation, if adopted, might be called socialism, were it to become permanent. Rogers did not much care what it was called; the times certainly warranted it. President Hoover did finally respond to the crisis by agreeing to support the creation of the Reconstruction Finance Corporation in 1932. Funded at two billion dollars, it was designed to save teetering banks and railroads, giving them loans to keep going. When many critics noted that this would hardly help common people, Hoover grudgingly agreed to allow some money to be used to support public works projects. By fall of 1932, these concessions by the president, meant to be temporary, had constituted far too little help, and they were far too late.

Rogers recognized the absolute folly of Hoover's efforts. He had seen the devastation in Oklahoma and Texas where share-cropping was common. He understood just how bad conditions had become for these people. Some had rioted, invading small towns, overpowering Red Cross officials, and stealing food. The most publicized incident occurred in little England, Arkansas, not far from where Rogers grew up. The suffering in the South became more apparent when hundreds of thousands of poor farmers simply left their dried-up farms. California suddenly realized the severity of the problem as roughly a million refugees came streaming into their state, most fleeing Texas, Oklahoma, and Kansas. The exodus from the "Dust Bowl," which began in 1930, continued into 1933. As they arrived on the West Coast, most without food and with very little clothing, Californians introduced a new word into the English language—the refugees were dubbed "Okies."

Americans slowly learned about the migration from news reports. Some pictures showed camps of Okies stretching haphazardly along the side of roads. A large number had moved into Los Angeles, a bustling city that only recognized the depressed economy in 1931, when the city council finally authorized several million dollars for relief. So many Okies reached Los Angeles from Oklahoma that they held a state picnic in June, where Oklahoma's new Governor, Alfalfa Bill Murray, was introduced by the master of ceremonies, Will Rogers.

Rogers liked Murray, a Democrat, but his introduction focused mostly on the twenty-five thousand Okies who now lived in Los Angeles. They were certainly not well-off. After braving the "desert" of the West in an old Model T car, as Rogers dramatically put it, "you could see punctures and blowouts written on every face." But they seemed less destitute than those poor farmers back in Arkansas, though a few had not been eating well. They had turned to harvesting crops, often picking cotton, vegetables, and fruit. They had often replaced Mexican laborers. California tried to help the Okies by passing a law that encouraged those Mexicans to return to Mexico. The state offered a free train ticket to any Mexican willing to move back south of the border.

Most Americans blamed President Hoover and the Republican Party for the Depression. That blame literally exploded after President Hoover dealt with the "Bonus Marchers," who invaded Washington during the summer of 1931. They wanted Congress to pay pensions earned for military service that were not due for another decade. Most camped out on the Mall, creating shanty-towns, some of which still remained by the summer of 1932. Just as the Olympics opened in Los Angeles during that summer, and the attention of the nation shifted to the West, Hoover ordered General Douglas MacArthur to remove the marchers who remained by force. MacArthur had fought alongside these men during World War I and Hoover assumed that his general would be firm yet careful in his efforts. MacArthur was neither, stepping to the head of four large tanks and forming up his troops in full battle gear. They swept through the camp, burning the shacks and driving out the marchers. One man died.

Hoover was understandably angry over the outcome, yet he had ordered the dispersal. The attack on the Bonus Marchers constituted a last straw for Rogers and many other Americans. Indeed, Rogers, back in California, could hardly believe the newsreels that showed the event in theaters. "I was just thinking of the effect of that being shown all over the world," Will wrote. "We can never go around preaching 'Disarmament' and 'Brotherly Love' any more." The trouble in Washington was repeated in many parts of the United States during the summer of 1932. Some 300 unemployed men stormed the food stores of Henryetta, Oklahoma, stealing bread. And across the rural lands of America, when banks tried to sell repossessed farms and machinery, crowds taunted the auctioneers to the point where the sales could not go forward. The country was coming apart!

While the country faced an awful Depression, the Rogers family settled into what can only be described as an idyllic lifestyle. The land that Will had purchased along with considerable beachfront property had declined in value as a result of the Depression, but he had paid for it. And in 1929 he elected to add onto the ranch house, which, by Los Angeles standards, was smallish. The new two-story addition had a dozen large rooms. Isolated and quiet, Will added to the ranch his own finishing touches, an immense U-shaped horse barn that housed 30 animals, and a polo field. While the family initially intended only to summer at the ranch, once the addition was finished, Will and Betty sold the Beverly Hills house and moved to the ranch permanently.

When not on the road, or working on films, Will and Betty entertained large groups of friends, many of whom stayed at the ranch. Most were involved in the film business. For several months each summer, they came to play polo. The group one afternoon included legendary producers Darryl Zanuck, Hal Roach, and Walt Disney, as well as movie stars Spencer Tracy and Robert Stack. Most, including the rather large Walt Disney, loved the polo matches. Will rode in his customary blue jeans and white shirt, racing up and down the field waving his mallet like a mad cowboy. His horsemanship was superb, but his polo talent only average. He missed easy shots and made the hard ones. To amuse his close friend Fred Stone, Will had two putting greens put in, one at each end of the ranch. While he never played golf, his course did attract yet another legend, Bobby Jones, who often came for dinner. When left to his own, however, Will always returned to his first love, roping. He could often be seen riding off with a rope in hand as if chasing a steer or headed down to the beach.

Will Rogers turned 50 when the Pacific Palisades house was built. His health remained good and he kept his weight down with considerable exercise. The new house had a splendid office that Will used to compose his daily and weekly columns. He wrote on a special typewriter that had only capital letters—this alleviated his constant struggle with capitalization. When home, he occasionally snuck away from his work to take long rides into the hills above the house. Just as frequently, he jumped in the car with his typewriter and rode out over the ranch to some secluded spot, where he composed his column in the back seat. Sometimes, he grabbed Betty and the two of them drove off for hours, usually at a high rate of speed (Rogers had a collection of speeding tickets, which he willingly paid). But Betty most enjoyed being a gracious and comely host. The household never lacked for friends.

There was, however, a cautious side to Will Rogers, especially when it came to his children. His children all were well adjusted but not overly ambitious. To his credit, Will refused to allow them to trade on his name. Bill, the oldest, graduated from High School in 1931 and, given his interest in journalism, Amon Carter gave him a temporary job at his Fort Worth paper, at a beginning wage. He later had a successful four years at Stanford, but Betty fretted somewhat about his future, not unlike Will's father had done so over him. Mary wanted to try acting, but Will convinced her to use a stage name instead of Rogers and coaxed her along slowly by arranging summer stock engagements. She later appeared in a few films, and married, but struggled with her family life.

Will encouraged Betty to accompany Mary while she performed on stage. This may have resulted from the arrival of a young, rather bashful, and exceedingly rich Howard Hughes, who came courting. Rogers was certainly relieved when Hughes wanted to talk with him about airplanes rather than run off with his daughter. Whether Hughes met young Katharine Hepburn while at the ranch is not certain; the two had a torrid and well-publicized affair a year or so later, which Mary was informed of while she was doing summer stock. Mary may have had more than a passing interest in the dashing Hughes, but the letters between Will and Betty remain murky on the subject.

Will's youngest son Jim loved horses as much as his dad. Will was able to help him in a protected way as well, since Will maintained a close relationship with the Kleberg family, who owned the largest ranch in Texas. Jim turned to cowboying for a while before entering college.

Ranch life on the California coast was not all fun and games. During the summer of 1932, Flo Ziegfeld came to stay. Old and dying, he had lost a fortune in the Crash of 1929 and could not care for himself. He had to turn to someone for help. Rogers took him in and paid the hospital costs. Ziegfeld passed away on July 22. Will covered the cost of the funeral and also helped take care of Ziegfeld's children who lived nearby. In a tribute, Rogers wrote that Ziegfeld "left something on earth that hundreds of us will treasure till our curtain falls." It was a simple badge that said: "I worked for Ziegfeld!"

Rogers could afford to help Ziegfeld. Will's contract with Fox called for making three pictures a year, at close to $200,000 a picture. This declined by half as the Depression wore on, but he still received a considerable income. Rogers' films remained farcical, one of the best of 1931 being his rendition of Mark Twain's famous time-travel novel *A Connecticut Yankee in King Arthur's Court* (1889). Rogers played the key character, Mark Morgan, who, after being hit on the head, found himself back in medieval England. Friend and then Governor of New York, Franklin Delano Roosevelt, wrote Rogers that he fondly recalled reading the novel as a child and wanted to see the picture. He asked Will if he could preview it at the mansion in Albany before its release. Roosevelt later wrote Will a kind note explaining how much he enjoyed Will's rendition of Morgan, adding a post salutation: "Oh, most excellent of philosophers!"

A new opportunity opened in 1930, when Rogers began a radio show. While sporadic at first, he signed a contract for $77,000 to do a weekly half-hour of radio. Ultimately, the Gulf Oil Company signed Will to do a Sunday evening broadcast. This paid $50,000 for the first two months, and after the show proved an immediate hit, Rogers' radio show became permanent. Rogers talked on the air about all sorts of issues, ensuring that he quit at

30 minutes by bringing an alarm clock into the studio. When the alarm struck, he said so-long, regardless of where he was in his monologue. When his first check arrived, he gave half of it to the Red Cross and the other half to the Salvation Army.

Rogers had less success dealing with other oil companies. Halliburton Oil of Houston had loaned him the airplane and pilot that he used on his 1931 charity tour—a tour for which he paid his own expenses. Some of their executives sent him a mean letter afterwards complaining of Will's unwillingness to mention their contribution during one of his radio broadcasts, which in fact was untrue. Rogers sent the CEO a signed check, telling him to fill in the amount needed for compensation. Nothing more was heard of the matter.

Worried that attendance would collapse as a result of the Depression, the organizers of the Olympic Games in Los Angeles turned to Rogers to help promote the contest in the spring of 1932. Will used the new medium of radio to do so, setting up one of the first world-wide broadcasts ever. He spent a half-hour on the air inviting all the various countries to send their athletes and spectators to Los Angeles. Given his world travels, he spoke at times in the language of the various countries. While attendance was down that summer, most organizers believed it was better than they had a right to expect.

While Will's radio talks were folksy and soothing to an audience that needed some homespun levity, invariably Rogers turned to politics. Given the virtual political chaos in Washington—shanty-towns had emerged across America that were dubbed "Hoovervilles"—by the fall of 1932 most Americans were ready for a change. The Democratic Party had enjoyed some victories during the November 1930 elections. A rising star in the party, Governor Roosevelt had started a state relief program in New York that became an excellent model for the nation. Democrats anxiously attacked Hoover's record, which by 1932 included a budget deficit of $2 billion, a collapsed economy, and massive unemployment. Some observers estimated an unemployment rate of nearly 50 percent in some areas of the country and the Gross National Product, or the measure of all manufactured goods and services, had dropped to about one-third of what it had been just three years before. There had been no prosperity around the corner.

Optimism abounded, then, among Democrats, as they went to Chicago for their convention in June. Roosevelt had put together a coalition that moved beyond Al Smith's mostly northern and wet urban support. Yet many thought Roosevelt and Smith would destroy each other, much like Smith and McAdoo had done in 1924. Rogers noted the feud in his weekly column and suggested that perhaps John Garner from Texas would gain from the scrape. The Hearst family, powerful in Democratic circles, supported Garner. Rogers' friend from Fort Worth, Amon Carter, definitely pushed Garner. The keys to the convention nomination became the South, where Garner seemed strong, and California, where Roosevelt had considerable support, including Rogers close friend, McAdoo.

Many Democrats, especially McAdoo, did not wish to see another rendition of the 1924 convention, where floor fights erupted. He began working behind doors with Rogers at his side, suggesting that Garner would make a good vice-president. The extent of Rogers' role is difficult to determine. For sure, McAdoo, Carter, and a number of other dignitaries, orchestrated the group that ultimately dragged Will Rogers to the convention podium for a speech. The crowd of 20,000 conventioneers went wild as Will took the rostrum. "I'm not a delegate," he began, "I have no political affiliation in this convention, no one paid my way here. So if I'm rotten I won't owe you anything." The crowd roared their approval. Rogers then suggested a need to end the squabbles over Prohibition; he prophesied that "as soon as they can get enough of the platform committee sober," they needed to tackle this one divisive issue. And they did, the Democratic platform finally came out for its repeal; Rogers had helped it along.

The political horse-trading went on as the favorite sons were all nominated. When the voting finally began, strong Democratic money-men like Joseph P. Kennedy, who supported Roosevelt from the start, and William Randolph Hearst, who considered Garner to be the best candidate, put their heads together and ultimately agreed on Roosevelt. Rogers, of course, knew the Hearst family well and certainly knew when their support changed from Garner to Roosevelt. He likely brought the news to Carter—who must have been terribly disappointed—and Garner, who then saw the handwriting on the wall. Garner joined the Roosevelt camp after the third ballot. Arch-enemy of Al Smith, McAdoo finally took the rostrum, after having won over Hearst, and thus California, and demanded that the deadlock end. On the fourth ballot, Roosevelt got the two-thirds majority vote that he needed and became the Democratic nominee.

In an unprecedented manner, FDR grabbed a plane in Albany, New York and headed to Chicago to accept the nomination in person. Taking the rostrum, he regretted that he was late: "I have no control over the winds of Heaven," his said, with a gigantic grin. He continued: "Ours must be the party of liberal thought, of planned action, of enlightened international outlook, and of the greatest good to the greatest number of citizens." These were views that Rogers had espoused since the fall of 1930. FDR then addressed the Depression. He wanted relief

From left: Governor Franklin Delano Roosevelt; James Roosevelt, his eldest son; senator William G. McAdoo; and Roosevelt's campaign manager James A. Farley react to Will Rogers' remarks at the Motion Picture Electrical Pageant in Los Angeles during Roosevelt's 1932 Presidential election campaign tour of the West Coast. (Will Rogers Memorial Museum)

for all who were suffering, then retrenchment in Washington to demonstrate responsible government, followed by reforestation, agricultural planning, bank reform, industrial recovery, and a reduction in the tariff. And he ended with a cheering ovation that could be heard outside the hall: "I pledge myself, to a new deal for the American people," after which the band played *Happy Days Are Here Again.*

Some days later, Will Rogers concluded in his column that Roosevelt's victory was a foregone conclusion. FDR won all but six states, compiling a 22 to 15 million-vote majority over rival Herbert Hoover. Rogers accurately predicted Roosevelt's victory or defeat in every state. States west and south of Pennsylvania went Democratic, as did those west of the Mississippi River, which had been terribly hurt by drought. Despite the success of Democrats, Rogers did his best to give Hoover some credit. Will speculated that Hoover insisted on running to affirm the integrity of his party. For him to remove his name "would be admitting that the Party had failed." "So another good man was sent out to bite the dust. I'll bet you that Mr. Coolidge would have ducked 'em if he had been in there." And then it would seem that Will Rogers could not help himself—Coolidge "would have 'Not Choosed' right in their face."

The Republican defeat constituted the passing of an era. The Depression had come to dominate America, and anything approaching "normalcy" had long since vanished. Hollywood, in terms of its substance and its impact on morality, had entered a new age as well. Many of Rogers' close friends found it difficult to deal with the change. While Rogers' wholesome and comical films made money, other stars of the previous decade suffered. Mary Pickford, who had been described by one critic as a "curly-locked Pollyanna," had refused to cut her long hair in the 1920s and accepted only roles that displayed her youthful innocence. By 1930 she had short locks and would appear on screen in any role she could get. Then "Silent Kal," or President Coolidge, fell from a heart attack on January 5, 1933. The politicians and actors who had constituted the era of the "Roaring Twenties" were fading.

Rogers offered a heart-felt obituary of Coolidge. He praised his contribution, admitting that he had a "great admiration" for him. Coolidge had invited Rogers to the White House, and later after

Coolidge left office, Rogers was a frequent guest at the Coolidge beach house. Rogers suggested that Coolidge had sensed the coming economic collapse, which explained his retirement from the Presidency. But had he proclaimed it from the tallest building, who would have listened? Many would have said, as Rogers put it, "what's the idea of butting into our prosperity." Coolidge remained silent, despite the massive speculation in stocks and the inflated values of some businesses. Whether he had sensed the deluge or not, Rogers captured the essence of the man in his final tribute—"He could put more in a line than any public man could in a whole speech."

While Coolidge's passing certainly did end an era, Roosevelt began a new one. The New Deal ushered in a gigantic change that dominated Rogers' column. And Rogers was posited to become a cheerleader for the new administration. He sensed that now was his opportunity to make a difference as a journalist. Nearly everyone in the Democratic Party was a Rogers' confidant, from McAdoo to Smith to the new Vice-President John Nance Garner. FDR felt so close to Rogers that on one occasion, when a parent from Oklahoma wrote the Hot Springs, Georgia hospital asking for help in financing a trip for his daughter for treatment, Roosevelt simply forwarded the letter to Will knowing that he would pick up the bill, and of course, Rogers did. Will Rogers would have inside information regarding the new administration that no other New York journalist could possibly match, regardless of their connections.

Perhaps inevitably, some journalists resented Rogers' insider information and his influence. Attacks on Rogers began when FDR was inaugurated. The first assault came from a columnist nearly as famous as Rogers—Walter Lippmann, the star columnist for the *New York World*, the main competitor to the *Times*. Lippmann suggested that Rogers lacked the knowledge to be allowed to comment on political and worldly affairs. He took aim at Rogers' consistent stand regarding the European debt. Rogers thought it should be paid; Lippmann and others wanted it cancelled. Uncharacteristically, Rogers defended himself vigorously against the attacks by striking back. "Where do these fellows get all their vast stores of knowledge. I never hear of 'em going any place . . . Those New York writers should be compelled to get out once in their lifetime." Rogers was a world traveler; Lippmann was not.

Rogers then made it clear that he intended to follow the next four years carefully, despite the critics. "We are living in a time when if one or the other of these partys don't start delivering an economic government to the people, they are both going out on their ears." Politics, Rogers thought, "was the best show in America . . . I hope I never get so old that I can't peep behind the scenes and see the amount of politics." And he would not allow his limitations to take him away from his journalistic endeavors, despite the suggestion of his critics that he lacked the necessary book-learning. "My lack of humor, lack of English, lack of good taste, and all the other things they accuse me of, is a lot of bunk." Rogers proudly proclaimed in his column that he intended to "get the truth." He had become quite proud of his journalistic abilities, though he fully admitted that there was always "some Baloney in it!"

6

Will Rogers and the New Liberalism

A dramatic political shift occurred in the United States in 1932. Americans had abandoned President Hoover's optimistic statements regarding economic recovery. Banks had closed in large numbers, savings accounts had been lost, access to credit had disappeared, and hope had vanished. Those Americans who read Will Rogers' column sensed a change in his views; while he had criticized the Hoover Administration early on for doing little to help the poor farmers of the Plains and the South, the Depression soon affected everyone in the country. Rogers, speaking for the American people, demanded that something be done, quickly to help all Americans.

Standard Republican economic philosophy of the 1920s and 1930s was based, to some extent, upon Say's Law, a formula derived from the nineteenth-century French economist Jean-Baptiste Say. It prophesied that there could be no "demand" without "supply." The more goods produced in an economic cycle—or supply—the more demand grew, the more goods sold, and thus, the more prosperity. Consequently, government should encourage production—through supporting the wealthiest people who invested in production—not create more money through inflation or give it to those who did not have it, which would only increase demand.

While Baptiste Say may not have been the first to espouse "supply-side" economic theory, he applied the idea in France of the 1820s, a rural country that imported large quantities of manufactured goods from Germany and England. Unfortunately, President Hoover's Secretary of Interior Andrew Mellon adapted the policy to the American industrial society of the 1920s. He convinced Congress to cut taxes on the richest Americans, who he theorized would then invest the funds and create more production, which, in turn, would increase demand and jobs. Henry Ford became a believer—although he briefly increased wages for his workers in 1930, suggesting a nominal belief in "demand" philosophy—as did most American industrialists.

Will Rogers, who watched the phenomena, initially had no economic answer for it, although he fretted over its favor for the rich in America. Such emotional arguments might sell a few papers, but they hardly made a dent on most advocates of the philosophy, who continued to believe in it into the 1930s. President Hoover encouraged middle-class Americans to spend their money, cut taxes, and tried to get production—or supply—moving again. But in the end, he failed to see the need to put money into the pockets of individual middle-, or lower-class, Americans, who he believed would benefit best by simply being encouraged to pull themselves out of the muck of unemployment or under-employment through their own efforts.

In the post-election months after Roosevelt's victory, Rogers slowly applied his cowboy philosophy to a number of these questions. He wondered in his columns, for example, whether smart men had not predicted the collapse. Coolidge presumably had all the answers. "He knew just to an inch how much American wind the financial balloon would hold and he got out just two days before it busted." Unfortunately, unlike Coolidge, Hoover "dident see the thing any more than poor Rin Tin Tin [a popular Hollywood dog]."

Then becoming more serious, Rogers argued that Republicans lost the election "five and six years ago." "They dident start thinking of the old common fellow [the consumer] till just as they started out on the election tour." Rogers then added a lament that has since become a classic, standard anti supply-side response: "The money was all appropriated for the top in the hopes that it would **trickle down** to the needy." Even if Hoover had given some to the poor, "at the bottom . . . the people at the top will have it before night anyhow." But, as Rogers believed, "it will at least have passed through the poor fellow's hands."

This idea became known as the "trickle-down" economic theory. Rogers coined the phrase for the first time in a September 1931 column, and used it several times thereafter. By the time FDR assumed the presidency, it had become standard jargon in discussions of the American economy and has since become the "liberal" response to "supply-side" economics. It offered a damning critique of Republican policy, which seemed callous and uncompassionate. What made Rogers' use of the term more compelling was his simple definition of it. "Republican's theory is that if you tax big incomes too much you will discourage a man from making so much for himself." Then Rogers noted that just such a high tax policy did not discourage wealth accumulation during World War I, though the tax rate for wealthy Americans reached 70 percent. Indeed, he argued, "some of the biggest fortunes were made at that rate of income tax . . . Any guy that's been lucky enough to have a bucket of water during this two-year drought shouldn't kick on handing out a drink."

The collapsed economy had other ramifications of which Rogers took notice. The burdens placed on private charities that Rogers consistently supported, were breaking down by fall 1932. The Red Cross was constantly out of money. State tax revenues declined, property taxes suffered as people lost their homes and businesses, and job "sharing," a solution offered by some industries and endorsed by President Hoover, only led to a situation where workers still having a job shared work hours, and accordingly, what little they brought home. Many members of the working class as well as sharecroppers were on the verge of starvation.

At the most hopeless of times, the late fall of 1932, Rogers wrote and published an open letter to newly elected President Franklin Delano Roosevelt. Since the letter was not aimed at FDR's economic advisors—soon to be dubbed the "Brain Trust"—it contained little economic philosophy and considerable fatherly advice. He encouraged Roosevelt to take care of his health and to smile while on camera—indeed, FDR became famous for his smile and the confidence it emitted. The American people wanted to see some hope, some indication from their leaders that conditions would improve. Rogers urged the newly elected president to make Europe pay its debts. And he ardently hoped that FDR's secretary of agriculture would distribute food to the needy. People's needs had to be foremost in any new administration. Rogers could hardly help adding some advice on foreign policy. The United States should disavow meddling in the business of other countries. "If Nicaragua wants to hold an election," he wrote, "send 'em your best wishes but no Marines." And he had much the same to say about Congress. "Kid Congress and the Senate, don't scold 'em . . . They are just children thats never grown up."

While Roosevelt might have quibbled with Rogers over the debt issue, the President embraced the new liberalism of the age, modern "Jeffersonianism," as intellectuals sometimes called it. The concept evolved out of the pre–World War thoughts of intellectuals like Herbert Croly, John Dewey, and Louis Brandeis, and such politicians as Rogers' close friend William McAdoo (who had urged Hoover to distribute food, to no avail) as well as John Nance Garner, Cordell Hull, Harry Hopkins, Francis Perkins, and Sam Rayburn, all individuals who eventually played key roles in the New Deal. FDR and these New Dealers believed generally that competition should be maintained in every aspect of business, big and small, but wherever competition led to monopoly, it needed to be broken up, regulated, or owned by the people. It was a pragmatic policy, one designed to use only as much government regulation as was needed.

This approach, which rejected "Supply-Side Economics," was outlined in leading academic journals, such as the *New Republic*. These articles offered some of the most insightful analysis of the troubles facing America, authored by intellectuals Charles Beard, Felix Frankfurter, Rexford Tugwell, and George Soule. All agreed that the 1920s had been an era of over-production, glutting markets, a decline in consumerism, and rampant and un-regulated speculation. The country needed a "demand-side" approach, which mostly saved capitalism. This was the "New Liberalism" of the age.

But the published charts of economists and intellectuals hardly reached the ears of the American people. The fallibility of supply-side economics, that sooner or later the flow of money to the consumer simply failed to match the supply of goods, thus causing layoffs and recession, and that banking speculation had led to catastrophe on Wall Street, was too complicated. Those authors espousing such leftist ideas as "collectivism" also received little attention. Academic exercises, then, failed to educate the people; Will Rogers, the "plain talker," did. He said simply that it was the moral duty of government to feed people and give them jobs, even if temporary ones. The vast majority of Americans accepted that argument by 1933.

Back in Pacific Palisades on New Year's Day, Rogers penned several thoughts regarding the issues at hand for his Daily Telegram. "I don't know what will be the first commission Mr. Roosevelt will appoint, but millions hope that it won't be the 'president of this concern,' or 'the head of that corporation,' but ten men who have been without work." At least, Rogers believed, the country would "get an original viewpoint." The government needed to place all of its attention on those out of work. While the year before Rogers' column had put the number of unemployed at 7,000,000, he now set the figure at 10,000,000. It was going up at a sickening rate. Those without jobs had sat "for three years listening to 'big men' solve their problems." Rogers then warned the new president, that if men without jobs were to "go to the dogs," they "at least should have a voice on the commission" that sends them.

By January 1933 everyone in the country pondered one simple question—what was this "New Deal" that Roosevelt had promised. While elated with the election results, Rogers toned down expectations. The lame-duck Congress had proved divisive. It appeared that Congress fiddled while the country suffered. Rogers took the nonsense in stride. Never very optimistic where politics was concerned, he expected the same from the new men about to enter Congress in March. But he did have faith in Roosevelt, who had plans.

Roosevelt took the oath of the Presidency on March 4, 1933, a time when unemployment—just those who were recorded to be without jobs—stood at 13,000,000 people. Rebellion loomed as men gathered on street corners and those with wealth cringed in their homes, fearing the worst. As Walter Lippmann, Rogers' old nemesis, said of the times: "At the end of February, we were a congeries of disorderly panic-stricken mobs and factions." In the midst of such turmoil, Roosevelt gave his inaugural speech, promising rapid change. That afternoon he closed the banks in America, by decree—many states had also closed the banks to prevent runs—and called Congress into emergency session. His actions started the "100 days"—a period of furious legislative action that resulted in 15 major new laws.

Early legislation attempted to secure and regulate the banking structure, bring back industry, reform agriculture, create jobs in massive numbers, and regulate the stock market. The administration, however, refused to abandon capitalism in planning the new economy. Instead, it wanted to lower interest rates and get capital moving again—the New Deal set out to save capitalism, not destroy it. Above all, as Rogers had so pointedly suggested, Roosevelt gave the country hope, which it decidedly needed.

Democrats had studied two major construction projects that had created jobs during the 1920s, the Muscle Shoals and Boulder Dams. Rogers had written about the dams; he thought them marvelous examples of American engineering. Many newly elected New Dealers were aligning with western Progressives, to develop massive public works projects similar to the earlier ones. They would put men to work. But the National Chamber of Commerce worried about the issue of ownership. If the government built them, would it also own and operate them?

Rogers had been skeptical about such "Socialistic" ideas at an earlier time, agreeing to some degree with the Chamber of Commerce. At one point he worried that dam construction would lead to huge government bureaucracy. "If politicians have their way," he wrote, "there won't be a foot of water in this country that's not standing above a dam." Yet, by 1933, Rogers had changed his mind; he saw no reason why the government should not own and operate dams. They ran the post office, he noted, and delivered "a letter from the North to the South Pole for 3 cents." Maybe the government should "build some more dams and roads," and own them for the public good. In these desperate times, Rogers was leaning toward any idea that would save the country.

Roosevelt's 100 Days of New Deal legislation contained massive, temporary work programs that built dams and many other structures. It changed the lives of millions of Americans. The most important of these were the Civilian Conservation Corps (CCC), the Federal Emergency Relief Act (FERA), the Works Progress Administration (WPA), and the Civil Works Administration (CWA). The CWA alone, ran very efficiently by Harry Hopkins, put 4.2 million people to work, laying 11 million feet of sewer pipe, building four hundred airports, and sending 50,000 teachers into rural schools, many in the poverty-stricken South. The dams that emerged along the Columbia and Sacramento River systems (the last ones were completed in 1941) alone provided forty times the electricity for the West Coast that had been available in 1933. While Republicans criticized them as being unnecessary, the power would later be absolutely essential in constructing the thousands of ships and planes that won the Second World War.

The New Deal also broke with Republican supply-side advocates when it came to farm policy. New Deal farm programs such as the Emergency Farm Mortgage and the Home Owners' Loan Acts, and the Agricultural Adjustment Act (AAA) helped farmers who could be saved, although the legislation did practically nothing for sharecroppers, most of whom had abandoned their shacks already by 1933. Mostly, the programs allowed farm families to stay on their farms rather than have banks take them over. And, the AAA paid subsidies to farmers to take land out of production—Will Rogers had advocated a similar plan many years before. This brought a slow recovery in prices paid for agricultural goods, and it signaled an end to what had been three years of "deflation." Critics of the program—ironically, liberals—pointed out that the problems in America were with under-consumption, or the fact that people were not eating well, not over-production. But the excess of agricultural production had been a problem during the 1920s when the economy was to some degree booming.

On the evening of March 14, after a flurry of activity, FDR sat down with America to give his first Fire-side Chat. Americans listened as he calmly, and in a fatherly tone, reassured them that the banks were now safe. Congress had already passed the Emergency Banking Act, insuring the money that investors put into banks. Americans quickly responded to the news, returning $600 million dollars of hoarded money to interest-paying accounts. A month later the figure was one billion dollars. Banks started to function again.

As a greatly relieved "brain trust" economist, Raymond Moley, later said: the act "saved American capitalism in eight days." Roosevelt also played a role as he finished his radio address with a strong, reasonable appeal: "Let us unite in banishing fear . . . together we cannot fail." Then Roosevelt went back to the radio and newspapers to hear what men like Will Rogers would say.

Will praised the speech not only for its simple language but also for its calming effect. "His message was not only a great comfort," Rogers noted the next day, "but it pointed a lesson to all radio announcers." When it came to a "big vocabulary . . . leave it at home in the dictionary." In the days that followed, Rogers joined the New Deal fight wholeheartedly. The newsreels quoted him frequently. A classic line came when Will was asked about the bank legislation. He said that the President had made banking simple and understandable, "even to the bankers." In yet another interview, Rogers expressed a belief that the whole country should support FDR. "If he burned down the capitol we would cheer and say 'well, we at least got a fire started anyhow.'"

The average American probably learned more about the New Deal from Rogers' column than any other source. "I am telling you the honest opinion," Rogers wrote in late March, "we've got the puncture [flat tire] fixed and are headed away. Of course I don't know when we may have another one, but it's a terrible relief to get this one mended . . . that's what Mr. Roosevelt has done for us." The President was getting things done, and in record time. He had put the country back on the path to "normalcy," a term Rogers now borrowed from the previous decade.

Rogers then offered an obituary of sorts for the Republicans: "Poor old Republicans," he began, "they weren't a bad bunch of fellows, just dumb." You could love a "dumb fellow" for certain, but you had to pity them at the same time. They now sat and watched "a guy come in and do everything in the world that they ought to have done years ago, but didn't think of doing." Roosevelt's actions, Rogers mused, had made many Republicans into Democrats—"You keep a Republican getting interest on his money and he doesn't care if it's Stalin of Russia who is doing it." There was much truth to Rogers' assessment as many moderate Republicans did come to support Roosevelt.

Rogers continued the theme of salvation in several columns that followed. He especially took FDR's side regarding the abandonment of the Gold Standard, passed at the same time as banking legislation, joining Walter Lippmann, who strongly supported the decision. Hoover had failed in various attempts to convince England to return to the standard, and as long as Europe rejected it, the American gold supply had to be protected. Indeed, just in the week before FDR's inauguration, European countries had exchanged one billion U.S. dollars for gold in New York. And the high interest rates that were required theoretically to protect gold virtually precluded any serious economic recovery.

Rogers explained the gold issue in a simplistic fashion to millions of readers who did not fully understand the implications of the decision:

> you can't stay on it [the gold standard], and have all these other nations off, for they gang on you and take it all away from you. You see they get a hold of our paper money and it says payable in gold. Well we always knew it said that, but we dident try to make the government prove it every time we got ahold of a ten dollar bill. But these Europeans, every time they got their clutches on some of our dough, they took that inscription on there, 'Payable in Gold,' serious, and our treasury had to shell out the hard money.

Again, somewhat like Roosevelt himself, Rogers did little to lay out the economic reality, but rather put the issue into words that the common American could understand. And Rogers used an old ally, sarcasm, in his praise for FDR's decision to abandon the standard, looking at it from the viewpoint of the common American: "That's going to be a terrible hardship to millions of us that was so used to handling gold every day." Those who wrote about it "as if they had lost an old brother" apparently had plenty of gold. It was, Rogers said, simply the abandonment of another "old Republican Doctrine." As for all the rest of America, "you can't take anybody off something they never was on." Lippmann, by contrast, took a more sophisticated tone; the government could either push for inflationary policies, and thus economic recovery, or support gold. He used a higher level of language to say it could not do both.

Rogers returned to the issue of gold on many occasions in his columns in the months that followed. The decision of going off of gold was directly related to inflating the economy, something that Rogers had some trouble understanding. John J. Raskob, a Democrat and a millionaire, tried to explain it to Rogers, and Rogers used the explanation in his column. Raskob argued simply that "money will be cheaper." Rogers used the phrase to create a dialogue: "cheaper than what?" It led to a simple answer, that common Americans would be able to get dollars once again. Bernard Baruch gave Will another lesson in economics in a letter later that fall. He noted that Roosevelt was walking a tightrope, trying to get three billion dollars into circulation. Baruch feared that this would devalue the dollar. Rogers responded to this lesson by relating the issue to the poor, who had trouble getting a dime, let alone a dollar. The banter in Rogers' columns regarding money always led to the argument that it was best to adopt policies that put dollars into the hands of the common man.

If inflation meant putting money into the hands of the poor, Rogers supported it. But he did see one practical aspect to the policy. The rejection of gold, the columnist noted, already had opened up new markets for American goods in the Far East. "When we went off the gold that did more good than all the other things we could have done." He then recalled the days he spent in the Far East just after England had abandoned the Gold Standard in 1931. They were underselling Americans by as much as "a third." "It's the fact," Rogers noted, "that our money is cheap and our stuff is within the reach of all buyers now for the first time in years." Once the dollar stabilized, as it did by fall of 1933, the issue left the front pages of the newspapers.

Congress passed the Agricultural Adjustment Act on May 12, 1933. Everyone in the gallery that day, including Rogers, understood that in order to get the farm bill, the Roosevelt Administration had to cater somewhat to western congressmen who came from states that produced large amounts of silver and wanted the government to buy it. The purchase of silver continued to be a difficult issue for the administration thereafter.

To some degree, silver and agriculture went hand in hand, as the prices of both had been deflated. Purchasing silver was obvious inflation—*a la* Democratic policies that went back as far as the late nineteenth century when the Populist supported "free silver"—that came at a time when the economy faced "deflation," or a decline in the value of commodities, especially in the farm belt. What made matters more complicated, there was no way to explain the farm legislation, which involved complicated formulas and figures. But Rogers generally supported it, despite the bill's long length and complications. "It gives relief to the farmer in so many complicated ways," he wrote, "that even if he [the farmer] received no relief at all, why, just trying to study it out will keep him so busy that he will forget he ever wanted relief."

The bill itself allowed farmers to take land out of production and receive a government subsidy for doing so. This seemed logical, yet the successful effort of western congressmen to tie increased silver minting to the farm bill itself resulted in considerable debate. It was clearly inflationary. Nevertheless, Rogers seemed to support the effort, in his usual comedic way. He particularly had fun tying the silver issue to what might happen when the country started selling farm produce to Europe. "Now you can well imagine the knickknacks we will receive," he started. "In other words, your wheat brought two of King George's teaspoons and one silver tipped Prince of Wales silver cigarette holder." An American farmer might work all summer, just to get "a salad bowl that had belonged to Mussolini!" As the Senate finally passed the bill, Rogers talked with Senator Borah just after the vote. "He was in a daze, poor man."

The farm bill mostly worked. Prices for farm produce rose 17 percent in the first six months of FDR's administration. Farmers could then start marketing their produce and pay for land and machinery rather than dumping eggs and milk along the side of the road or leave wheat un-harvested in the field. For Rogers, who had fought for farm support for so many years, it demonstrated that the Roosevelt Democrats who had taken over Congress were doing something. Rogers even supported taking land out of production—"It don't do any good to plow under every third row if you are going to raise more on the other two that you did on the three." The success of the farmer was driving him to "the poor house"; production had to be cut.

By late June, Rogers seemed convinced that all New Deal programs were working. Even the banks, he proclaimed, "were picking up." Rogers gave evidence: "they are raising their blinds up in the day time, and are making some loans." Will Rogers surprisingly stopped poking fun of Congress. He had always described it as a do-nothing body. Under Roosevelt, it accomplished the un-accomplishable—it ended Prohibition. Rogers' only concern rested with the conundrum that might result: "there will be about that many bootleggers out of work that will constitute the next big economic problem!" Actually, the legislation added jobs, those associated with manufacturing beer and liquor.

The end of Prohibition came in steps. The Eighteenth Amendment of the Constitution, adopted in 1920, gave Congress and the states concurrent power. In other words, the federal government recognized that fundamentally the amendment would have to be enforced by state authorities in order for it to work. This generally did not happen, and the new legislation, adopted by the Democratic Congress in early 1933, allowed states to determine the degree to which they wanted enforcement. When state after state legalized first beer, then stronger alcoholic beverages, Congress ultimately passed a new amendment that the states then ratified allowing for the production, transportation or importation of alcohol across state lines. Prohibition had finally ended. Rogers, never a supporter of Prohibition, enjoyed the changed mood. He could hardly help himself: "California is so wet Tuesday that they arrested a guy for bathing in water instead of native wine."

During most of the early days of the New Deal, the Rogers family remained in California. Will worked on his radio addresses and did movies. He did host a celebrity roast or two typically held at a hotel in downtown Los Angeles. His presence at the roast for Walter Winchell in July of 1933 was memorable. Winchell had gained fame as a "scandal" reporter whose gossip column was read by millions. He had destroyed the careers of a number of notable men and women. Rogers rather reluctantly went to the rostrum to open the affair, announcing to the audience: "I came here for the same reason that all the rest of did . . . I was afraid not to come."

His correspondence over the summer and fall of 1933 also continued to involve helping old friends, some of whom had suffered losses. Rogers became involved in a unique exchange of letters with Grace Coolidge, consoling her on the loss of her husband, the former president. These letters reveal rather surprisingly that Will Rogers and Calvin Coolidge were close friends, despite their political differences. Rogers regretted not being able to attend the funeral, but he later found time to visit the former President's wife.

When Rogers' weekly column meandered from politics, it often centered on those close friends who he had met and kept. Eleanor Roosevelt decided to travel across the country, inaugurating what would become her increased role as the eyes and ears of the administration in the hinterland of America. And to Rogers' delight, she chose to land in Fort Worth, where Rogers and Amon Carter were waiting, intending to meet her and accompany her on the final leg of her journey to Los Angeles. While she must have received one of Carter's famous cowboy hats, she was never photographed in it. Once in Los Angeles, Eleanor spent the day speaking and greeting people, to the amazement of all concerned. She charmed everyone, though she had not slept for nearly thirty-six hours.

After the obligatory public appearances, Eleanor, her son Elliott, Carter, and a few others, including Betty and Will Rogers, dined at the home of Franklyn Lane, Jr., the son of one of Woodrow Wilson's cabinet officials. As the event progressed, the party turned to discussing Franklin Roosevelt's bout with polio. Eleanor divulged that once the disease had been diagnosed, Franklin's strong-willed mother wanted him to accept his condition in life and leave public office (he had been Under Secretary of the Navy under President Wilson). Eleanor refused to allow him to do so which caused some wrangling. She demanded that he fight on, seeking help at Warm Spring, Georgia, where the waters helped alleviate the pain.

As Rogers got into the story the next day in his column, his adoration of the Roosevelts and their commitment to public service clearly rose above all the typical banter and sarcasm. He revealed how FDR, while on vacation, had gone swimming in frigid waters, and awoke the next day "totally paralyzed." But like the Depression, FDR had conquered the disease. "He has learned through years of hard struggle, experience, and advice, just exactly how to take care of himself." Indeed, Roosevelt had turned the affliction into an advantage. "He claims that his affliction saves him at least a third of the energy and time of any other man," Rogers reported. He did not have to get up to open the door, or to shake a man's hand. "Right there you have a touch of his philosophy and good cheer."

In one story, Rogers had revealed what many of Roosevelt's inner circle initially wished to keep hidden. Yet Eleanor's role in discussing it openly at the dinner suggests that both she and her husband knew that Will Rogers would use it in his column, in a sympathetic and politically useful fashion. Stories had been circulating about FDR's health, some of which had not been flattering. Rogers' revelation worked. It seemed to satisfy newspaper reporters and their cameraman, regardless of their political persuasion, who ignored his disability, never revealing it through photographs. Rogers then was setting the record straight for the nation. He depicted a President who had overcome a terrible, crippling disease, much like the nation would overcome the Depression. He also portrayed the President as one who was on the side of the people; a powerful opponent of the rich and banker class who had, with their greed, brought on the Depression.

Through the summer of 1933, Rogers repeated this theme time and again. Money, for the most part, was "the one thing bout [about] the Democrats that make 'em different from the Republicans." Roosevelt had defied the money interests, though he had saved the banks. "With a Republican," Rogers argued, "there is just something about his make-up, that the richer the man, the less he should be watched, the bigger the industry, the wider open it should run." It went against Republican principles, Rogers mused, "to stop a guy from making a big killing, even if he is robbing a bank. They claim you are 'Hamstringing Big Business.'" The lessons that Rogers provided for his readers were really quite simple—the New Deal was all about controlling competition, so that big business did not crush the little man, much as the New Freedom advocates had argued some years before. Rogers simply put the concept in a much more understandable format.

Yet the New Deal at times passed pro-business legislation, and Rogers did come to question the more controversial programs that FDR endorsed. For example, FDR continued and greatly expanded the Reconstruction Finance Corporation (RFC). This agency had been created in the last year of the Hoover Administration with a budget of two billion dollars. Rogers had commented on Hoover's signing of the bill in January of 1932 by noting that the money was earmarked "to relieve bankers' mistakes." "You can always count on us helping those who have lost part of their fortune," Rogers wrote, "but our whole history records nary a case where the loan was for the man who had absolutely nothing." A month later, Rogers equated the agency to classic "trickle-down" economic theory. "Water goes down hill," he wrote in a simple example, "but gold or money goes uphill." The agency gave money to banks that simply paid off what they owed to other banks, or purchased other banks and did little to alleviate the Depression. "You can drop a bag of gold in Death Valley," Rogers continued to rant, "and before Saturday it will be home to papa J. P. [Morgan, a banker]." Under Hoover, who refused to allocate RFC funds to private industry, the agency accomplished little.

FDR saw potential in the RFC. Once taking over, he placed the agency under the direction of Rogers' friend Jesse Jones, an immensely successful banker and developer from Houston. It turned out to be one of FDR's best decisions. Jones had a pragmatic view of the world, rather than an idealistic one, much like Roosevelt. He had perhaps too much "Texas charm," however; Jones loved profanity, spoke the unfiltered truth too frequently, and was distinctly out-of-place with the brain-trust book readers who headed up most of FDR's agencies, but he possessed a sense of security that few others could match. He had made fortunes in Texas—Rogers later reported that he built every building in Houston over two stories tall—and he had kept most of his money even during the stock market crash. He was a man to be reckoned with, not unlike his close friend Will Rogers.

Jones discovered that a few banks would take government loans in exchange for stock but use the money conservatively to shore up their own debt. This had occurred under Hoover, who put no requirements on the government loans, and it helped no one except bankers. The central cause of the Depression was the loss of financial liquidity that had been inherited from the

Hoover years. Jones tried to solve the problem suggesting the need—or perhaps threatening—to loan money directly to industry, bypassing the banks. Rogers thought such strategy might just work: "the banks will about be so humiliated that they will be the first ones to borrow all that Jesse has." This would eventually help industry recover.

But a month later, the problem still persisted—the banks simply were not expanding credit. Rogers again poked fun at them. He noted in a column that his friend Jones had invited him to attend the annual Chamber of Commerce dinner in Washington, D.C. Rogers and Jones sat quietly as speaker after speaker from what Rogers described as the "Orchid Club" took the rostrum and recited the "constitution and bylaws" of the organization, which was to "keep government out of business." Quietly, Jones noted on the back of the menu card just how much money each banker in the crowd owed the federal government, passing the list on to Rogers. Jones then spoke to the bankers, warning them openly that nearly half of them represented banks that were teetering on bankruptcy. His agency would lend them money in exchange for preferred stock, but they needed to get that money into the economy. Few banks had taken the government up on the proposition. Indeed, by July 1933, only five had responded to Jones' request.

Jones' rather undiplomatic handling of bankers led to opposition to his role as director of the RFC. Bankers demanded of Roosevelt that he be replaced—by a New York banker, of course. Roosevelt refused. Nevertheless, the President did not wish a fight with bankers. Indeed, he pleaded with them to cooperate with the government: "Private business can and must take up the slack," the President told them. But the bankers remained stubborn, determined to defy the New Deal and its lending policies. Roosevelt then took Jones' advice. He planned to lend money directly to industry through the RFC, charging a small interest.

Such a policy would have greatly benefitted southern and western businesses—the heads of which Jones knew intimately. They needed cash and often lacked the friendly connections with New York bankers necessary to get it. By late fall, however, the administration offered a new strategy—it required that any bank that wished to partake of the new program of government insurance, or the Federal Deposit Insurance Corporation's guarantee of deposits, needed to have a "Certificate of Solvency." FDR then made it clear that certificates likely would go only to banks that participated in the RFC program. This broke the bankers' back, as the Manufacturers Trust accepted twenty-five million dollars in federal money, in exchange for stock, in October. Others quickly followed. By 1935, the federal government owned roughly a billion dollars in the preferred stock of about half the banks in the United States. Many avoided bankruptcy only because of Jones' decisive leadership and the President's faith in him.

Rogers had an inside seat to all this maneuvering. He later confirmed that Jones had given him New Deal secrets, such as just when the government would leave the Gold Standard, well before they became public. Yet he kept his comments regarding the ongoing fight between the bankers and the New Deal at modest levels. Likely he felt that somehow he might betray the trust that Jones had shown in him by revealing the most gory details. Rogers learned, for example, that after a few banks finally capitulated to the RFC in early October, others apparently decided on fighting to the bitter end. "To show Roosevelt his financial scheme don't suit them," Rogers rather obliquely began in a November column, "they are unloading government bonds and securities by the bushel." Rogers clearly thought such a move disgraceful and un-patriotic. But he held his pen down. Rogers said he could not recall, "but wasn't they [the bankers] the fellows that the government was helping so much not long ago?" Will thought bankers should pray every night—"God bless mama and papa, and all my family, and interests, and Roosevelt."

A year later, when a New York banker who partially owned the studio that Rogers was filming in for Fox came into his dressing room, the banker openly accused the actor of complicity in the administration's pressure on banks. Rogers had certainly written columns that sided with his friend Jones and had chided bankers. The banker openly charged Rogers with "being an inflationist." But Rogers denied the charge and leveled a blistering rebuttal in his column. "If industrialist and business men didn't start investing and helping the President, and not keep hollering for a guarantee of the value of their money, they would force the President to do the very thing that they kept hollering and asking him not to do."

Most New York bankers knew that Rogers had sat right next to Jones during the tense goings-on in the summer of 1933, and they likely understood exactly what that threat meant—direct government lending to businesses above and beyond the railroads, which had already received some support. Rogers, for his part, finally abandoned the debate in one last dig at the banking establishment. In one of his columns he wrote: "The R. F. C. is the most business-like run thing in Washington." And it too had been a wonderful success under Roosevelt.

Rogers' trust in Jones was certainly deserved. Jones went on to expand the power and influence of the RFC to unprecedented levels, at times doing exactly what bankers feared most. Jones brought under the umbrella of his agency the Commodity Credit Corporation, an agency organized under the AAA, to get funds into the hands of farmers. Other funds from the RFC went to finance the Rural Electrification Administration. This agency purchased electrical equipment to bring power to rural areas. The RFC Mortgage Company designated funds, which bankers allocated, for new home owners and RFC funds eventually went to 89 railroad companies, most of which were teetering on bankruptcy. In a simple sense, the RFC provided more funds for the re-industrialization of America than all the New York banks combined. And of the ten billion dollars or so that it invested by 1938, nearly all of it was repaid to the government in later years.

While Will Rogers strongly supported the work of the RFC, perhaps because of his close contacts with its administrator, he was less supportive of the National Industrial Recovery Act, which created the National Recovery Administration, or the NRA, though General Hugh Johnson, a fellow Oklahoman, became its director. FDR and other members of his "brain trust" recognized that it could quickly put people to work, save the railroads and banks with an infusion of capital, and bring back agriculture, rather easily, but without the recovery of industry, the New Deal would fail. Between 1929 and 1933 the total value of finished products had fallen from 38 billion dollars to just 17. The private construction of buildings had declined to roughly 20 percent of the construction level before the crash. Roosevelt's answer to the problem was the NRA.

Under director Johnson, an energetic, brilliant, but somewhat unstable administrator, the NRA organized business by suspending the anti-trust legislation that had prohibited business consolidation. The idea came from Rogers' old friend Bernard Baruch, whom he had first met while performing for the *Follies*. Indeed, Johnson had worked with Baruch during World War I to maximize American industrial capacity through the War Industries Board. Many leading businessmen agreed that "economic planning" through trade associations (mostly illegal under the law) would help reignite industry. Other, more liberal, New Dealers feared that too much industrial self-regulation would not be good; they wanted more authority vested in the government, through licensing systems, for example. The final bill that emerged from both ideas contained an organization of businesses into trade groups, but also provided for so-called "Codes of Conduct," which constituted "voluntary" regulation. In addition, it offered some guarantees to labor, in the form of "collective bargaining," providing labor with federal recognition for the first time in history—maximum hours limitations, and minimum wages.

Rogers initially voiced support for the program, mostly because of the people that Roosevelt put in charge of the new agency. "Barney Baruch," as he called him, was a close friend of Will Rogers. Baruch had convinced the president to select Johnson to administer the agency. "Well, the President couldn't have appointed a wet nurse for any more needy group of people than the 'big ones,'" as Rogers put it. But the reality of establishing codes of conduct brought the entire experience into question, or so Rogers thought. He wondered if Johnson could control the "big ones," or prevent them from garnering too much power.

Just a month later, the papers reported that Frank Phillips, of Phillips Petroleum, and many other oil men were then in Washington to meet with Johnson. "The oil men were going to draw up a code of ethics," Rogers mused. If it had been said that "the gangsters of America were drawing up a code of ethics, it wouldn't have sounded near as impossible." In essence, Rogers had suddenly learned that each industry would write their own codes, determining the bottom figure that workers would be paid (minimum wage), working conditions, and the number of hours laborers toiled at their jobs. There were benefits; the codes supposedly would end child labor in America.

Rogers had experience with oil men, and he laughed at the notion that they would ever be ethical. In reality though, the oil industry was also suffering; it had even asked the Secretary of Interior, Harold Ickes, to nationalize the energy sector of the economy, with the hope of getting a set, regulated, price for a barrel of oil. And Johnson had no choice but to use oil men to write the codes; he lacked the experienced bureaucracy necessary to do so. In what Rogers saw as more frivolity, Johnson had concluded that it would have been unconstitutional to force businesses to abide by the codes. He hoped to accomplish this by making it the patriotic duty of American industrial leaders to enforce them.

Accordingly, industrial leaders in America wrote their own codes—for steel, textiles, clothing, oil, automobiles, food processing, and the like. Meanwhile, Johnson worked ferociously on a campaign to make the codes part of American culture. He created a symbol, the "Blue Eagle," which came to represent compliance with the codes. A massive propaganda campaign then ensued in which housewives were instructed not to purchase or allow any products in their homes that were not stamped with the Blue Eagle. Johnson incessantly traveled the countryside preaching the need to honor the Blue Eagle. Many industrialists quickly complied, but not all. Henry Ford, while publically compliant, privately said that he would not have "that Roosevelt buzzard" attached to any of his cars. On the other hand, Ford's motor company was not in any danger of bankruptcy.

Despite Ford's response, for a brief time during the fall of 1933 and into the next year, support for the Blue Eagle took the country by storm. Parades and speeches honored the symbol. Merchants put the symbol in their windows, agreeing not to sell anything that was not constructed under the codes. Over 250,000 Americans paraded down Fifth Avenue in New York in support of the Blue Eagle. Even Herbert Hoover—who would soon charge Roosevelt with being a "Communist"—signed a pledge of support for the eagle. Will Rogers watched in utter amazement as this patriotic outcry for the Blue Eagle unfolded— perhaps Johnson's ideas had not been so frivolous. "If this NRA works out," Rogers wrote, "it will just show you, you don't have to have war to make folks patriotic."

Roosevelt's popularity also brought respect for, as Ford called it, "the buzzard." When Charles Schwab reported to the President that his stockholders had refused to allow the eagle to be implanted on their steel, Roosevelt called him aside and asked if he had looked out for his stockholders when he had quietly given multi-million dollar bonuses to several of his managers. Fearing the wrath of a popular president, Schwab relented. The "Big Men," as Rogers called them, were, at least temporarily, on the run.

Rogers had considerable fun with the code mania that hit America, and naturally wondered where comedians fit into the scheme. "I am working day and night since almost yesterday with this fellow Johnson on a code for comedians." Johnson, Rogers factitiously claimed, concluded that as far as "trade connections," comedians belonged with "Senators and Congressmen." Naturally, Rogers objected, promising to carry his fight all the way "to the people." The code that Johnson was writing "would give work to more Senators and Congressmen" to the exclusion of comedians. Indeed, senators and congressmen were often quite a bit funnier than comedians, or so Will saw it.

Rogers' assessment held some truth. A few large industries dominated the code writing, to the detriment of smaller competitors, but not always. In the textile mills and the coal mines, smaller operators took over the codes, prompting complaints from larger firms. Price fixing also occurred, under the direction of the larger industries, though NRA administrators tried to prevent it. By 1935, the codes were so un-obstructive and overwhelmingly controlled by big business that even the Chamber of Commerce endorsed them. Two steel companies, U.S. Steel and Bethlehem (Charles Schwab's company) determined the prices for all steel products in America! While some industries recovered under the codes, the Supreme Court ruled the codes unconstitutional in 1935 when it examined how they were administered within the oil industry, the very group that Rogers had singled out. By then, many larger industries had consolidated control over their businesses, corporate mergers being a common result, and the fear of bankruptcy had come to an end. The NRA also brought to an end most child labor, it established maximum hours and minimum wages, and it created the mechanism that allowed for collective bargaining for labor, although more legislation would be necessary to institutionalize labor reform.

The NRA's contribution to the labor movement may have been far more significant than its assistance of industry. Previous to the law, labor unions had been outlawed and frequently broken up by state or local governments. After the creation of the NRA, union membership grew quickly, especially in the automobile, textile, and trucking industries. In Minneapolis, this led to open violence in the spring 1934, as unionized truckers shut the city down. A group of upper-class businessmen organized an opposition group, meeting in the most fashionable part of the city, Lowry Hill. Armed, these men hired others and banded together with the police to break the strike. When union men tried to prevent a truck from moving, Police and so-called "special officers," armed with shotguns fired into the crowd, killing two men and wounding over sixty. A young reporter for the Minneapolis *Star*, Eric Sevareid, later noted: "I [then] understood deep in my bones and blood what Fascism was."

Given the times and events, such as the shoot-out in Minneapolis, in some parts of the country the struggle to unionize gained support. In San Francisco, several unions gained confidence under the new law, in particular, the International Longshoreman, headed by the feisty Harry Bridges. He demanded that shipping companies negotiate a new contract, and when they refused to honor the new collective bargaining law, Bridges' longshoreman went on strike in May 1934. The strike constituted a real test of the new NRA law; the city sent in police to break up the strikers which brought on a "general strike." This shut the city down. By July, strikers and police battled to control the docks, and finally, the governor called out the National Guard. Several men died in the melee.

Roosevelt, perhaps sensing the coming storm, had taken a cruise to Hawaii to inspect the fleet aboard the *USS Houston*, leaving the problems to his Secretary of Labor, Francis Perkins, and Johnson. As the trolleys stopped running in San Francisco, other sympathetic strikes hit the nation. Dock workers in Seattle slowed their work, and in Toledo, workers shut down the

Electric Auto-Lite Company and the private Toledo Edison Company. Fearing the same disorder as in Minneapolis and San Francisco, the governor of Ohio sent in the National Guard. The strikers stood their ground, throwing bottles and bricks—and mostly breaking windows. Strikers across the land were demanding fair, collective bargaining.

Where labor had strong organization, and solidarity, some success came. The longshoremen in San Francisco attained some of their demands in 1934, due in part to the intervention of the Roosevelt Administration. The steel and automobile industries, however, witnessed more violence and less progress. Rogers' friend Henry Ford violently opposed labor organization and charged leaders with being "Communists." Ford fought union-ism throughout the 1930s; he even hired hundreds of "thugs" to beat up union officials in Dallas, where he built a new assembly plant. Several were killed.

The Roosevelt Administration formed the National Labor Relations Board to solve such problems in June 1934. But it lacked the teeth to enforce NRA regulations until February of the next year, when New York Senator Robert Wagner introduced a new bill. Wagner, a leading New Dealer, believed that "the fair distribution of purchasing power upon which permanent pros-perity must rest" came only through collective bargaining. Unlike the NRA codes, which had been voluntary, his bill mandated collective bargaining and it outlawed "company" unions, which companies used to suppress real labor organization. The Wagner Labor Relations Act passed that summer; it became one of the lasting legacies of the New Deal.

Many Americans remained convinced that labor agitators were "un-American." A few critics were convinced that they were foreign "socialists" or "communists." Will Rogers, while perhaps more sympathetic than most, like many Americans struggled to understand the administration's new, liberal policies toward labor. Rogers first addressed the issue in an October 1933 column, at the onset of labor trouble in America. He likely expressed the views of most Americans:

> It must be terribly discouraging to Mr. Roosevelt after eight
> months of hard work to try to get people a job to have

'em strike the minute they get it . . . If American labor would work while their case is being arbitrated, they would have the gratitude of our President and the sympathy of everybody.

The steel workers' strike appeared more destructive, at first, than the others. Rogers failed to understand that the Steel and Tin Workers' unions hoped to rid the industry of bogus company unions that did the bidding of the companies, which the Wagner Act would ultimately outlaw.

Rogers had never had much contact with union workers or their families. To his credit though, Rogers decided to see first-hand the great "general strike" in San Francisco. He caught a train to the city and spent two days walking through its streets during the aftermath of what had been a serious conflict, in the spring of 1934. To his amazement, it was "a quiet, restful, old city" in which "nothing happens." Two days later, his whole sense of the situation had changed. While he admitted that "no doubt" the "Reds," or Communists, had been influential in the strike—Bridges refused to deny his connection to the Communist Party—"the thing was not, as some try to make you believe, 100 percent one-sided." Indeed, the strikers "had some just kicks, and plenty of fair-minded people of San Francisco were in sympathy with 'em." His surprise originated from the general belief held by many Americans that unions were the product of foreign agitation, an old idea that held little credence.

To some degree, seeing the strikers in action reaffirmed Rogers' total faith in New Deal policies as well as in the common sense of Americans in general. In his column, he compared the situation with the general strike that he observed in London in 1926, a strike that exhibited the "level-headed" nature of the people of that city. There had been no violence and a fair settlement. Despite the violence in San Francisco, Rogers tried to draw a parallel with the British strike. "I tell you we are not so nutty," Rogers began. "It was as quiet as the British. The only thing that went haywire was the headlines in the out-of-Frisco papers." In the end, Rogers could not find blame with anyone, not even the "Communists." Struggling, he concluded that maybe that "darn Dillinger" was responsible for the mess. John Dillinger was a famous bank robber who had continued to evade the FBI. "That fellow should be deported," Rogers mused, not the strikers in San Francisco, as some had suggested.

Just as Rogers was completely committed to the New Deal, however, a new crisis arose that brought an impassioned plea. FDR had suddenly and almost without warning canceled all air mail contracts with the fledgling cross-country aviation companies that Rogers had so passionately supported. The issue evolved around a scandal that began during the Hoover Administration in which three companies received over 90 percent of the contracts, subsidies that almost certainly guaranteed their success in difference to other, smaller air transport firms. When the scandal broke, though Roosevelt had simply inherited these contracts, he canceled them and ordered the army to fly the mail. Rogers read the story out of Washington the next day, saw the danger in FDR's decision, and promptly entered the fray. Unlike labor disputes, Rogers likely knew more about the air mail business than anyone in the country.

For the first time, Rogers openly disagreed with FDR's decision. "What's all the hundreds of airplane pilots and the thousands of people who make an honest living in the airplane business going to do?" he asked. "It's like finding a crooked railroad president, then stopping all the trains." In a rather somber fashion, Rogers then predicted the outcome: "You are going to lose some fine boys in these army flyers who are marvelously trained in their line but not in night cross-country flying, in rain and snow." To see how bad the situation really was, Rogers hopped on a plane to travel across the country, hoping to gather as much information as possible and perhaps change some minds in Washington. It was late February of 1934 and once hitting the Plains, he stopped at airport after airport, interviewing people and getting the inside story.

In Grand Island, Nebraska, Rogers found a small collection of Army Air Corps pilots huddled in a shack near the runway. "Glad they didn't start the army fliers out on this route till morning," he noted in his *Daily Telegraph* column, "it's a tough night." Those pilots, he went on, "are just kids . . . I preached and pled with 'em if it got tough to turn around and go back . . . Don't try to show how brave you are." He then spoke directly to FDR in his column. "Mr. Roosevelt, I believe it would be great good if you would warn 'em that you don't expect the service [delivered by] the level-headed old experienced regulars." All along the route, Rogers sought out army officers, including Major Hap Arnold, who headed the air corps effort. Rogers intervened in behalf of the pilots. Within a week, Rogers had mounted a one-man crusade to end what he considered foolishness. He blamed the administration and Congress. "Hurry up and get busy, Congress," he wrote while in Omaha, "straighten the whole thing out. All of you say you want to. Well, then do it."

Rogers had been on planes around the world. He understood that Army Air Corps flyers were good at what they did, but they had no experience at judging the storms that hit the country during February and March, or the perils that came with flying through the Rocky Mountains. Army pilots had little training for bad weather or night flying and no instruments in their planes. Rogers' worst fears soon materialized. Within a few days of starting his trip, an army plane crashed and burned in Idaho; the pilot died. Another hit a mountain in Utah. More crashes occurred and nearly a dozen pilots died in a brief few weeks. It was bad news for aviation in general and worse news for the government.

Critics mounted their attacks on Roosevelt, the New Deal, and his foolish decision. Eddie Rickenbacker, an air corps hero of World War I, who then ran Eastern Airlines, called FDR's actions "legalized murder." "Slim," or Charles Lindbergh, another airline executive with Pan American, wrote Roosevelt an open letter criticizing his decision and demanding congressional hearings. Congress obliged. The administration was on the defensive as never it had been in the past. Just three weeks after ordering the army to take over the mail, Roosevelt ordered a stand down, and he asked Congress to draft new legislation to fix the air mail contract system. The bill reached the President's desk by mid-March, 1934.

Rogers felt vindicated and promptly praised the President in his column. "Everybody cheers the President's air mail move." Then, Rogers turned to vindicating the Air Corps pilots who had tried to implement the order. "Most criticism of the army flier is going to be very unjust. He is taught to fight in the air. When he fails at that, then criticize him. He didn't hire out as a postman!" And then addressing the critics of the administration, Rogers mused: "Eddie Rickenbacker did mighty well for us in the last war, and he had never delivered a letter in his life."

For others, the outcome was less positive. As historian Arthur M. Schlesinger, Jr., observed: the Roosevelt Administration "was shaken by the experience." Many Americans were left with serious reservations about the Army Air Corps and its ability to perform. Wars were not always fought in perfect weather. To some degree, the event spotlighted Rogers' old friend Billy Mitchell, who testified to the need to overhaul the air corps. Ironically, it hurt the reputation of Charles Lindbergh, who was perceived as the "front man" for the airline industry. Lindbergh became more conservative in later years, moving to Europe briefly. Unfortunately, he allowed his friendship with Herman Gehring, the head of Hitler's air force, and several other Nazi leaders, to be filmed. The pictures were not well received a few years later in the United States.

Will Rogers had put the air mail conflict behind him by summer of 1934. A new election was looming, and many New Deal reforms would be scrutinized by candidates running for Congress in the so-called "off year." For Rogers, it was a time of reckoning, for he had said early on that if the Democrats would not solve the massive problems in America, they deserved to be thrown out of office. In late June, as the candidate lists appeared, he addressed that very issue, in a column entitled "But Where is Good Government." Conceding that there is "not a type of government that [we] can point to with complete pride," he still strongly defended Roosevelt. "This man Roosevelt is racking his brain, and all the other best ones, to help us out." Despite the fact that the country had not yet fully recovered from the Depression, Roosevelt was "doing a mighty fine job." As the votes came in, more New Dealers won Congressional seats than in 1932. The people—and Will Rogers—stood behind the New Deal.

Despite the victory for New Dealers, another side of the 1934 elections reflected the political cautiousness of Will Rogers. In California, the Socialist Upton Sinclair was running for governor. Sinclair's fame came from the publication of his 1906 book

The Jungle, which stressed the abusive nature of the Chicago packing industry on labor and proposed a political solution—socialism. In California, the race generated incredible interest. The heads of the movie studios banded together with business leaders in a desperate effort to defeat Sinclair. Rogers studiously avoided this fight though his son, Will Jr., worked for Sinclair. FDR also sat out on the sidelines and Sinclair ultimately lost in a close race. Rogers simply was not a Socialist and neither was the President.

A new opportunity for Rogers to immerse himself in foreign policy came when a brief revolution broke out in Cuba. The Roosevelt administration sent a young ambassador named Sumner Welles to the island. He disliked the dictatorship that had emerged from the revolt—and was willing to use American influence to depose it—but he discovered that the political void after the revolution was being filled by a group of military sergeants, including the future dictator of Cuba, Fulgenico Batista. Welles and other New Dealers were convinced that at least some of the parties involved supported democratic government. Welles concluded a new agreement with the "revolutionary" regime, which ended American hegemony under the Platt Amendment of 1901. This congressional act had allowed American intervention in Cuban affairs.

As Rogers saw the situation, the Cuban mini-crisis was the first test of FDR's new Latin American policy. The president had called it the "Good Neighbor Policy," in which the United States agreed to stop using "gun boat diplomacy" in Central and Latin America. In August of 1933, Rogers roared with approval as the new events transpired in Cuba: "about the best thing we can do in Cuba is to let Cuba take care of Cuba." In the weeks that followed, he hit the theme over and over again in his columns. The only reason we had intervened in Cuba, he noted, was to control their sugar. "Take the sugar out of Cuba and we would no more be interested in their troubles than we would a revolution among the Zulus."

Another foreign policy issue presented itself when Germany left the League of Nations and began rebuilding its military. "Poor old League never had a chance, for it had no power," Rogers wrote. Pledges to stay out of war were equally as foolish, as were so-called economic boycotts, Rogers thought. Rogers pointed out that if the nations of the world had truly wanted to get Japan to leave Manchuria, a serious economic boycott would have done the trick. But no country had the stomach to force the issue. Japan and Russia were staring each other down, both determined to start a war. The problem, Rogers felt, was the same in Europe. Germany and France were at it again, like "two old Tomcats whose tails are tied over the fence." It was just a question of time before one would "pounce on the other."

Rogers' foreign policy views had not changed when the Democrats came into power. Indeed, he was a more determined isolationist, more so than anyone in the country. In February 1934, he started his column with "Lotsa headlines today." Mussolini had troops "camped on the Austrian Border." Hitler said nothing, as he was too busy "moving troops" himself. Supposedly, France backed Austria, and Japan anticipated the Soviet Union's joining the fracas. Such entanglements had helped start World War I. But what of America? Rogers had simple advice for President Roosevelt: "shut your front door to all foreign ambassadors running to you with news. Just send 'em these words: Boys, its your cats that's fighting, you pull 'em apart."

Of course, in hindsight, much of what Rogers believed about America's role in world affairs in 1934 might appear ill-considered. Isolationism had led to a strong block of congressmen who by the mid-1930s opposed appropriations for modernizing the American military, just at a time when Fascists had taken over in Germany and Japan. Both of these foreign governments were becoming extremely militaristic and bent on conquest. Yet Rogers' brand of isolationism rejected the argument that the country should stop building up its military. Many committed isolationists believed that strong military forces would only guarantee American involvement in some future war. Rogers, on the other hand, expected conflict and argued for a strong military in order to keep America safe.

Believing as he did that observing firsthand the countries involved always provided the best information, Will decided on yet another trip around the world. He wanted to assess the Asian problem, to revisit Manchuria and see the extent to which

Japan and Russia were about to commence fighting, and then travel westward across the Soviet Union into Europe. He departed San Francisco by ship on July 22, 1934, this time taking Betty and sons Bill and Jim along.

Now a world traveler of renown, Rogers was a celebrity who everyone on board ship recognized. Knowing that Rogers had frequently commented on the ability of John Dillinger, the bank robber, to elude the FBI, the ship's radio operator woke Will up in the middle of the night to announce that Dillinger had finally been killed. He had attended a movie one evening and one of his female companions turned him in for the reward money. Rogers column, which he telegraphed the next day, celebrated the gangster's demise: "Guess it's like Armistice Day . . . The better element warned him to stay away from those movies . . . Cable me at once (your expense) what picture it was got him. Hope it was mine."

Traveling leisurely west, the Rogers visited Hawaii, and while there, had dinner with President and Mrs. Roosevelt. Undoubtedly, Rogers filled the President in on the San Francisco strike that had been mostly settled. But if FDR let Rogers in on any secrets, Will neglected to report them. The President apparently remained mum on the independence movements in the Philippines and the Hawaiian Islands, two issues that Rogers was greatly interested in. FDR's trip had been a vacation. He did leave Will with a cute recital likely meant for the press: "Will, don't you jump on Japan! . . . You just keep them from jumping on us."

This banter, though considered by reporters as nothing more than presidential humor, possessed some reality, as Roosevelt's government continued the policy of non-recognition, arguing with Japan relative to its invasion of the Asian mainland. On one side trip, Rogers took time to visit the Navy base at Pearl Harbor and Henderson Field, the army air field near Schofield Barracks. Almost as an afterthought he prophetically concluded: "If war was declared with some Pacific nation we would lose the Philippines before lunch, but if we lost these [the two bases] it would be our own fault." The Philippines would be lost to Japan in the war just seven years in the future, and the American bases in Hawaii destroyed, but not captured.

Once in Japan, Rogers found plenty of interesting people to talk with. He dined with Prince Fumimaro Konoe, soon to be Prime Minister of Japan. Konoe came from the most important family in Tokyo and served the government between 1937 and 1940, trying in vain to rein in the Japanese Army. Rogers also talked with other newspaper men and walked through the streets of the city. Japan, he concluded, was going to build more naval ships whether the United States liked it or not: "They want a bigger navy and I think I will let 'em have it." Rogers' point fit his laissez-faire views on world politics: we could not prevent a Japanese build up and should prepare to deal with it. The fascination with baseball and golf in Japan, however, Rogers believed to be a good omen. With the arrival of golf courses, Rogers mused, one witnessed "the beginning of a nation's commercial decline."

Heading next to Korea and thence on to Manchuria, Rogers' column became yet another travelogue, complete with modest political commentary. Once landing in Mukden, he noted that while most countries of the world had failed to recognize the Japanese regime, or puppet government, "I recognized it the minute I got into the hotel here." Unfortunately, the situation had not changed since his former visit three years before. Fighting had not broken out; it looked as though "we're going to have peace over here all week long." To escape the boredom, Will, Betty, Bill, and Jim grabbed the train into the Soviet Union, entering eastern Siberia and passing by Lake Baikal. The land reminded Rogers of home in an earlier era with its treeless plains, lack of fences, and high grass, grass that was "up to your stirrups." He liked the country although his sons were nearly bored to death.

Will seemed somewhat tense on the trip, this being the first time he had taken his family into the forbidding territory of the Soviet empire. While slowly chugging along through the eastern Siberian steppes, he noticed that Jim was reading a novel, *Mutiny on the Bounty*. Will grabbed it out of his son's hands and threw it out the window. He had ingratiated himself with the Soviet government by not mentioning or bringing into the country anything that might be construed as "western." After spending several days in Moscow in a cramped hotel room, the boys were likely glad to head back to Los Angeles, alone.

Rogers had pandered to the Soviet Union in a number of articles published after 1930. Soviet leaders reciprocated by allowing him to fly south all the way to the Black Sea. He also spent time with Ambassador William Bullitt, who had received his post after the Roosevelt Administration had diplomatically recognized the Soviet government. Rogers noted the tremendous construction effort in Moscow, being surprised to see women doing much of the labor. He also praised Soviet military aviation, which his friend Wiley Post had encouraged him to observe. He visited the old Stock Exchange in St. Petersburg—the city being renamed Leningrad at the time—and offered a joke to the New York bankers. "Would hate to tell you what it [the building] is now. Boys, you better behave!" Rogers would learn nothing of the Soviet oppression of small farmers, or Kulaks—or at least he never published it—who lost their lands under the five-year plans.

After side trips into the Scandinavian countries, Betty and Will reached London where they visited old friends and rested. Entering the third month of travel, and anxious to get home, they departed by ship for New York in late September. Upon returning to the American scene, Rogers set out to compare the recovery in Europe with that in the United States. Americans, who had embraced the New Deal, were far ahead, or so he believed.

The American economy was on the rise. By January 1935, Ford was rehiring workers for his auto plants and Wall Street witnessed a slow recovery. Once back in California, Will wrote his customary New Year's column, which for the first time in many years, was positive. In the "old deal," he started, the President sat around waiting for Wall Street to do something. Under FDR, the President set the agenda and got the country moving again. The only negative had been the cost of recovery—the country was eight billion dollars in debt. "Well," Rogers announced, "it goes for relief, and there is nobody can legitimately kick on that." Besides, the New Deal advocate explained, it was only half as much per person (some $270 a taxpayer) as the debt in England. The country seemed on the mend by early 1935.

During these years of slow recovery, 1933 to 1935, Rogers worked hard at his movies but found it difficult to meet all his obligations and his columns often suffered. While he traveled extensively on mostly short trips, this also contributed to columns that were less informative and more gossipy. A second distraction came when he moved into his Fox Studio bungalow for four or five weeks to do a movie. There were often ten to fifteen visitors a day who demanded his attention. In one afternoon he saw an ambassador, a U.S. Senator, and several reporters, then dined with friends Amon Carter and Fred Stone. Rogers was a man who could command a private dinner with the president, and others craved the same attention of him. Given this crush of activity, he demanded that the studio stop filming at 4:30 every afternoon.

Will's weekly radio program added more work. The National Broadcasting Company (NBC) offered his show in nearly every market in America by 1933. The show was hugely popular. The only redeeming aspect—or perhaps liability—was that Rogers did the program live without a script and at times, he was tired from filming all day. He would pick a topic and stick with it throughout the show. Interestingly, on one occasion he discussed the disgraceful treatment of American Indians by the government. While he toned down the criticism while on the radio, Rogers had strong feelings about the issue that he had vocalized on only one previous occasion. Years before, he became livid with anger in front of family friends when someone brought up President Andrew Jackson who had been responsible for Indian Removal in the 1830s. On the radio, he combined humor and history, making the story more palatable.

On another program, he reminisced about ranch life. Unfortunately, perhaps as a result of the fatigue that Betty observed, he discussed "The Last Roundup," a popular song that cowboys sang while at work, what Will called "a nigger spiritual." His use of the term surprised many American listeners and critics deluged NBC with negative mail. Rogers explained the next week that he had grown up with Black Americans, some of whom had raised him. He apologized and tried to explain that he found the treatment of Black Americans in the South to be unacceptable. At times, Rogers radio work revealed the more passionate side of Will Rogers, unlike the columns that were more impersonal and calculated.

The many films that Rogers did during this two-year stretch made money, but none won awards. His characters often were idyllic—a bachelor farmer, or a small-town widower, sometimes a public figure, but never an unemployed victim of the times. They offered the audience an escape from the realities of the Depression. *The County Chairman* (1934) and *Life Begins at Forty* (January 1935) were good examples. When viewed by someone outside the United States, it would have been difficult to conclude that anything was amiss in the country. Their success—his films always made well over a million dollars for Fox—convinced the studio to renew Rogers contract in 1935 for another ten films. Will remained the star attraction at the studio, his only rival a young girl who had captivated America, one Shirley Temple.

Some of Rogers' films did not escape criticism. Similar to *The County Chairman* and *Life Begins at Forty*, in *David Harum* (1934), Rogers plays a young man who finally leaves the big city during the economic panic of 1893 to find a job as a horse trainer in the countryside. The young man reveals a rural America filled with optimism, a clarion call to those in America who feared the future of the New Deal. The critics noted the lack of reality, even for a rural setting. Rogers failed to respond to them, although he did at one point ask Fox for more complex scripts. The studio sent him several hundred and asked Will to pick one. He apologized and sent them back.

One film that made considerable money for the studio but also romanticized country living was *State Fair* (1933). Drawing on the large participation in rural America at that time for such gatherings, the film also offered Rogers a more demanding role, one replete with comedy and substance. He played Abel Frake, a farmer who bought his prize pig named Blue Bell, whom he often talked to, to the fair. The rather slim plot evolved around the competition for prizes that both Abel and his wife, who made pickles spiced with Abel's brandy, won. Will's role, his affection for this very large pig, touched middle America. Rogers was overly human, as one reviewer called it, and divorced from his usual "Homespun Philosopher" role.

Two uncharacteristically controversial and somewhat dark films that Rogers made during this time were *Dr. Bull* and *Judge Priest*, both released in 1934. In *Dr. Bull*, Rogers met and worked with Director John Ford for the first time. Ford was more intense than any director of that time, making films with messages rather than merely just entertaining audiences. In *Dr. Bull*, Rogers played a crotchety old country doctor who disliked many of his patients, whom Ford portrayed as complainers and slackers, indicative perhaps of many Americans during the Depression. This was not the idyllic America that Rogers had represented in earlier films. When the townspeople came down with typhoid, and a number died, Dr. Bull was called in to explain the peril. He offered up little in the way of sympathy and simply dismissed their criticism that somehow he had failed them: "I've seen a hundred people die, and none of them seem to mind it," his character, Dr. Bull dryly said.

Ford allowed Rogers some sentimentality in *Dr. Bull*—and he had a girl friend for the first time on screen. His second film with Ford, *Judge Priest*, while unveiling a more harmonious society— Kentucky in the 1890s—depicted a more unjust, racist view of American society than anything that Rogers had done previously. Rogers starred alongside the famous Black actor Stepin Fetchit in a story about the prosecution of a stranger who unexpectedly came into town. While the background of the Old South in the film was almost reminiscent of *The Birth of the Nation*, with its grotesque clan, the story ended on a high note with Judge Priest acquitting the stranger. Yet this was not exactly the way that Ford wished for the production to end.

During the filming, director Ford called upon Rogers to do a scene in which he castigated the townsfolk for preparing to lynch an innocent Black man. Lynchings, while declining in number in the South, were still occurring at this time and Rogers lit into the dialogue, in what Ford himself called "the most scorching things you ever heard." With this scene, the film became convoluted—it contradicted the folksier sentiment that characterized race relations in most films of this age. To Ford's surprise, the studio cut perhaps Rogers' most provocative diatribe regarding race, suspecting that it would not play well in the South.

Arguably, *Judge Priest* was Will Rogers' best film—Ford thought it one of the finest he ever directed. And it revealed a Will Rogers who had finally come to speak out about the evils of segregation and lynching in the South, though the scene never reached theaters. Rogers never said much about the effort thereafter, but it likely bothered him. In his films, he hid behind comedic characters, and the one opportunity to say something meaningful about race had dissipated. But the film industry was simply too new to America to become a serious source of social criticism, at least in 1934. And a direct critique of race relations, or criticism of it in his columns, was simply not in Will Rogers' character. Such confrontation films would not be possible for sometime.

Whenever possible, Will Rogers wanted to escape from Hollywood, much like his audiences wished to avoid the troubles of the Depression. A good outlet was Fort Worth where his friend Amon Carter kept a suite for him at a downtown club. There, he had fresh clothes and a chef who prepared food to his liking. Rogers had apparently met Frank Hawks while in Fort Worth, a famed aviator who had set many of the world's high-speed records for planes. Fort Worth had become somewhat of a center for aviation, at least in the Southwest, and while hanging around its airport, Rogers also had met aviator Wiley Post. Rogers had featured Post in his columns on several occasions, particularly after Post and Harold Gatty had flown around the world in 1931.

As Post's aviation star rose, he convinced one of the large national airlines to finance a trip, via Alaska, into the Soviet Union, supposedly planned for the summer of 1935. Post intended to pioneer an air mail route across Siberia. After finishing yet another picture, Rogers heard of the scheme and rushed to Burbank, California, where he convinced Post to take him along. Will had just been in the Soviet Union the year before and Betty opposed the trip, but she was busy at the time, trying to help Mary with her acting career that had taken her to New England.

Post, certainly a natural pilot, was more skilled as a mechanic than as an engineer; nevertheless, he decided to enlarge a Lockheed Orion plane to fit the task for the rugged trip. He extended the fuselage, put in a larger 550-horsepower engine and propeller, and added pontoons. In the process, the plane became several hundred pounds heavier. While a prescription for disaster, the Department of Commerce issued the plane a restricted license—it could not legally carry passengers—and with Rogers in tow, Post left for Alaska. Will Rogers had flown thousands of miles in airplanes, and he fully understood the

Juneau, Alaska, 1935. Will Rogers stands on the wing of the Lockheed Orion-Explorer in which he and pilot Wiley Post made their ill-fated trip. (Will Rogers Memorial Museum)

importance of weight distribution. Despite the changes made to the plane, however, Rogers also had an abiding trust in Post, a fellow Oklahoman, who had flown around the world.

Post hurried the trip along, leaving San Francisco as quickly as arrangements could be made with the Soviet consul general's office for the right to cross into their country. Post almost certainly knew that the pontoons had made the plane too heavy, and another inspection by the commerce department likely would have grounded it. On taking off, he made Rogers move to the very back of the plane to even out the weight. At one stop along the way, Will was handed some cookies as he prepared to get back into the plane. He laughed, and shouted that while they were good, he intended to throw them out if the plane could not get off the ground. It did, several more times.

Once at Fairbanks, the next trip should have been across the Bering Sea. But here Rogers interceded. He wished to visit Point Barrow, the northern-most town in the nation. He knew of a legendary fur trader there named Charlie Brower, and he wanted to interview him. By this time, Rogers was paying most of the bills, as the aviation company that had originally financed Post had reneged on the deal. Anxious to get this new part of the trip over, Post determined to take off on the afternoon of August 14 from Fairbanks, though the weather reports from Barrow were terrible. There was zero visibility. Post headed west to the ocean, and then turned north to hug the coast into Point Barrow. Post got lost, retraced his route, and eventually landed some fifteen miles south of the point.

A few Eskimos came up to the plane and Rogers spoke with them, inquiring where they were. After being convinced that Point Barrow was to the north, he climbed back in and closed the door, and the plane took off. It rose from the small lake without trouble, but then the engine failed. It fell rapidly, nose first, crashing into the edge of a pond. Both Wiley Post and Will Rogers died on impact. The Eskimos pulled the bodies from the wreckage and wrapped them in white shrouds.

Will Rogers, circa 1934. (Will Rogers Memorial Museum)

Epilogue

Will Rogers had never spoken of death, other than to obliquely make fun of it. "If the world comes to an end," he once quipped, "I want to be in Cincinnati. Everything comes there ten years late." When Eskimos recovered his body, they noted a sheepish grin on Rogers' face. They tenderly took Will and Wiley out of the plane, placed them in a canoe, and brought them back to their village, all the while singing death songs in their own language. Rogers surely would have approved of such an end. Will and Wiley were then taken to a nearby Indian hospital. As the news spread across America that Rogers was dead, newspapers reported the story with black, gilded headlines.

The news caught up with Betty and daughter Mary in New England. Phone calls offering condolences and assistance overwhelmed them. Mary talked with Charles Lindbergh, who put the resources of Pan American Airlines at her disposal. One of Lindbergh's pilots flew to Alaska to recover the bodies. Betty and the family flew back to California to meet the plane. Amon Carter asked if he might travel north to sit beside his old friend on the return leg to Los Angeles; Betty agreed. Carter never really got over the loss of his friend Will Rogers. The nation grieved as well; Vice President Garner adjourned Congress. American flags flew at half-mast.

The funeral of Will Rogers occurred in Los Angeles at the Hollywood Bowl on a bright August day. Over 100,000 people passed by the coffin before interment at Forest Lawn Cemetery. Bells rang out in Rogers' honor in hundreds of churches across the land. A Protestant minister officiated, but a Catholic priest spoke as well, and a Yiddish performer sang "The Kaddish," a Hebrew mourning chant. The event was broadcast by radio all across America. Back in Oklahoma,

Cherokee Indians danced a death song as the California service came to them over the airwaves. Everybody in America claimed Will Rogers as their own. Messages of condolences were read from Roosevelt, Garner, Hoover, Rockefeller, the Prince of Wales, Lady Astor, and even Charles Schwab.

Over the next four years, many different groups and states unveiled memorials dedicated to Rogers' life. Betty eventually donated the ranch in Santa Monica to the state of California for a State Park, which remains today. Congress and the state of Oklahoma helped build a large museum and library at Claremore, Oklahoma honoring the state's fallen son. It consists of a rambling, ranch-style house, public park, and museum. Rogers' friend Jesse Jones spoke at the dedication, and President Roosevelt joined by radio. In 1944, at Betty's death, her will stipulated that she and Will should rest together in a new crypt at the museum.

Amon Carter was determined to honor his fallen friend. He hired artists to capture his image in oil, and he had not one but two marvelous bronze statues completed of Rogers on his famous horse, Soapsuds. One was sent to the museum in Claremore. It was likely at Rogers' insistence that Carter started collecting western art, buying up an entire collection of Charles Russell's work at one point, which he later put in his Fort Worth museum, where the second statue of Will on horseback is found across the square. Carter also approached the Secretary of Interior to ask for WPA funds to construct an auditorium/coliseum in Fort Worth to be named after Rogers. When Secretary Harold Ickes, not a friend of rodeo or western art, turned the project down, dubbing it a "cowshed," Carter went directly to the president. James Farley, a close friend of both Rogers and Carter and a member of Roosevelt's cabinet, agreed to intervene.

Unbeknownst to Carter, Farley had already made some headway on funding the memorial when Carter showed up at the White House to make his pitch. Farley cautioned an anxious Carter to wait quietly outside while he approached President Roosevelt in the Oval Office. Rather suspiciously, Farley left the door ajar just enough so Carter could hear Farley say "Amon wants to build a cowshed to honor Will Rogers!" Carter, beside himself, burst into the room, nearly screaming, "Now, gawd-dammit, it's not a cowshed!" Immediately, Farley and Roosevelt collapsed with laughter, knowing full well that Carter would take the bait. Carter got his project, a massive structure with two large coliseums separated by a tall obelisk; it remains in use today, offering trade shows and rodeos to the people of Texas. No doubt the incident, so political, so humorous and yet so typical of the types of people that Rogers cultivated and enjoyed, would have brought a smile to his face.

Certainly that is one of the legacies of Will Rogers—he brought smiles to people's faces even at the height of the Depression. But as years passed after his death, his role as a journalist and even his Hollywood career as an actor faded. By the late 1930s, conservatives were even claiming Will Rogers as one of their own. Herbert Hoover cited Rogers as an example of "a splendid American who sprang from the soil recently won in the westward march of civilization." Other chamber-of-commerce–types in Colorado Springs built a monument to him. Inside the tower, large paintings depicted soldiers killing Indians and police suppressing strikes in an effort to recast Rogers as one who played a role in "winning the west." And his movies, which Fox promptly put in a vault and never released again—for fear that such action would be seen as exploiting Rogers' sudden death—further broadened a collective haze that overshadowed this marvelously interesting man and his life.

But this is not Rogers' real legacy. In reality, he extolled a populism in America that fell short of endorsing a cooperative commonwealth. Author Larry May has called it a "radicalism of tradition." In particular, Rogers became a spokesman for the rural common farmer and the poor, the urban masses who were out of work, as well as for the capitalistic system which Rogers believed had offered most of these people some opportunity in the past. But he did so without embroiling himself in the debate, increasingly common during the Depression, which placed class against class. Rogers abhorred the notion of class warfare. He believed that the rich should pay more in income tax that such a system did redistribute wealth, and that supply-side economics simply did not work. But he also believed in the right of individuals to control their destiny, and accordingly, saw Prohibition as a stupid imposition on those rights.

While Rogers at times revealed a fascination with dictators—indeed he never did have an open argument or fight with anyone—he disliked demagogues, particularly those who knew little about world affairs. He barely mentioned in his columns the two most famous demagogues of the Depression, Senator Huey Long and Father Charles Coughlin. Rogers espoused strong isolationist views, urging presidents to stay out of foreign wars and praising the fact that the creator had put the Atlantic and Pacific Oceans in their present locations just so that the United States could stay out of such conflicts. Yet he saw the need to maintain a strong military, both a navy and an army. He expected the Second World War to come in his lifetime, a prediction that he missed by only four years. Rogers was a pragmatist, not an ideologue, and he very likely would have revised many of his views regarding world conflict in the late 1930s, when Germany and Japan prepared to immerse the entire world in war.

Certainly Rogers became a cheerleader for the New Deal, even before it was visualized by Franklin Delano Roosevelt. When Congress debated Social Security in early 1935—about the time Rogers left for Alaska—Will prematurely endorsed it, and just before his death, called it "the greatest thing we ever could have." Roosevelt signed the legislation creating the system a day before the plane crash that killed Rogers. While the New Deal very likely would have been successful without Will Rogers' support, it was seen as a salvation among the lower and middle classes in America thanks in part to his cheerleading. As friends nominated Will Rogers for president at the 1932 Democratic Convention, Roosevelt went out of his way to make sure that it remained a joke. The future president recognized the power and influence of this man, Will Rogers, and once in office, both Roosevelt and his wife went out of their way to court Rogers, meeting Will and Betty for dinner while even on vacation.

Above all, Will Rogers helped mold the common perception of the emerging modern liberal philosophy in America. In many ways, the country had positioned itself to be "His America" at his death—a compassionate land where men of power and influence still led the nation, a capitalistic land, but a land as well where the power of government was finally un-leashed to help not only American business and banking but the American people as a whole. On the other hand, Will Rogers saw the need to renew traditional values, indeed to praise them and preserve them, whether exemplified by honest labor or honest banking; at the same time, he promoted political and social change, such as the sort where the wife of a newly elected Black congressman could have tea with the First Lady in the White House.

Perhaps the nation has so little memory of Will Rogers because what he stood for is so mainstream in America today. As bashful as he often was, Rogers would have liked it that way.

Study and Discussion Questions

Introduction: Will Rogers and "His" America

1. What was Will Rogers' world view? In what ways did it reflect the sentiments of the "common man" in the first third of the twentieth century?

2. What made Rogers so appealing to the American public?

Chapter 1: Will Rogers, the Opening Act

1. Describe Will Rogers' views toward race. In what ways were these views a reflection of the time and place in which he grew up?

2. Explain Rogers' humor. In what ways did Will Rogers' humor reflect his mother's Cherokee roots?

3. Explain the U.S. government's policy towards the Cherokee. How did changes in Indian policy affect Rogers and his family?

4. How did Will's early world travels challenge, reaffirm, or complicate his views of race, America, and himself?

5. Much of Rogers' early success came from playing the role of a cowboy from "Injun Territory." Where did he perform? What sort of audiences did he entertain? How did his act shape or reaffirm his audiences' views of "the West"?

Chapter 2: The Pursuit of Fame

1. Describe early twentieth-century social and political ideas about Indians. What was "Social Darwinism?" Why did Will Rogers stop referring to himself as the "Cherokee Kid?"

2. When and why did Rogers re-embrace his Cherokee roots? Did this affect his view on "Indians" in general?

3. As Rogers transformed his show from a novelty act to a comedy routine, his favorite topics to joke about became politics and politicians. What sort of individuals did he poke fun at? Why did his audiences find this so appealing?

4. In 1908, Betty Blake agreed to marry Rogers. Explain the adjustments both Betty and Will had to make in order for the marriage to succeed. How did their marriage defy the conventions of the Victorian Age?

5. During the 1910s, the United States underwent some profound changes. How did the Harlem Renaissance and groups such as the Society for American Indians challenge Americans' thinking about race? How did Rogers react to these and other Progressive institutions and movements?

Chapter 3: The Renaissance

1. Describe the metamorphosis of Will Rogers from "a one-dimensional comic and writer who covered politics at a superficial level to a confident commentator on the rich, the industrial entrepreneurs of the age, European royalty, . . . and especially the common man." What events and individuals played key roles in this transformation?

2. The "Roaring Twenties" was a time of great social change. What were some of these changes? To what degree did Will Rogers' "graduate education" at the Lummis house influence his views of 1920s culture? How did Rogers react to the growing cynicism of the age?

3. In what way did Will Rogers' friendship with Hays affect the movie industry in the 1920s?

4. Throughout the 1920s, Will Rogers increasingly poked fun at the growing hypocrisy and immorality he saw within American society. Which individuals and institutions were his favorite targets? Why?

5. What issues dominated the 1924 election for Republicans? For Democrats? How did Rogers portray each party?

Chapter 4: A Liberal in an Illiberal Age

1. In what ways did Will Rogers' participation in Wagner's tour through the Midwest mark a "turning point" in his career?

2. What is liberalism? In what ways was 1920s society becoming increasingly "illiberal?" How did this growing sentiment affect Rogers' comedy and writing?

3. Will Rogers traveled extensively during the 1920s. How did his travels abroad and in the U. S. affect his views of American politics at home? How did his travels affect his views regarding American involvement in world politics?

4. During the 1920s Will Rogers became increasingly enamored with flying. Why did he become such a champion of aviation, particularly the development of an Air Force? Why was Congress so slow to act on this idea?

5. By 1926, Rogers was becoming more skeptical of America's ability to improve itself. What were the reasons for his growing pessimism? How was Will's pessimism reflected in his columns? How did he attempt to cope with his growing disillusionment?

Chapter 5: Will Rogers, the Journalist

1. By 1926, Rogers increasingly came to view himself as a journalist. His Daily Telegram graced the front page of scores of newspapers and his influence continued to grow. What was it about Rogers that caused the American public to embrace him in the way that they did?

2. What caused the Stock Market Crash in 1929? What were the effects of the crash? Why did it take Will Rogers and the American public some time to realize the implications of the "crash"?

3. Why did Will Rogers agree to do a series of charity shows in the South? How did Rogers' tour through the South affect his views regarding government intervention in the economic crisis?

4. Who were the Okies? The Bonus Marchers? How did the plight of these and other groups reaffirm Will's increasing critiques of the government and big business?

5. How did Calvin Coolidge's death signal the end of an era? In what ways did the election of Franklin Roosevelt begin a new era?

Chapter 6: Will Rogers and the New Liberalism

1. A "new" liberalism emerged in 1932. What were the characteristics of this "new" liberalism? Who were the major players?

2. Roosevelt's first "100 days" were marked by a flurry of new legislation. What were some of the New Deal programs created during this time? What was the goal of these programs? How, specifically, did these programs seek to accomplish their goals?

3. Despite the popularity of Roosevelt's New Deal, its programs were not without critics. Who objected to the New Deal? What reasons did they give? Which programs did Rogers himself question?

4. Will Rogers' around-the-world trip in 1934 would ultimately be his last. How was this trip different from his earlier voyages abroad?

5. How did Will's movie roles in the 1930s differ from his earlier ones?

Epilogue

1. How did Will Rogers, a self-proclaimed cowboy from "Injun Territory," come to speak for the common American by the 1930s?

2. What was "Will Rogers' America?" What is his legacy?

3. Though not well remembered in the twenty-first century, when he died in 1935, nearly the entire nation mourned his death. Why?

A Note on the Sources

Much has been written about Will Rogers, most of it in the two to three decades after his death. These studies extensively cover his early years in Oklahoma, his family life, his work in motion pictures, and his network of friends. For whatever reason, these authors focus mostly on his humor and give little attention to the significant impact that Rogers had on politics, his first love. The best of the early biographical attempts include Jake G. Lyons, *Folks Say of Will Rogers* (1936); Spi Trent, *My Cousin Will Rogers* (1938); Betty Rogers, *Will Rogers, His Wife's Story* (1941); and Donald Day, *Will Rogers* (New York, 1962). More-recent studies have helped flesh out his career, especially in vaudeville and film. These include Bryan Sterling, *The Will Rogers Scrapbook* (1976) and Frances N. Sterling, *Will Rogers in Hollywood* (1984). By far, the best new biographies are Ben Yagoda, *Will Rogers, a Biography* (1993) and Ray Robinson, *American Original, A Life of Will Rogers* (1996).

Recently, the University of Oklahoma Press undertook the monumental task of publishing the most significant aspects of Rogers' correspondence, much of it found in the Will Rogers Museum in Claremore, Oklahoma. This effort resulted in Arthur Frank Wertheim and Barbara Bair, eds., *The Papers of Will Rogers*, Vols., 1–3 (1996–2001) and Steven K. Gragert and M. Jane Johansson, eds., *The Papers of Will Rogers* Vols. 4–5 (2005–2006). The published newspaper columns that Rogers wrote were edited by James M. Smallwood, as *Will Rogers' Weekly Articles*, Vols. 1–6, covering 1922–1935 (1980–1982). Earlier, Smallwood also edited *Will Rogers' Daily Telegrams*, Vols. 1–4, covering 1926–1935 (1978–1979). Other Will Rogers primary material is included in Albert and Charles Boni, *Letters of a Self-Made Diplomat to His President* (1926); Steven K. Gragert, ed., *More Letters of a*

Self-Made Diplomat (1982); Joseph A. Stout, Jr., ed., *Convention Articles of Will Rogers* (1976); and Steven K. Gragert, ed., *Radio Broadcasts of Will Rogers* (1983).

There are a number of books and essays of note that have been helpful in shaping this author's views on Rogers' life. They include Larry May's chapter "'My Ancestors Did Not Come Over on the Mayflower': Will Rogers and the Radicalism of Tradition," found in *The Big Tomorrow: Hollywood and the Politics of the American Way* (2000); Robert Allen Warrior, *Tribal Secrets: Recovering American Indian Intellectual Traditions* (1995); Loretta I. Winters and Herman L. DeBose, *New Faces in a Changing America: Multiracial Identity in the 21st Century* (2003); John Lowe, "Theories of Ethnic Humor: How to Enter, Laughing," *American Quarterly* Vol. 28, No. 3 (1986); Ron Jenkins, *Subversive Laughter: The Liberating Power of Comedy* (1994); A. Joseph War, "Prayers Shrieked to Heaven: Humor and Folklore in Contemporary American Indian Literature," *Western Folklore*, Vol. 56, No. 3/4 (1997); and Michael Medved, *Hollywood vs. America: Popular Culture and the War on Traditional Values* (1992).

The literature on the social and cultural history of this age is voluminous, especially writings on early vaudeville and its impact on America. While Rogers started his career as a vaudeville performer, the industry changed dramatically after 1915, when silent films took over many small vaudeville theaters. Rogers survived by entering a new genre of entertainment, identified generally as the "entertainment revue." Some of the sources consulted for this study of Will Rogers' early career in entertainment include Lewis Erenberg, *Steppin' Out: New York Nightlife and the Transformation of American Culture 1890–1930* (1981); Charles Castle, *The Folies Bergère* (1985); Robert W. Snyder, *The Voice of the City: Vaudeville and Popular Culture in New York* (1989); M. Alison Kibler, *Rank Ladies: Gender and Cultural Hierarchy in American Vaudeville* (1999); Shirley Staples, *Male-Female Comedy Teams in American Vaudeville, 1865–1932* (1981); Andrew L. Erdman, *Blue Vaudeville: Sex, Morals and the Mass Marketing of Amusement, 1895–1915* (2004); and Edward L. Larson, *Summer for the Gods: The Scopes Trial and America's Continuing Debate Over Science and Religion* (1997).

A host of studies have influenced the author's views on the politics and foreign policy of the age, including "the Roaring Twenties," the Great Depression, and the New Deal. See William E. Leuchtenburg, *The Perils of Prosperity, 1914–1932* (1958); Roderick Nash, *The Nervous Generation: American Thought, 1917–1930* (1970); Mark Thompson, *American Character: The Curious Life of Charles Fletcher Lummis and the Rediscovery of the Southwest* (2001); David M. Chambers,

Hooded Americanism: The History of the Ku Klux Klan (1965); Jerry Flemmons, *Amon: The Texan Who Played Cowboy for America* (1998); Robert H. Ferrell, *American Diplomacy in the Great Depression* (1957); Jules R. Benjamin, *The United States and the Origins of the Cuban Revolution* (1990); Richard H. Pells, *Radical Visions and the American Dreams* (1973); Daneila Spenser, *The Impossible Triangle: Mexico, Soviet Russia, and the United States in the 1920s* (1999); Arthur M. Schlesinger, Jr., *The Coming of the New Deal: The War on Poverty of the 1930s* (1958); David M. Kennedy, *Freedom From Fear: The American People in Depression and War, 1929–1945* (1999); Roger Biles, *The South and the New Deal* (1994); Michael E. Parrish, *Anxious Decades: America in Prosperity and Depression, 1920–1941* (1992); and Wendy L. Wall, *Inventing the "American Way": The Politics of Consensus from the New Deal to the Civil Rights Movement* (2008).

As a check on the many "gags" that Rogers invented, a very useful listing with dates (but without commentary), is Reba Collins, ed., *Will Rogers Says* (1993).

Index